Hellenic Studies 62

DIVINE YET HUMAN EPICS

Recent Titles in the Hellenic Studies Series

The Web of Athenaeus

Eusebius of Caesarea
Tradition and Innovations

The Theology of Arithmetic
Number Symbolism in Platonism and Early Christianity

Homeric Durability
Telling Time in the Iliad

Paideia and Cult
Christian Initiation in Theodore of Mopsuestia

Imperial Geographies in Byzantine and Ottoman Space

Loving Humanity, Learning, and Being Honored
The Foundations of Leadership in Xenophon's Education of Cyrus

The Theory and Practice of Life
Isocrates and the Philosophers

From Listeners to Viewers
Space in the Iliad

Aspects of History and Epic in Ancient Iran
From Gaumāta to Wahnām

Homer's Versicolored Fabric
The Evocative Power of Ancient Greek Epic Word-Making

Christianity and Hellenism in the Fifth-Century Greek East
Theodoret's Apologetics against the Greeks in Context

The Master of Signs
Signs and the Interpretation of Signs in Herodotus' Histories

Eve of the Festival
Making Myth in Odyssey 19

Plato's Counterfeit Sophists

Kleos in a Minor Key
The Homeric Education of a Little Prince

Plato's Counterfeit Sophists

Multitextuality in Homer's Iliad
The Witness of the Ptolemaic Papyri

http://chs.harvard.edu/publications

DIVINE YET HUMAN EPICS

REFLECTIONS OF POETIC RULERS FROM ANCIENT GREECE AND INDIA

Shubha Pathak

Center for Hellenic Studies
Trustees for Harvard University
Washington, DC
Distributed by Harvard University Press
Cambridge, Massachusetts, and London, England
2014

Divine Yet Human Epics: Reflections of Poetic Rulers from Ancient Greece and India
by Shubha Pathak

Published by Center for Hellenic Studies, Trustees for Harvard University, Washington, DC
Distributed by Harvard University Press, Cambridge, Massachusetts, and London, England
Production: Ivy Livingston
Cover design: Joni Godlove
Printed by Edwards Brothers Malloy, Ann Arbor, MI

LIBRARY OF CONGRESS CATALOGING-IN-PUBLICATION DATA

Pathak, Shubha, 1972- author.
Divine yet human epics : reflections of poetic rulers from ancient Greece and India / by Shubha Pathak.
pages cm -- (Hellenic studies ; 62)
Includes bibliographical references and index.
ISBN 978-0-674-72675-8 (alk. paper)
1. Epic poetry, Greek--History and criticism. 2. Epic poetry, Indic--History and criticism. 3. Kings and rulers in literature. I. Title. II. Series: Hellenic studies ; 62.

PA3106.P38 2014
883'.01--dc23

2013049497

For my menfolk,
with love

Contents

Acknowledgments

I STARTED WRITING THIS BOOK when I was a graduate student at the University of Chicago Divinity School. There, I found welcome support for my comparative project, even though the scholarly norm tended increasingly toward highly specialized studies. In my wider-ranging intellectual interests, I was encouraged by Wendy Doniger, my dissertation advisor, and by Anthony C. Yu and Laura M. Slatkin, the other members of my dissertation committee. I am grateful to all three of them for helping me to envision what my work could be.

I finished writing this book as an assistant professor in the Department of Philosophy and Religion at American University, where a much-appreciated junior-faculty teaching release afforded me the time and resources to complete most of my manuscript. I would like to thank the AU colleagues who made my leave a reality. After drafting my manuscript, I was fortunate to find at Harvard University's Center for Hellenic Studies another set of sympathetic readers willing to see what my cross-cultural comparative inquiry would reveal. I am truly thankful to Gregory Nagy, Leonard Muellner, Casey Dué, and the other scholars on the CHS editorial board for their faith in and feedback on my work. I also am indebted to the anonymous reader of this work's initial manuscript for offering thoughtful criticism of it, to Jill Curry Robbins for tirelessly guiding this project through the production process, to Joni Godlove for interweaving the Greek and Indian textile images that I found in the Victoria and Albert Museum's online repository into her stunning design on this book's cover, to Ivy Livingston for expertly reformatting and typesetting my revised manuscript, and to Valerie Quercia for carefully copyediting it.

Somewhat more removed from but no less vital to the completion of this monograph were my wonderful menfolk: my father, Ambadas Pathak; my husband, Jim Blenko (who assembled its indices); and my brother, Sujay Pathak. I dedicate this book to them in deep gratitude for their limitless love and steadfast support.

Note on Texts and Translations

THE CLASSICAL SOURCES that I have cited are found in the following editions, unless otherwise specified:

The Kauṭilīya Arthaśāstra, ed. and trans. R. P. Kangle, 2nd ed., 2 pts. (Bombay, 1969–1972).

Dhvanyāloka of Ānandavardhana, ed. and trans. K. Krishnamoorthy (Dharwar, 1974).

Herodoti Historiae, ed. Karl Hude, 3rd ed., 2 vols. (Oxford, 1927).

The Homeric Hymns, ed. T. W. Allen, W. R. Halliday, and E. E. Sikes, 2nd ed. (Oxford, 1936).

Iliad, ed. David B. Monro and Thomas W. Allen, 3rd ed., vols. 1–2 of *Homeri opera* (Oxford, 1920).

The Kāvyamīmāṃsā of Rājaśekhara Edited with the Madhusūdanī Commentary by Sāhityāchārya Paṇḍit Madhusūdana Miśra, ed. Madhusudan Sharma, 3 pts. (Benares, 1931–1934).

The Mahābhārata, ed. Vishnu S. Sukthankar, S. K. Belvalkar, and P. L. Vaidya, 19 vols. (Poona, 1933–1966).

Maitrāyaṇī Saṃhitā: Die Saṃhitā der Maitrāyaṇīya-Śākhā, ed. Leopold von Schroeder, 4 vols. (Leipzig, 1881–1886; repr., Wiesbaden, 1970–1972).

Manu's Code of Law: A Critical Edition and Translation of the Mānava-Dharmaśāstra, ed. and trans. Patrick Olivelle, with the editorial assistance of Suman Olivelle (Oxford, 2005).

Nāṭyaśāstra of Bharatamuni with the Commentary Abhinavabhāratī by Abhinavaguptācārya, ed. R. S. Nagar, with the assistance of K. L. Joshi and M. A. Vedalankar, 4 vols. (Delhi, 1981–1984).

Odyssey, ed. Thomas W. Allen, 2nd ed., vols. 3–4 of *Homeri opera* (Oxford, 1917–1919).

Pindari carmina cum fragmentis, ed. Bruno Snell and Herwig Maehler, 2 vols. (Leipzig, 1971–1975).

The Vālmīki-Rāmāyaṇa, ed. G. H. Bhatt and U. P. Shah, 7 vols. (Baroda, 1960–1975).

Śatapatha-Brāhmaṇam, ed. Ganga Prasad Upadhyaya (New Delhi, 1998).
Scholia vetera in Pindari carmina, ed. A. B. Drachmann, 3 vols. (Leipzig, 1903–1927).
The Taittirīya Brāhmaṇa of the Black Yajur Veda, ed. Rājendralāla Mitra, with the assistance of several learned *paṇḍitas*, 4 vols. (Calcutta, 1855–1870; repr., Osnabrück, 1981).
Taittirīya Saṃhitā with the Padapāṭha and the Commentaries of Bhaṭṭa Bhāskara Miśra and Sāyaṇācārya, ed. N. S. Sontakke and T. N. Dharmadhikari, 3 vols. (Poona, 1970–1990).
Hesiod. Theogony, ed. M. L. West (Oxford, 1966; repr., 1997).
Claudii Aeliani Varia Historia, ed. Mervin R. Dilts (Leipzig, 1974).

I have transliterated with diacritical marks both the Greek and the Sanskrit quotations in this comparative study so that they will be more accessible to readers who are not familiar with the original scripts of these languages, but still will be easily recognizable to readers who are. The transliterations of the quotations are accompanied by translations that are mine unless otherwise indicated. I generally have used the Latinate forms of Greek names, except in cases where the Latinizations appear less frequently in contemporary scholarly literature than do the Greek forms (for example, I refer to the *Odyssey*'s hero as "Odysseus" rather than as "Ulysses").

Introduction

Defining Epics through Comparison

AN EPIC IS AN EXTENSIVE POEM that has been composed in an elevated style, that treats a pivotal epoch in the past of a particular people, and that endures because it both entertains its audiences and educates them on issues of ultimate importance. But the images that the term "epic" now evokes—mighty heroes who face fierce foes while traveling to exotic realms in search of special powers—reveal that a rather narrower definition of epic has prevailed in the minds of its users. At some point in its long history, the epic category collapsed into a class of adventure story. Consequently, the critics who employ this category emphasize aspects of epics that concern quests for faraway rewards rather than consolidations of holdings at home, clashes with enemies from outside rather than reconnections with beloved insiders, and aspirations to divine dominion rather than acceptance of human impotence.

Yet a corrective to such critical shortsightedness lies in epics themselves, for these poems portray what happens at home as well as away from it, and thus offer insight into living resignedly with human frailty in addition to striving mightily for the divine. In fact, four poems that have had among the greatest influences on critical conceptions of epic feature figures whose own poetic efforts sharpen the contrast between divine ease and human difficulty. These characters are kings or kings-to-be who appear in the Greek *Iliad* and *Odyssey* and the Sanskrit *Rāmāyaṇa* and *Mahābhārata.*

Those who listen to these singing kings—Achilles in the *Iliad*, Odysseus in the *Odyssey*, Kuśa and Lava in the *Rāmāyaṇa*, and Nala in the *Mahābhārata*—learn that their songs reflect the epics in which they are embedded. These songs thus reveal the epics' perspectives on their respective religious ideals, *kléos* (or heroic glory) in the case of the Greek poems and *dharma* (or righteousness) in the instance of the Sanskrit ones. Each pair of epics comprises an "affirmative" epic that exhibits the divine ease with which a core ideal is achieved and an "interrogative" epic that demonstrates the human difficulty with which the same ideal is attained.

Reconceptualizing the *Iliad* and *Rāmāyaṇa* as affirmative epics and the *Odyssey* and *Mahābhārata* as interrogative epics requires relinquishing earlier ideas of what the Greek and Sanskrit epics were. These ideas emerged from the epics themselves, from classical criticism of these works, and from their modern reinterpretations. Tracing the progression of both Greek and Indian notions of epic, then, is possible. But the culturally distinct developments of these epic ideas do not show what they share simply by virtue of being human creations.

So, examining Greek and Indian epic categories separately in the manner of Hellenists and Indologists is not enough. These categories—and therefore the poems that have given rise to them—must be brought together so that they may be reconsidered in light of their mutual illumination. Such comparisons of epic categories and of epics from two different cultures can inform a reformulation of the more general notion of epic that encompasses them. This reconception of epic offers insight into the cross-cultural problem of bridging the human/divine divide on which any poems of this genre center.

To reformulate the category of epic, then, I will study not only how this category came to be applied to the *Iliad* and the *Odyssey*, and to the *Rāmāyaṇa* and the *Mahābhārata*, but also how the performances of poetic kings in these works refine Greek and Indian ideas of epic. My study comprises three comparisons, the first two of which I will make in methodological support of the third. First, I will compare the different ways in which the Homeric epics and the Cyclic epics, two sets of poems composed in ancient Greece, have been classified by their premodern and modern interpreters, my aim being to explain why it was the Homeric poems rather than their Cyclic counterparts that shaped premodern and modern notions of epic. Second, I will compare the distinct histories that the Homeric epics and the Sanskrit epics have had with the term "epic," so that I may clarify the respective contributions that these pairs of poems have made to the epic category. My third and central comparison actually is a meta-comparison, a comparison of two comparisons. I will begin by comparing the poems performed by kings in the *Iliad* and the *Odyssey*, continue by comparing analogous accounts offered by monarchs in the *Rāmāyaṇa* and the *Mahābhārata*, and end by comparing interculturally the outcomes of these two intracultural comparisons. My purpose in doing so will be to shed light on the different and similar ways in which the ancient Greek and Indian poems depict epic composition in their portrayals of poetic rulers.

The three comparisons that compose my study are of three different types based on three different assumptions about how the comparanda of concern are interrelated.[1] The assumption underlying my first comparison is that the poetic inheritance common to the Homeric epics and the Cyclic epics reflects

1 Classicist Gregory Nagy (2005:71–72) has taken a similar threefold approach to different comparanda.

the derivation of these two sets of works from the same source. In my second comparison, however, I assume that the classification of the Homeric epics has influenced that of the Sanskrit epics because interpreters of the Greek poems have interacted with interpreters of the Sanskrit ones. Yet I assume no such interaction between the royal poems in the *Iliad* and *Odyssey* and those in the *Rāmāyaṇa* and *Mahābhārata*, assuming instead that the Sanskrit accounts could have arisen independently of the Greek ones.

Issues concerning genetic comparisons that assume an inheritance common to the comparanda, diffusionist comparisons that assume influence among the comparanda, or analogical comparisons that assume the independence of the comparanda have been discussed in disciplines as disparate as political science, anthropology, comparative literature, classical studies, religious studies, and art history. As I keep in view what scholars in these fields have identified (sometimes unconsciously) as potential problems posed by genetic, diffusionist, and analogical approaches, I, a historian of religions, will propose solutions to these problems that will allow me to adopt these approaches fruitfully.

The Inheritance, Influence, and Independence of Epics

The nature of what is shared by epics being compared, as well as the extent of their pre-existing interconnection, varies between the three major types of comparative studies considered here. An "independence study" requires that such epics share simply the scholarly category in which they have been placed—the category that indicates why a scholar has associated these perhaps otherwise unconnected works with one another. In contrast, an "influence study" presumes that the authors or critics of already interconnected epics share a history of having interacted with one another, though the epics themselves may belong to different literary and cultural traditions. In still further contrast, an "inheritance study" holds long-interconnected epics to share a literary and cultural source, as in the case of the Homeric epics and the Cyclic epics.

The genesis of the Homeric and Cyclic epics

Examining the etymology of the English word "epic" reveals its roots in Archaic (ca. 800–500 BCE) Greece, where its etymon was applied to two types of poems: the *Iliad* and *Odyssey* of Homer and the poems composing the Epic Cycle. The similarities between the Homeric epics and the Cyclic epics in style and subject matter stem from their outgrowth from the same body of heroic poetry present in an even earlier Geometric (ca. 900–800 BCE) Greece.

In assuming that the traits shared by the Homeric and Cyclic epics reflect their descent from the same source, I am undertaking a genetic comparison. This kind of comparison was made most famous (and infamous) by late-nineteenth-century comparative mythologists who regarded the similarities that they saw among sacred stories related in different Indo-European languages as evidence of a shared Indo-European inheritance.[2] This legacy was held to be one of location as well as literature, of space shared at one time by the groups responsible for the sets of stories being compared.[3] Indeed, the comparative mythologists' presupposition of a common Indo-European space was shared by their admirer Wilhelm Scherer, a philologist and literary critic who incorporated their project into his comparative poetics as the first of three types of relations that he treated: "The first kind deals, as a rule, with comparative mythology, ... and the Indo-European area entailed by the parallels drawn above ... may also belong there."[4] The two other relation types that Scherer goes on to characterize correspond to the diffusionist and analogical approaches to comparison.

Genetic comparisons are appealing now, as in the nineteenth century, because they rely on linguistic data that can be analyzed systematically. The usefulness of such information was affirmed early on by political historian Edward A. Freeman:

> It is not safe to set down any instance of likeness as being necessarily a case of an inheritance from the common stock, unless we have some corroborative evidence besides the likeness itself. We have the highest degree of such corroborative evidence whenever Comparative Philology steps in to help us. If two distinct nations of the Aryan family—or, by the same argument, if two distinct nations of any other family—have a common institution called by a common name, and if the likeness is plainly not a case of imitation or borrowing from one another, such an institution may be set down without any kind of doubt as being a clear case of common inheritance from a common stock.[5]

In my own inheritance study, I assume that the Homeric and Cyclic epics came to be called by the same name because they shared features passed down to

2 Thompson 1946:371, 372. For discussion of the disastrous repercussions of comparative mythology, see Lincoln 1999:64–75.

3 Debates over the existence and location of the Indo-European homeland are examined extensively in Mallory 1989.

4 Scherer 1893:704: "*Die erste Art behandelt in der Regel die vergleichende Mythologie, ... und der arische Theil der oben ... angestellten Vergleichungen mag auch dahin gehören.*" All translations are my own unless otherwise noted.

5 Freeman 1873:61.

them from their common poetic predecessors. But this resemblance between the Homeric and Cyclic epics cannot be confirmed, for the Cyclic poems no longer exist. Any information about the Epic Cycle must be gleaned from the criticism composed about it. Thus, as I will discuss in Chapter 1, ancient critics clearly used the same term to classify the Cyclic poems and the Homeric poems, but the common characteristics of these poems no longer can be compared directly. Their "likeness" is accessible only through the assessments of their earlier interpreters, even as "corroborative evidence" of this similarity between the Homeric and Cyclic epics exists in their shared classification. Therefore, my genetic comparison differs from the kind that Freeman has in mind, not only in considering literary works produced by speakers of the same language, but also in being limited by a lack of comparanda themselves rather than by a lack of evidence of how they were classified by their early critics.

The absence of the Cyclic epics at present is not an impediment to my genetic comparative study, but rather its central subject. After observing that these no longer extant poems have been categorized in the same way as their Homeric counterparts, I will explain how the absence of the Cyclic works has led modern critics to assume that ancient interpreters were correct to assess the Cyclic epics as poems inferior and ancillary to the *Iliad* and *Odyssey.* As a consequence of modern critics' uncritical acceptance of this assumption, the defining characteristics of the Homeric rather than the Cyclic poems have informed the modern conception of the epic genre. This Homerically informed notion of epic has shaped the study of poems composed after the *Iliad* and *Odyssey* in areas other than Greece, as I will show in my second comparison.

The diffusion of the Homeric and Sanskrit epics

In my second comparison, I will inquire into the reasons why the *Rāmāyaṇa* and the *Mahābhārata*—poems composed largely between 200 BCE and 200 CE in Sanskrit, a language having no etymon for the word "epic"—nonetheless came to be called epics. My aim is not to identify which elements of these Sanskrit poems were contributed by the Homeric works as they made their way from Greece to India with soldiers, traders, and other travelers, but instead to understand how modern interpreters' Homerically informed idea of epic influenced their similar categorization of the *Rāmāyaṇa* and the *Mahābhārata.*

In distinguishing the classificatory influence that modern readers of Homer have had on modern readers of Vālmīki and Vyāsa from the spread of epic narratives over time and space, I draw upon a distinction that literary critic G. Gregory Smith drew for the discipline of comparative literature between "the antiquarian and genealogical facts of authorship" (which include "the influence of individual authors and books on other authors and books") and "the folklore bases" of literature (that is, the collections of tales that have traveled the world over with their tellers).[6] Although Smith calls attention to the authors of literary works while I am spotlighting their interpreters, we both single out individuals interested in these works, in an effort to discern the influences that these individuals have had on one another.

Yet, in studying the influence of readers of the *Iliad* and *Odyssey* on readers of the *Rāmāyaṇa* and *Mahābhārata*, I will do well to heed the warnings of scholars studying those who have tried to trace the faceless spread of stories across cultures.[7] Those who claim to have followed the movement of narratives from the place of their creators to the place of their appropriators, and who thus have invested heavily in establishing the direction of story diffusion from one society to another, tend to make too much of the tale-lender's contribution and the tale-borrower's obligation. These tale-trackers—like their fellow diffusionists, who have been assessed by historian of religions Jonathan Z. Smith[8]—are susceptible to overvaluing what they see as the source and to undervaluing what they see as the receiver, and therefore to asserting the superiority of the source tradition over the receiver tradition in the manner described by historian of religions David M. Freidenreich.[9] For example, folklorist Stith Thompson does little to discount the possibility that "stories usually proceed from culturally higher to culturally lower peoples" when he uses the phrases "diffused from an original center" and "versions close to the archetype" just prior to his discussion of this proposition.[10]

Art historian Partha Mitter sees a similar obeisance to the supposed source in some of the reports of early Western travelers to India who recorded their reactions to the art there. In contrast to those beholders for whom "Indian art consisted of nothing but irrational monsters and horrific demons[, t]he other[s] saw the elegance and grandeur of the temples as clearly proving their classical origins. Some even went so far as to find historical links with Alexander."[11] The cognitive bridges that these explorers quickly built between India and Greece

6 G. G. Smith 1905:1.

7 This anonymous transmission of tales is captured by the second sort of relation that Scherer (1893:704) addressed in his comparative poetics: "The contents of short stories and fairy tales provide the best-known example of the second kind." [*Für die zweite Art geben die Novellen- und Märchenstoffe das bekannteste Beispiel.*] On the grounds of this statement, Germanist and comparative literary critic Ulrich Weisstein (1973:188) argues that Scherer's poetics had "a home base in folklore."

8 J. Z. Smith 1978:243.

9 Freidenreich 2004:83.

10 Thompson 1946:438, 437, 438.

11 Mitter 1992:47–48.

suggest that the venturers would have subscribed to this belief in the original's unsurpassability: "We should add—and this again is true of organic nature as well as of human affairs—that all forms show themselves in their purest state at the point of their origin, before they have undergone the changes which later befall them. The leaf of the fern is more fully formed than that of the higher plants which must relinquish the stage to the glory of the blossom. Similarly certain forms of art, the representations of human beauty and the poetic genres of epic, lyric, and drama found their perfect shape among the Greeks."[12] Like the aforementioned sightseers who managed to peer at the Parthenon though far from Athens, advocates of the diffusionist approach may fall prey to the prejudices that the later form of an artifact can be flawless only if it is a facsimile of the original, and that this imitation is interesting only insofar as it preserves its paradigm.

In order not to privilege any archetype as I adopt a diffusionist approach to comparing critics' designations of Homeric and Sanskrit poems as epics, I will study not only the influence that the epic categorization of the *Iliad* and the *Odyssey* has had on the modern reception of the *Rāmāyaṇa* and the *Mahābhārata*, but also the influence that the epic categorization of these Sanskrit poems has had on the originally Greek epic category itself. Even though the *Iliad* and *Odyssey* predate the *Rāmāyaṇa* and *Mahābhārata* by centuries, the Sanskrit poems—despite being different enough from each other to designate themselves in different ways—were coupled by medieval Indian critics who recognized the poems' common characteristics. Moreover, once the *Rāmāyaṇa* and *Mahābhārata* were paired by modern Western readers as epics, these works contributed their intracultural commonalities to the epic category.

But, at the same time that the Homeric and Sanskrit poem pairs differ from each other in their culturally informed constructions of what constitutes an epic, these coupled compositions portray poetic kings in ways that evince intercultural similarities and intracultural disparities with regard to the representation of epic creation. The similar manners in which bardic rulers—and thus the poems that they compose—differ across the *Iliad* and the *Odyssey* and across the *Rāmāyaṇa* and the *Mahābhārata* form the center of my third comparison.

The analogy of the Homeric and Sanskrit epics

As I examine the resemblances between the Greek and Indian epic representations of singing kings, resemblances that remain prominent in the face of the kings' striking unlikenesses, I will assume that these correspondences reflect the common human condition of the epics' authors. Their shared human concerns

[12] Snell 1953:261.

probably account best for the commonalities between the composers' limnings of kings performing poems, given the wide temporal and cultural divides that separate the Greek and Indian epics. The *Rāmāyaṇa* and *Mahābhārata*, which were composed several centuries after the *Iliad* and *Odyssey* (which date approximately from 750 to 700 BCE), take as their topic not the Greek ideal of *kléos*, but the Indian ideal of *dharma*.

By comparing first the Homeric epics' portrayals of poetic rulers, and next the Sanskrit epics' depictions of such figures, and finally the results of these two comparisons, I will make an analogical metacomparison. Thus, I will regard any patterns that persist across the Greek and Indian epics as ensuing from what Freeman and anthropologist Edward B. Tylor termed "independent invention,"[13] such trends being "the fruit of like circumstances leading to like results."[14] Such correspondences, therefore, constitute "the likeness of analogy."[15]

The grounds for such similarity among data likely to be historically independent are broader than those underlying data related through common inheritance or geographical influence. Whereas genetic comparisons rest on similarities reflecting slight divergences from a single cultural source, and diffusionist comparisons are based on commonalities stemming from the sharing of materials across cultures that is associated with migrations, analogical comparisons are founded on parallels that transcend the accident of actual human contact. Thus, in the apparent absence of intercultural interaction that could account for the connections between cultures, the analogical comparativist herself identifies those aspects of shared human existence that are most salient to the comparison that she has constructed. As she selects and connects her comparanda "for ... her own good theoretical reasons,"[16] she is free from the stricture of having to gather evidence specifically to establish the inheritance or influence linking her comparanda. But, at the same time, the comparison that she constructs must reveal something important about the comparanda. Her comparison must provide some type of useful information about the comparanda apart from their interconnection through a shared inheritance or direct influence. Her study of her comparanda's independence must offer

13 Freeman 1873:17; Tylor 1878:373, 376.

14 Freeman 1873:17.

15 Freeman 1873:74. Explorations of this type of relationship have been fixtures in the field of literature. In 1893, Scherer (1893:704) assured his readers that "[t]he third kind [of relation for which he accounted in his comparative poetics] w[ould] be present in the non-Indo-European parallels above" (*Die dritte Art wird in den außerarischen obigen Parallelen vorliegen*), i.e. those that did not ensue either from inheritance or from influence. By 1971, "analogy studies" of the sort Scherer foresaw had appeared frequently enough to afford fodder for the doctoral dissertation of comparative literary critic Michael Eugene Moriarty (1971).

16 J. Z. Smith 1990:115.

insight into them that is different from that afforded by investigations of their inheritance or influence, for "[t]he value of any analogy," including that at the heart of her comparative analysis, "is dependent upon the depth and richness of its implications."[17]

In my own independence study, I aim to interpret the poems by (and about) bardic rulers that the Greek and Sanskrit epics incorporate. The rulers' portrayals of their respective religious ideals reflect the methods that the epics themselves employ to instill these ideals. The heroic attainment of *kléos* in the Greek epics and of *dharma* in the Sanskrit ones poetically addresses two common human concerns: namely, how people face the inevitability of their mortality, and how they act morally in the face of ever-present immorality. These concerns number among what theologian David Tracy has termed "religious questions," which are

> the most serious and difficult questions, both personal and communal, that any human being or society must face: Has existence any ultimate meaning? Is a fundamental trust to be found amidst the fears, anxieties and terror of existence? Is there some reality, some force, even some one, who speaks a word of truth that can be recognized and trusted? Religions ask and respond to such fundamental questions of the meaning and truth of our existence as human beings in solitude, and in society, history and the cosmos. ... Lurking beneath the surface of our everyday lives, exploding into explicitness in the limit-situations inevitable in any life, are questions which logically must be and historically are called religious questions.[18]

Such "religious questions," as historian of religions Wendy Doniger has described, "recur in myths" and treat such topics as why human beings exist and what happens to them after they die.[19]

The particular ways in which singing kings treat these types of religious issues within the Homeric and Hindu epics clarify why the epics have their kings sing, and how the epics reflect in these royal songs on the religious reasons for their own invention. This invention of epic in ancient Greece and India is understood best by an analogical comparison. Even if the kings' accounts of epic invention could be connected genetically or by diffusion, such connections would not evidence the aspects of epic invention in which I am most interested. Understanding the enduring appeal of the solutions that the Greek and Sanskrit epics advance to their existential problems (the inevitability of mortality and

17 Moriarty 1971:140.
18 Tracy 1981:4.
19 Doniger 1998:65.

the ubiquity of immorality, respectively) within and without their poetic kings' accounts is too broad an interpretative purpose to be realized by interconnecting linguistically the occasional epic incident common to Greek and Sanskrit or by attesting materially the ancient travel of epic tales between Greece and India.

So, to keep in sight the epics' parallel efforts to address their audiences' religious concerns, I will take up an analogist's telescope instead of a geneticist's microscopes or a diffusionist's movie camera. An analogical comparativist, by conceiving of categories in an effort to fathom the flood of data before her, devises a way to view everything of interest to her, taking up the telescope of intercultural comparative analysis to see as a whole the components that a genetic comparativist would see only separately through the microscopes of intracultural contextual analyses.[20] If a genetic comparativist would move between intracultural microscopes through which she would observe aspects of Greek and Sanskrit epics connected by a common linguistic inheritance, then a diffusionist comparativist would carry a movie camera because she would aim to document the spread of epic stories from one culture to another.

In adopting an analogical approach, I do not deny that connections between ancient Greece and India at the microscopic level of linguistic genetics and at the readily observable level of geographical diffusion may lie behind, and thus account for, the epic likenesses reflected in the human analogies that telescopists draw when they peer from afar at the poems. Instead I assert that analogists, who look through their telescopes at these texts as wholes rather than in parts, view something new about these works, by virtue of having a broad focus. This type of perspective is instructive even in instances where the objects of study have no common origin or history of contact.

Defining Greek and Sanskrit Epics via Identity, Metaphor, and Ideals

Even though my study of the Greek and Sanskrit epics does not rely on their relation by inheritance or influence, I will adopt the aforementioned methods of geneticists and diffusionists as I consider the categorizations of these poems in their premodern and modern contexts. In Chapter 1, I will examine the etymology of the word "epic" in advance of arguing that, because this term originated in ancient times as an appellation for the *Iliad* and the *Odyssey*, the statement today that these texts are epics amounts to an identity. In Chapter 2, I will exchange my microscope for a movie camera in order to track modern critics'

[20] For this figure of double vision, I am indebted to Doniger (1998:chap. 1, "Microscopes and Telescopes").

transfer of the term "epic" from Greek works to Sanskrit ones, and thereupon to explain why saying that the *Rāmāyaṇa* and the *Mahābhārata* are epics amounts to making a metaphor.

After investigating how premodern and modern scholars have invented the Greek and Sanskrit "epics," I will compare the royal poems embedded in these works and thus their religious inventions. In Chapter 3, I will interpret the poems of Achilles and Odysseus, heroes of the *Iliad* and *Odyssey* whose own coming *kléos* is symbolized by their identification with poets (who would celebrate them), but whose triumphal and piteous poems mirror the two men's distinct means of achieving their ideal (conquering another country versus defending one's own kingdom). In Chapter 4, I will study the poems of Kuśa and Lava and Nala—rulers whom the heroes of the *Rāmāyaṇa* and *Mahābhārata* hear as they attempt to demonstrate *dharma*, but whose narratives' exultant and sorrowful characters forecast that righteousness will spread readily across Rāma's cosmos, but will be restricted within Yudhiṣṭhira's realm.

In the conclusion that trails this pair of comparisons, I will recontextualize the epic pairs, turning back briefly to their textual traditions in order to explain intercultural differences (and intracultural similarities) between the pairs' portrayals of their respective religious ideals. Yet I will emphasize the intercultural similarities (and intracultural differences) between the dyads' depictions so as to recategorize the *Iliad* and *Rāmāyaṇa* as "affirmative epics" that exhibit the ease with which their core ideals are achieved, and the *Odyssey* and *Mahabhārata* as "interrogative epics" that show that these ideals are attained only with tremendous difficulty. I will end by asserting that affirmative and interrogative epics arose simultaneously—first the *Iliad* and *Odyssey* in Greece, and then the *Rāmāyaṇa* and *Mahābhārata* in India—in order to offer their audiences alternative models of religious accomplishment, and that the persistence of these poems till today demonstrates the immense appeal of their complementary instructional approaches, an appeal that modern self- and social-psychological theories make clearer.

1

The Epic Identity of the *Iliad* and *Odyssey*

Pindar and Herodotus' Lofty Legacy

THE HOMERIC AND HINDU EPICS appeal to their audiences as religious instructors by dint of addressing important existential issues in entertaining manners. Each pair of poems offers a couple of complementary solutions to a particularly pressing human problem. Because these solutions are found in the accounts that the epics place in the mouths of their poetic kings, accounts that mirror the epics in which they occur, understanding the relationship between the coupled epics in which the kings' songs are embedded provides insight into the epics' distinct approaches to their central existential concern. Illuminating the similarity that connects each epic with its partner simultaneously casts into relief the contrasts that exist between them.

The connection between each pair of contrasting epics originates with the poems themselves and is reinforced by their early readers. Hence, examining how each epic set represents itself and how its self-representation informs its designation by its early exegetes makes sense. This designation continues today to influence not only interpretations of the epic set itself, but also the conceptions that literary critics offer of the epic genre.

The earliest influence on critical conceptions of epic is the portrayal that the *Iliad* and *Odyssey* present of their interrelationship. The poems' self-reflection shapes the Classical (ca. 500–323 BCE) Greek notions of epic that found modern ideas of this kind of literature, and that thus must be taken into account in any classificatory study of the epic genre's representative works.

The *Iliad* and *Odyssey*'s Single Self-Understanding

A contemporary critic who parallels the *Iliad* and the *Odyssey* enters an exegetical tradition as old as the works themselves,[1] for they attest their own association.

1 I assume that the Homeric epics were composed more or less simultaneously in the latter half of the eighth century BCE, because problems with definitively dating these texts preclude me from arguing that the affirmative *Iliad* preceded the interrogative *Odyssey*.

Appropriately, the *Iliad* (an account of earlier events) introduces the appellation for such stories as itself, while the *Odyssey* (which picks up the *Iliad*'s plot line) pushes for its own place under this umbrella term.

In the *Iliad*, Achilles' father figure Phoenix calls up *kléa andrȏn* (men's glorious deeds) at a point in the poem when the inclusion of Achilles' own acts among these illustrious exploits appears to be at risk. Seeking to convince the soldier to set aside his anger at his commander Agamemnon and to return to combat, Phoenix plays on Achilles' aspiration to prestige:

> *nûn d' háma t' autíka pollà didoî, tà d' ópisthen hupéstē,*
> *ándras dè líssesthai epiproéēken arístous*
> *krinámenos katà laòn Akhaiïkón, hoí te soì autȏi*
> *phíltatoi Argeíōn· tȏn mḕ sú ge mûthon elénxēis*
> *mēdè pódas· prìn d' oú ti nemessētòn kekholȏsthai.*
> *hoútō kaì tȏn prósthen epeuthómetha kléa andrȏn*
> *hērṓōn, hóte kén tin' epizáphelos khólos híkoi·*
> *dōrētoí te pélonto parárrētoí t' epéessi.*
>
> But now [Agamemnon] is giving you many things at once, and has promised more to come,
> and has sent men to entreat you,
> having selected the best among the Achaean army, the men who are
> dearest to you of the Argives. Nullify neither their appeal
> nor their approach, though before that no one could blame you for being angry.
> To this effect, too, we have heard the glorious deeds of men of yore—
> warriors who, when waves of anger washed over them,
> would be propitiated by presents and open to persuasive words.
>
> *Iliad* 9.519–526

In trying to steer Achilles back to his storied trajectory, a path to poetic immortality, Phoenix aligns the *Iliad*—an inchoate account from his perspective because Achilles has yet to attain in battle the *kléos* that the *Iliad* is being composed to celebrate[2]—and earlier tales that already have been entrenched within his society's world view. By placing Achilles, the *Iliad*'s protagonist, on

2 Classicist Andrew Ford (1992:109) makes a similar point while analyzing the epic poem that Phemius performs in the first book of the *Odyssey*: "The fundamental character of epic as poetry of the past is reversed when it appears in the looking glass of epic. What were the 'fames of men' for Homer's audience were fresh rumor and recent news for the heroes; the literate's trope would be to say that the faded parchments we keep in museums were the daily newspapers of old. And this makes sense, for it is an appropriate glorification of these men greater than we to

a par with characters known for their *kléa*, Phoenix implicitly adds the poem in its future full form to this repository of records of renown as he attempts to persuade the hero of the *Iliad* to reenter the Trojan War and thus to make possible the completion of this poem's presently suspended composition.

The *Odyssey* argues for its own classification as one of the *kléa andrôn* as it portrays a poetic performance:

> *autàr epeì pósios kaì edētúos ex éron hénto,*
> *Moûs' ár' aoidòn anêken aeidémenai kléa andrôn,*
> *oímēs tês tót' ára kléos ouranòn eurùn híkane,*
> *neîkos Odusêos kaì Pēleḯdeō Akhilêos,*
> *hṓs pote dērísanto theôn en daitì thaleíēi*
> *ekpáglois epéessin, ánax d' andrôn Agamémnōn*
> *khaîre nóōi, hó t' áristoi Akhaiôn dērióōnto.*
>
> But, when their desire for food and drink subsided,
> the Muse incited the singer to sing of men's glorious deeds
> from that song whose glory at that time reached widespread heaven,
> namely, the quarrel between Odysseus and Peleus' son Achilles—
> how they once wrangled at the gods' bountiful banquet
> with violent words, and the king of men, Agamemnon,
> exulted at the idea that the best of the Achaeans were wrangling.
>
> *Odyssey* 8.72–78

This conflict between Achilles and Odysseus symbolizes that the *kléa andrôn* encompass the *Iliad* and the *Odyssey* alike, as Nagy has hinted: "The quarrel between Achilles and Odysseus in the first song of [Phaeacian singer] Demodokos, viii 72–82, dramatizes the antithesis of two inherited central themes built into the *Iliad* and the *Odyssey*, namely, the qualifications of [their heroes] Achilles and Odysseus respectively for the title 'best of the Achaeans.' Their epic actions are striving to attain what is perhaps the most distinctive heroic epithet that the **kléos** of the Achaeans can confer upon a mortal. In the first song of Demodokos, the poet—or let us say Demodokos—comments not only on the *Odyssey* but also on the *Iliad* itself."[3]

Nagy's characterization of Achilles' and Odysseus' quintessential actions as "epic" raises the question of when the *Iliad* and *Odyssey* began to be regarded as

say that, just as their own deeds and lives are destined to become the stuff of immortal poetry, so the poetry they prefer comes closest to these deeds."

3 Nagy 1999:59. An earlier version of the following two paragraphs has appeared in Pathak 2013:36–37.

epics rather than as *kléa andrôn*. In response, some people, even without examining any evidence, may sense that these poems are inextricable from the idea of epic. For most readers schooled in the Western tradition, for instance, the *Iliad* and *Odyssey* epitomize epic poetry, as they are the first epics that students of this tradition encounter (though perhaps in abridged form).[4] These students' assumption is borne out insofar as the Homeric poems have taken precedence etymologically, as well as experientially. The English word "epic" ultimately derives (via the Greek adjective *epikós*) from the Greek noun *épos*,[5] the meaning of whose plural form, *épea*, expanded by neology to encompass "epic poetry or poem" in addition to "words." More precisely, *épos* in the late eighth century BCE was "used widely in Homer to designate words, in contrast to *mûthos*, which applies instead to the content of the words."[6] However, by the early fifth century BCE, *épos* had come in its plural form to mean epic poetry as well, as attest works of the lyric poet Pindar (518–ca. 440 BCE) and the historian Herodotus (ca. 485–425 BCE).[7]

Pindar and Herodotus: Exegetes Identifying the *Iliad* and *Odyssey* as Epics

Nagy has noted that, "[a]s in the songs of Pindar, the figure of Homer is treated as the ultimate representative of epic in the prose of Herodotus (e.g. [*Histories*] 2.116–117)."[8] I would go a step further to stress that the foremost epic exemplars for both Pindar and Herodotus were Homer's *Iliad* and *Odyssey*. Although Pindar and Herodotus each count among Homer's epic compositions at least one component of the Epic Cycle (a number of now-lost poems that were composed separately circa the seventh century BCE, but were subsequently collected as accounts of the creation of the gods, the Theban War, and the Trojan War), the *Iliad* and *Odyssey* are the paradigmatic epics in the eyes of these two later authors.

Pindar's praise of the *Iliad* and *Odyssey*

Pindar, for example, styles the athlete Timodemus after performers of this epic pair, explicitly connecting the extensive compositions that the Homeridae

4 Summaries of the *Iliad* and *Odyssey* include those prepared by mythographer Thomas Bulfinch (1912:220–232, 241–262) and by classicist Edith Hamilton (1942:178–192, 202–219) for their popular mythological compendia. An even briefer account of the epics that is addressed to even younger readers appears in children's book authors Ingri and Edgar Parin d'Aulaire's (1962:183–184) *Book of Greek Myths*.

5 *Oxford English Dictionary* 1989–2013, s.v. "epic, *a.* and *n.*"

6 Chantraine 1984–1990, vol. 1, s.v. "*épos*": "*employé largement chez Hom. pour désigner les paroles, à côté de* mũthos *qui s'applique plutôt au contenu des paroles.*"

7 Liddell, Scott, and Jones 1940 (hereafter cited as LSJ), s.v. "*épos*," IV.a.

8 Nagy 1990a:215.

ultimately will articulate with the run of wins that this competitor eventually will amass, and implicitly likening his own ability to immortalize Timodemus poetically through praise to these Homeric rhapsodes' potential to memorialize illustrious heroes by reciting epics. Thus, *Nemean* 2 begins:

> *Hóthen per kaì Homērídai*
> *rhaptôn epéōn tà póll' aoidoí*
> *árkhontai, Diòs ek prooimíou, kaì hód' anḗr*
> *katabolàn hierôn agṓnōn nikaphorías dédektai prôton, Nemeaíou*[9]
> *en poluumnḗtōi Diòs álsei.*
>
> Just as the Homeridae,
> singers of epic poems pieced together,
> start out for the most part with a prelude to Zeus, so too this man
> has begun to collect victories in the sacred contests of Nemea
> in Zeus' celebrated sacred grove.
>
> *Nemean* 2.1–5

That the word *epéōn* (epic poems) in this passage's second line alludes to the *Iliad* and *Odyssey* is indicated by the scholia to *Nemean* 2.1d, whose description of the aforementioned rhapsodes includes "[t]he expression *hekatéras tês poiḗseōs* 'each of the two poems[,' which] implies that the *Iliad* and the *Odyssey* are meant."[10]

Moreover, Pindar refers to events in these epics as he parallels himself to Homer, the prototypical epic poet,[11] in *Isthmian* 4:

> *kaì krésson' andrôn kheirónōn*
> *ésphale tékhna katamárpsais'· íste mán Aíantos alkán, phoínion tàn opsíai*
> *en nuktì tamṑn perì hôi phasgánōi momphàn ékhei paídessin Hellánōn hósoi*
> *Trṓiand' éban.*
>
> *all' Hómērós toi tetímaken di' anthrṓpōn, hòs autoû*
> *pâsan orthṓsais aretàn katà rhábdon éphrasen*
> *thespesíōn epéōn loipoîs athúrein.*
> *toûto gàr athánaton phōnâen hérpei,*

9 Like classicist-poet Richmond Lattimore (1976:103), I read *Nemeaíou* with the rest of line 4 rather than with line 5. (In fact, C. M. Bowra [1935], the classicist who edited the text on which Lattimore's translation is based, includes no comma between the words *prôton* and *Nemeaíou*.)

10 Scholia to *Nemean* 2.1d, quoted in Nagy 1996b:84n56.

11 If Homer is "the protopoet whose poetry is reproduced by [a] continuous succession of [such] performers" as the Homeridae (Nagy 1996a:76), then Pindar seeks a spot at the end of this line.

eí tis eû eípēi ti· kaì pánkarpon epì khthóna kaì dià pónton bébaken
ergmátōn aktìs kalō̂n ásbestos aieí.
prophrónōn Moisân túkhoimen, keînon hápsai pursòn húmnōn
kaì Melíssōi, pankratíou stephánōm' epáxion,
érneï Telesiáda. tólmai gàr eikṓs
thumòn eribremetân thērō̂n leóntōn
en pónōi, mē̂tin d' alṓpēx, aietoû há t' anapitnaména rhómbon iskhei·
khrḕ dè pân érdont' amaurō̂sai tòn ekhthrón.
ou gàr phúsin Oariōneían élakhen·
all' onotòs mèn idésthai,
sumpeseîn d' akmâi barús.

And the skill of inferior men
overtakes and overthrows the mightier man. No doubt you know of the might of Ajax, which he slew bloodily late
at night with his own sword, being blamed as a result by all of the Greeks' sons who traveled to Troy.

But Homer has honored him among people,
having gotten straight and recounted his every heroic act in the measured verse
of divine epic poems for successors to sing.
For, if someone says something well, it issues forth as an immortal utterance;
and over the earth full of all kinds of fruit and through the sea has ranged
the splendor of noble deeds, never to be extinguished.
May I gain the grace of the Muses so that I may ignite this torch of song
for Melissus too—for this offshoot of Telesiadas, a wreath worthy of his boxing-and-wrestling contest.
For in courage his heart resembles
those of roaring lions
in the thick of fighting, but in craftiness he is like a fox, which stays the swoop of an eagle by tumbling to its back.
The man must do anything to enfeeble his enemy.
For he was not allotted Orion's size,
but rather summons scorn on sight.
His strength, however, makes him hard to combat hand-to-hand.

Isthmian 4.34–51

I have translated the word *epéōn* in line 39 as "epic poems" in order to emphasize the sources that supply Pindar with the material from which he fashions his own poetic persona. He begins this passage by citing the suicide of Ajax depicted in the *Aethiopis* (scholium to *Isthmian* 4.58b), but quickly contrasts with the warrior's demise his heroism highlighted in the *Iliad* and indicated in the *Odyssey*. Thus, although Pindar—like most of his colleagues—probably attributed the *Aethiopis* and other Cyclic epics to Homer, he associated Homer's expertise as an epic author with the *Iliad* and *Odyssey*.

Pindar's privileging here of the *Iliad* over the *Aethiopis* has been discussed by classicist Frank J. Nisetich, who traces Ajax's suicide to the *Aethiopis* and his praise to the *Iliad*.[12] Indeed, in its assessment of the warriors in the Achaean army, the *Iliad* ranks Ajax second only to Achilles, the epic's hero (*Iliad* 2.768–769, 17.279–280). Yet, I disagree for two reasons with Nisetich's assertion that the Homer whom Pindar esteems so highly in the *Isthmian* excerpt above is the poet only of the *Iliad*.[13] First, even in the *Odyssey*, after the Trojan War has ended, Ajax—in the eyes of Odysseus, the epic's own Achaean hero, no less—continues to rate right below Achilles, as Nisetich himself acknowledges.[14] Second, and more significantly, the hero whom Homer "has honored" (*tetímaken*) in *Isthmian* 4.37 is not simply Ajax, as Nisetich argues,[15] but also Odysseus.

The hero's double identity here hinges on an ambiguity in *Isthmian* 4 to which its scholiasts have attended (scholia to *Isthmian* 4.58c–d; 4.63a, b–c). The inference that Homer is said to have immortalized Ajax in *Isthmian* 4.37 follows from Pindar's portrayal of Ajax's self-destruction in the same poem. After explaining that Ajax has incurred the Achaean army's censure by taking his own life, Pindar about-faces to emphasize how Homer has restored the warrior's reputation (*Isthmian* 4.35–42). Pindar thus contrasts Ajax's blame by the army to his praise by Homer.

Yet Pindar also may be opposing the stealthy shrewdness of Ajax's physically overmatched opponent Odysseus in the *Iliad* and the *Odyssey* to the poetic publicity that Homer provides for Odysseus in these epics. Appropriately, Pindar initially only intimates Odysseus' surreptitiousness, by advancing an aphorism ("... the skill of inferior men / overtakes and overthrows the mightier man. ..." [... *krésson' andrôn kheirónōn / ésphale tékhna katamárpsais'·* ...] [*Isthmian* 4.34–35]) that the encounter of Ajax and Odysseus in *Iliad* 23.700–739 instances. Here, the two take part in a wrestling contest in honor of their deceased compatriot Patroclus, and Ajax appears at first to have the upper hand—both literally and

12 Nisetich 1989:9.

13 Nisetich 1989:9–11.

14 *Odyssey* 11.469–470, 550–551, cited in Nisetich 1989:9.

15 Nisetich 1989:13.

figuratively—once he has hoisted Odysseus. Odysseus, however, surprises Ajax by hitting him on the back of his knee so that he falls backward; and, not long afterward, Achilles intercedes and awards the same prizes to both warriors. Their next confrontation, which occurs after Achilles' death (and thus without his intervention), is much more one-sided. As Odysseus recalls in *Odyssey* 11.543–551, he and Ajax vie for Achilles' arms; the contest judges—a group of Trojan men and Athena, the goddess of wisdom and war who is known in the *Odyssey* for her partiality to Odysseus—grant him the weapons; and Ajax dies as a result (as the *Aethiopis* makes explicit). Although Odysseus does not describe himself deceiving Ajax in their second struggle, Pindar seems to presume such a stratagem, elaborating the outcome of this engagement—Ajax's suicide—immediately after alluding to Odysseus' underhandedness in their first one. In fact, in Pindar's own retelling in *Nemean* 8 of Ajax and Odysseus' second conflict, the poet accuses Odysseus of swaying the contest judges (who are Achaeans rather than Trojans) with his lies (*Nemean* 8.25–26). The reason Pindar recasts the judges as Achaeans can be inferred from the contrast that Nisetich draws between the Homeric and Pindaric accounts of the contest. On the basis of the scholia to *Odyssey* 11.547, Nisetich deduces that "Agamemnon asked the Trojan captives named together with Athena as judges in line 547 who had hurt them more, Ajax or Odysseus; presumably, Athena moved them to name Odysseus. There is not much room here for the operation of Odysseus' rhetorical skills, of which Pindar makes so much in *Nemean* 8."[16] Pindar, in his quest to demonstrate Odysseus' deceit, thus alters the identity of the judges so that Odysseus has an audience likely to be receptive to his deceptive report of his heroic deeds.

In keeping, then, with the furtiveness for which Odysseus is known, Pindar places him at the periphery of *Isthmian* 4, centering instead on the unfortunate Ajax. And, even when acknowledging Odysseus' acclaim, the poet omits this hero's name (*Isthmian* 4.37). But Pindar makes two motions toward Odysseus. First, Pindar hints in line 39 that Odysseus' heroism extends through "epic poems" (*epéōn*), through the *Iliad* as well as the *Odyssey*. Indeed, if Iliadic Ajax, after his death, appears memorably in the *Odyssey* as Odysseus attempts to reconcile with him (this appearance occasioning Odysseus' remembrance of their last dispute), Odyssean Odysseus advances to the fore in the *Iliad* while still alive. For instance, as Nagy has noticed,[17] even though Odysseus—along with Ajax—originally is assigned to follow Phoenix in the Achaean embassy sent to soothe Achilles after Agamemnon has insulted him, Odysseus ends up at its lead (*Iliad* 9.168–169, 192).

16 Nisetich 1989:17.

17 Nagy 1999:49–50.

Pindar also points to Odysseus by commenting in *Isthmian* 4.40–42 on the persistence and pervasiveness of poetry, for in Pindar's characterization of poetic speech as immortal and spanning the fruitful earth as well as the sea are compressed several of the images that an incognito Odysseus himself once employed in *Odyssey* 19.107–114. Here, disguised as Aethon the beggar, he tells his wife, Penelope, that her glory reaches heaven—as does that of a righteous king for whom the earth produces grain; the trees, fruit; and the sea, fish. This king's identity is evinced by Odysseus' earlier avowal that his own glory extends to heaven, and by the abundance of his orchards (*Odyssey* 9.20, 24.336–344).

For his part, Pindar, by suggesting in *Isthmian* 4 that his patron Melissus has two faces (both Odysseus' and Ajax's), can exalt through imitation the *Odyssey* as much as the *Iliad*. Pindar's perspective on the parity of these epics also informs his equal address in *Isthmian* 4.45–47 of Melissus' leonine bravery and vulpine craftiness, for the poet's focus here on his patron's "heart" (*thumòn*) and "cunning" (*mē̂tin*) harks back to the Homeric opposition between the heroes of the *Iliad* and the *Odyssey*. While Achilles is labeled "lionhearted" (*thumoléonta*) and likened to a "lion" (*léōn*) that "has given way to its great power and bold heart" (*... megálēi te bíēi kaì agḗnori thumō̂i / eíxas ...*), Odysseus is tagged not only as *polúmētis* (crafty in many ways), but also as *poikilomḗtēs* (crafty in various ways) (*Iliad* 7.228; 24.41, 42–43; 1.311; *Odyssey* 2.173; *Iliad* 11.482; *Odyssey* 3.163)—an even more meaningful epithet in light of the fact that *poikílos* (subtle) is among "[t]he most common adjectives applied to the fox."[18]

Even though Pindar alludes to the opposition between Achilles and Odysseus in the course of characterizing Melissus, the poet prefaces his praise by commenting on the conflict between Ajax and Odysseus, because it is better suited to the immediate purpose of the poem—honoring Melissus for his military prowess. The bouts between Ajax and Odysseus in the *Iliad* and *Odyssey* pit brawn against brain. While these epics oppose Achilles and Odysseus on a similar basis (the distinction between their respective attributes of *bíē* and *mē̂tis* being a topos treated by Nagy[19]), the heroes' sole face-off—an altercation in *Odyssey* 8.75–77—is verbal rather than martial, and thus is less appropriate than Ajax and Odysseus' encounters as an emblem of Melissus' capabilities in combat.

The only other evidence of Pindar's employment of the plural form of *épos* to indicate a particular epic occurs in the *Varia Historia* of Roman writer Aelian (ca. 170–235 CE), who cites Pindar's pronouncement that "[Homer,] lacking the means to marry his daughter off, gave her the *Cypria* epic to have as her dowry" (*[Hómēros] aporō̂n ekdoûnai tḕn thugatéra, édōken autē̂i proîka ékhein tà épē tà Kúpria*)

[18] Detienne and Vernant 1978:35.

[19] Nagy 1999:45–49, 61, 147, 317–321.

(Pindar fragment 265, quoted in *Varia Historia* 9.15). Although the original context of Pindar's comment currently is unavailable, this fragment probably is not part of anything tantamount to his treatment of the transmission of the *Iliad* and *Odyssey*. Unlike the aforementioned excerpts from *Nemean* 2 and *Isthmian* 4, which evince Pindar's efforts to procure for himself the prestige of performers of the *Iliad* and *Odyssey*, his remark on Homer's handing down of the *Cypria* (a Cyclic epic) seems simply to be a statement of fact. If, from Pindar's perspective, the *Iliad* and *Odyssey* are immortal poems on a par with their prefacing prayers to Zeus (the king of the gods), the *Cypria* is a commodity in a human transaction. Pindar thus places the *Iliad* and *Odyssey* in a celestial sphere consonant with his own lofty poetic aspirations, but relegates the *Cypria* to a mundane realm consistent with quotidian concerns. Hence the relevance of classicist Edward Fitch's assertion "To say that Pindar knew and followed the *Cypria* and held the *Cypria* to be Homeric is not to affirm that the *Cypria* was as great as the *Iliad* [or, for that matter, the *Odyssey*], or that Pindar was undiscerning."[20]

Herodotus' attribution of the *Iliad* and *Odyssey*

The *Iliad* and *Odyssey* also are elevated above Cyclic epics in Herodotus' *Histories*, albeit in another way. While he does not distinguish what he sees as the best epics from others in the *Histories* on the basis of literary merits,[21] he conveys his preferences through his attribution of the epics.[22] The power of attribution has been theorized by philosopher Michel Foucault, for whom "an author's name ... serves as a means of classification," as it "can group together a number of texts and thus differentiate them from others" because of being one of the determinants of "[t]he meaning and value attributed to [a] text."[23] The appellation whose ascription carried such a cachet in Herodotus' time was "Homer," as the *Histories* make clear. Although Herodotus credits the contemporaries Hesiod and Homer[24] with "creating genealogies of gods for the Greeks, giving those gods their names, specifying their spheres of influence and skills, and indicating their appearances" (*poiḗsantes theogoníēn Héllēsi kaì toîsi theoîsi tàs epōnumías dóntes kaì timás te kaì tékhnas dielóntes kaì eídea autôn sēmḗnantes*) (*Histories* 2.53.2), Homer

20 Fitch 1924:65.

21 Pfeiffer 1968–1976, vol. 1:44–45.

22 As classicist Barbara Graziosi (2002:168) has observed, "discussions about authors were a powerful way of expressing thoughts about [Archaic epic] poetry, especially at a time in which written texts were not the focus of attention."

23 Foucault 1977:123, 126.

24 By Herodotus' reckoning, Hesiod and Homer belong to the ninth century BCE, preceding him by no more than four centuries (*Histories* 2.53.2). Most scholars today, however, would place Hesiod's poetry after Homer's, in the early seventh century BCE. For perhaps the most vociferous dissenting view, see M. L. West's (1966:46–47) prolegomena to the *Theogony*.

seems to have a stronger hold on this historian than does Hesiod. In Herodotus' eyes, Homer's expertise applies to the everyday and the exotic alike.

More precisely, Herodotus reports in *Histories* 7.161.3 that *Iliad* 2.552–554 was cited by the Athenian representative in the Greek delegation sent to Sicily before the Greeks defeated the Persians at sea at Salamis in 480 BCE, in support of his opposition to Sicilian command of the Athenian navy. In this excerpt from the *Iliad*, the Athenian leader Menestheus is praised for his military prowess:

> *tō̂n aûth' hēgemóneu' huiòs Peteō̂o Menestheús.*
> *tō̂i d' oú pṓ tis homoîos epikhthónios génet' anḕr*
> *kosmē̂sai híppous te kaì anéras aspidiṓtas·*
>
> what is more, these [young Athenian men] were led by Peteus' son,
> Menestheus.
> And there was no man at all on earth
> who could array horses and shield-carrying men as he could ...
>
> *Iliad* 2.552–554

In referring to this passage, Herodotus' Athenian delegate evokes *Iliad* 2.556 (where Menestheus is said to have led a force of fifty ships) and thereby counters the inferior alternative of Sicilian supervision.

In addition to mentioning this Athenian referencing of Menestheus' heroism, Herodotus himself adduces *Odyssey* 4.85 to bolster his belief that Scythian bovines are hornless because they are subject to harsh weather (*Histories* 4.29). Herodotus thus contrasts the frigid Scythian climate with the heat in Libya, "where lambs become horned soon after they are born" (*hína t' árnes áphar keraoì teléthousi*) (*Odyssey* 4.85). In a comment on *Histories* 4.29, classicists W. W. How and J. Wells opine that "H[erodotus] uses Homer as [thei]r [English] ancestors used the Bible, to prove everything."[25] Indeed, Herodotus' references to the *Iliad* and the *Odyssey* for his culture's last words on Athenian authority and cornute physiology, respectively, lend credence to classicist Eric A. Havelock's concept of the "Homeric Encyclopedia"—his idea that "in the compendious epic[s] of Homer [are] contained all philosophy and all history and all science."[26]

Like Pindar, Herodotus does not denote only the *Iliad* and *Odyssey* with the plural of *épos*. Yet the historian differs from the poet in his means of setting apart these epics from their Cyclic counterparts. Whereas Pindar reserves for the *Iliad* and *Odyssey* the kind of praise that he hopes that his own compositions will

25 How and Wells 1912, vol. 1:4.29n.
26 Havelock 1963:61, 292.

elicit eventually, Herodotus regards the two poems as the only epics that Homer authored indubitably, and thereby calls into question Homer's connection to the Cyclic poems. For example, Herodotus observes that Homer has mentioned the Hyperboreans in the *Epigoni*, but quickly qualifies this statement with the phrase "if in fact Homer composed this epic" (*ei dḕ tõi eónti ge Hómēros taûta tà épea epoíēse*) (*Histories* 4.32). In the case of the *Cypria*, moreover, Herodotus does not merely interrogate, but rather altogether denies, Homeric authorship: "[T]he *Cypria* epic is not by Homer but by someone else" (*ouk Homḗrou tà Kúpria épeá esti all' állou tinós*) (*Histories* 2.117).

Herodotus' suspicions about the origins of the Cyclic epics suggest that "the Homeric epics" (*tõn Homēreíōn epéōn*) whose recitation he says King Cleisthenes cuts off in his city, Sicyon, "because the Argives and Argos are exalted almost throughout them" (*hóti Argeîoí te kaì Árgos tà pollà pánta humnéatai*) include at least the *Iliad* and the *Odyssey* (*Histories* 5.67.1): "[T]he constant use [in the *Iliad* and the *Odyssey*] of 'Argives' for Greeks, and the position of Agamemnon as overlord of Sicyon, would be an offence to Cleisthenes, [even if] it [is] ... probable that H[erodotus] here [in *Histories* 5.67.1] ... refers to the Thebais[, a Cyclic epic] which began *Árgos áeide, théa, poludípsion* ['Sing, goddess, of parched Argos ...'], and to the Epigoni[,] in which Adrastus must have played a great part."[27] Although Adrastus the Argive, whose worship Cleisthenes seeks to stop in Sicyon (*Histories* 5.67), figures prominently in the *Thebais* as well as in the *Epigoni*, Herodotus was less likely to ascribe to Homer these epics than the *Iliad* and the *Odyssey*. Moreover, Adrastus also appears in *Iliad* 2.572, as Sicyon's first king.

Another way in which Herodotus highlights the Homeric composition of the *Iliad* and *Odyssey* is by coining terms for this type of poetry and its maker.[28] Herodotus invents the new genre name as he speculates that Homer heard the story of how Proteus had hosted Helen of Sparta in Memphis, but did not include this tale in the *Iliad* "because it was not as well suited to an *epic poem* as the other [story] of which he did make use" (*ou gàr homoíōs es tḕn* epopoiíēn *euprepḕs ẽn tõi hetérōi tõi per ekhrḗsato*) (*Histories* 2.116.1 [emphasis added]). Herodotus dubs Homer an "epic poet" (*epopoiòs*) in the course of citing his praise of Athenian power in the *Iliad* (*Histories* 7.161.3). The application of these two new terms (*epopoiíē* and *epopoiós*) in connection to the *Odyssey* as well as to the *Iliad* is implied both by Herodotus' inclusion of Odyssean as well as Iliadic passages as he presents Homer's references to Helen's stay in Egypt, soon after employing the word *epopoiíēn* (the singular accusative form of *epopoiíē*); and by the similar way in which Herodotus relies on the *Odyssey* for rhetorical support as he does

27 How and Wells 1912, vol. 2:5.67.1n.
28 LSJ, s.vv. "*epopoiía*," "*epopoiós*."

on the *Iliad*, whose source he sees as the aforementioned *epopoiós* (*Iliad* 6.289–292 and *Odyssey* 4.227–230, 351–352, quoted in *Histories* 2.116.3–5). In How and Wells' estimation, the Odyssean extracts "are probably interpolations," as Herodotus does not go on to discuss them.[29] But, even if Herodotus himself did not adduce any of the *Odyssey* to demonstrate what an epic poem entailed, the fact that some redactor of his deemed Odyssean material appropriate to incorporate into his description is telling. If, in this regard, "the question to ask is not where the disparate elements originated, but why they were put together, and why kept together,"[30] at least one answer is that, in light of the remainder of the *Histories*, the *Odyssey* exemplifies Homer's epic poetry no less than does the *Iliad*, and thus contains the kind of plot elements that Herodotus would have expected to find in one of Homer's epic poems.

Herodotus, by adding forms of the verb *poiéō* (to make) to the noun *épos* to create the compounds *epopoiós* and *epopoiíē*, emphasizes the process of producing epic poems and thus calls attention to their composer, Homer. Thus, in Herodotus' eyes, as in those of his precursor Pindar, Homer appears already to have assumed the cloak of a "culture hero" whose existence has been explained by Nagy:

> For the ancient Greeks, ... Homer was not just the creator of epic par excellence: he was also the culture hero of epic itself. Greek institutions tend to be traditionally retrojected, by the Greeks themselves, each to a protocreator, a culture hero who is credited with the sum total of a given cultural institution. It was a common practice to attribute any major achievement of society, even if this achievement may have been realized only through a lengthy period of social evolution, to the episodic and personal accomplishment of a culture hero who is pictured as having made his monumental contribution in an earlier era of the given society. Greek myths about lawgivers, for example, whether the lawgivers are historical figures or not, tend to reconstruct these figures as the originators of the sum total of customary law as it evolved through time. So also with Homer: he is retrojected as the original genius of epic.[31]

And, just as Homer is the paragon of epic poets for Pindar and Herodotus, the *Iliad* and *Odyssey* are their ideal epics.[32]

[29] How and Wells 1912, vol. 1:2.116.4n.
[30] O'Flaherty 1973:12.
[31] Nagy 1996b:21.
[32] An earlier version of the current chapter's remainder has appeared in Pathak 2013:37–43.

The Ongoing Elevation of the *Iliad* and *Odyssey* in the Twentieth Century

The emphasis that Pindar and Herodotus place on this pair of poems echoes in recent criticism. Twentieth-century critics, like the early exponents of Homer, single (or perhaps double) the *Iliad* and *Odyssey* out from the Greek epic corpus, with labels as lofty as "the noble epithets"[33] that the two poems themselves employ. On epic epithets, classicist G. S. Kirk comments: "The use of conventional decorative epithets is an essential part of the Greek epic style, and lends to the Homeric poetry much of its rich and formal texture. Each individual character, object or event is treated as a perfect member of its species, and is expressed in the way determined as best for the species as a whole. This tendency to describe individuals in generic terms implies a certain way of looking at things: a simplified, synthetic way."[34] Seen in such a way, the *Iliad* and *Odyssey* are "great epics,"[35] "monumental compositions"[36] of "influence."[37]

In comparison suffer their successors, the Cyclic epics. In the current absence of these works, contemporary critics assume that ancient exegetes assessed the poems correctly. On this assessment, the Cyclic epics are dismissed as being derivative: "Aristotle, Callimachus, and everyone else who mentions the Epic Cycle poems remark on their obvious inferiority to the Homeric poems. They seem to have been composed in order to create a chronology in epic narrative of all the events from the origin of the world to the death of Odysseus, which is what we might call the end of the heroic period."[38] Earlier, Kirk similarly asserts that these works were "designed [expressly] to fill gaps left by Homer, ... to fill in those aspects of the Trojan adventure not described in the Iliad or Odyssey."[39]

Seeing the Cyclic epics simply as supplements to the *Iliad* and *Odyssey* allows their modern readers to elevate this pair of earlier poems above subsequent works. From the perspective of these interpreters, not only were the Cyclic epics "clearly inferior to the *Iliad* and *Odyssey*," but the "distinction between Homeric and Cyclic [works] ... was due to the exceptional genius that went into the creation of the two Homeric epics."[40] This perspective thus proceeds from the assumption that the *Iliad* and the *Odyssey* are *magna opera sui generis*, the acme

33 Crotty 1994:159.
34 Kirk 1962:80.
35 Kirk 1962:159, 265; Griffin 1977:39, 52; Thalmann 1984:182.
36 Nagy 1999:15; Redfield 1983:218; Pucci 1987:18.
37 Griffin 1987:86.
38 Beye 1993:30.
39 Kirk 1962:98, 254.
40 Griffin 1977:52, 53.

of all poetic compositions past and to come: "The utter collapse of the creative epic spirit as shown in the poetry of the Epic Cycle, if we base our opinion of the merits of these poems on the estimate of competent ancient authorities, shows that Homer had no successors. The Iliad and the Odyssey represent the golden age of epic poetry, and golden ages are always brief."[41] At least part of the luster of the Homeric poems is lent by their "Panhellenic" outlook. While the Cyclic epics take up topics local to particular city-states, the *Iliad* and *Odyssey* meld the traditions of these areas into an amalgam that reflects local colors in the light of close examination, but that combines them to emit a characteristic spectrum.[42]

Yet separating the Homeric epics radically from their Cyclic counterparts uproots both sets of poems from the common ground of their shared mythological tradition. While both the Homeric and the Cyclic works likely grew at least partly independently out of an older body of heroic stories, considering the *Iliad* and *Odyssey* as this corpus' crowning glory requires reconceiving and relocating the Cyclic epics as limbs newly added to connect the Homeric canopy to its onetime trunk. In this misguiding light, the Cyclic poems seem to have been transplanted after the fact, as missing links between the Homeric epics and their narrative antecedents. More likely, however, the Cyclic epics are the younger offshoots of a largely separate branch belonging to the same storied tree.[43]

Misconstruing the relationship between the Homeric and Cyclic epics as one of sheer dependence of the latter on the former offers the distinct advantage of pinpointing in the *Iliad* and *Odyssey* the pinnacle of the ancient Greek poetic tradition. To this effect, classicist Cedric H. Whitman suggests that, in spite of subsequent literary production, the Homeric epics endure as their culture's most prominent representatives: "In the long run, both *Iliad* and *Odyssey* contributed their share to the perfecting of what we call the classical spirit. Embodying as they do the polarities of that spirit, they remain for us the archetypes of the Classical, the Hellenic."[44] In the eyes of yet other readers, including classicist Charles Rowan Beye, the influence of the Homeric epics is even wider, crossing cultural and temporal divides. Thus, "for [these] literary historians and theorists the very notion of epic poetry ultimately derives from the Homeric texts."[45]

41 Scott 1921:243.

42 On this striking contrast between the Homeric and Cyclic epics, see Huxley 1969, Finley 1978:73, and Nagy 1999:7–8 and 2005:85, 86.

43 Burgess 2001:1, 5, 174–175, 134–145, 154–156. For an overview of the differences between the Homeric and Cyclic epics, see Burgess 2005:350–351.

44 Whitman 1958:309.

45 Beye 1993:x.

But, although Whitman and Beye consider the *Iliad* and *Odyssey* to be prototypes, these critics do not claim that the poems possess no predecessors. While Whitman emphasizes the immense contribution that the *Iliad* and *Odyssey* have made to ancient Greek culture, he acknowledges their own debt to earlier works. In a later study, he states: "Homer's poems bear on every page the tokens of oral composition within a traditional verse medium reaching back for centuries into the unexplorable dimness of the Indo-European past."[46] By the same "tokens," Beye allows that "one may argue that the Greeks inherited epic poetry in dactylic hexametric rhythm from their Indo-European ancestors," even after he has identified the Homeric works as the source of the epic idea.[47]

The *Iliad* and *Odyssey* thus imitate as well as innovate, as their identification as epics implies. As a particular kind of composition, the *Iliad* and *Odyssey* resemble poems that preceded them, but at the same time have brought to the literary world something new that has become inextricable from the idea of what an epic is. This apparent paradox of originary model poems made in the mold of older ones usefully highlights the constructed character of the Homeric compositions' archetypicality. Recognizing that the *Iliad* and *Odyssey* themselves have poetic ancestors, in spite of being represented as the first forebears of a poetic tradition, reveals that interpretative pains have been taken to portray the Homeric poems as prototypes. This portrayal probably arose from two attributes of the *Iliad* and *Odyssey*. First, they are the earliest attested works of ancient Greek literature, so critics studying this corpus conveniently see these extant compositions as its head and ascribe an identity to this body on the basis of the poem pair's features. Second, the *Iliad* and *Odyssey* have long inspired aesthetic appreciation, and thus seem to be suitable exemplars for subsequent literary efforts.[48] Even if somehow recovered and proved to precede the Homeric poems, the Cyclic epics would be hard pressed to dethrone them as standards of artistic beauty, because—no matter what current critics beheld—they probably would still heed the dissatisfaction with the Cyclic poems that has been resounding for centuries.

The longstanding influence that the *Iliad* and *Odyssey* have had on later literary composition and criticism explains why identifying what these works contribute to the conception of epic that they inaugurated is important. This conception—which would serve as a standard of composition and comparison

46 Whitman 1982:92.

47 Whitman 1982:92; Beye 1993:5.

48 If imitation is the sincerest form of flattery, then the Homeric poems have been complimented constantly as primary epics by the conscious composition of secondary, tertiary, quaternary, and quinary epics on the Homeric pair's basis over succeeding centuries. For a survey of such developments, see Preminger et al. 1993, s.v. "EPIC."

not only for ancient Greek authors and exegetes, but also for their counterparts in later periods and other lands—can be clarified by applying philosopher Panayot Butchvarov's idea of generic identity.

Generic identity and the Homeric epics

"Generic identity" is a relationship between the quality of one individual and the quality of another, such that the characteristic specific to each quality (and thus not possessed by the other) depends logically on the characteristic that these qualities share (i.e. their generic characteristic). In the "classical example of [the] generic identity ... of an equilateral [triangle] and an isosceles triangle," the generic characteristic common to the qualities of these figures (which are equilateral triangularity and isosceles triangularity) is triangularity itself, and the specific characteristic of each quality (having three equal sides in the case of equilateral triangularity or having two equal sides in the case of isosceles triangularity) is contingent on the generic characteristic (triangularity). Therefore, equilateral triangularity and isosceles triangularity are generically, though not specifically, identical.[49]

This account of generic identity applies to the classification of the *Iliad* and *Odyssey* as epics. "Iliadness" and "Odysseyness," the respective qualities of the Homeric poems, share "epicness," their generic characteristic; and the specific characteristics of these qualities—namely, being unique to the *Iliad* and being unique to the *Odyssey*—are a subset of epicness.

Also pertinent to the equation of epic poetry and the Homeric texts is another aspect of generic identity: the fact that the quality of an individual has a generic characteristic means that this quality must have only one of a limited range of specific characteristics. Stated another way, the quality's generic characteristic must manifest as one of the specific characteristics that the quality can possess. Take, for example, triangles again: "[W]hile an instance of being a figure enclosed by three lines need not be an instance of equilateral triangularity, it must be an instance of *some* one of the logically possible species of being a figure enclosed by three lines, i.e., the lengths of its three sides must be proportioned in one of the several ways which alone are logically possible. It cannot be an instance of triangularity unless it is an instance ... of equilateral or isosceles or scalene triangularity."[50] For those who see epic poetry and the Homeric works as being synonymous, the generic characteristic of epicness is instantiated in Iliadness or Odysseyness. Epicness, or the conception of epic that originates with the Homeric works, is constructed from the attributes common

[49] Butchvarov 1966:163–164, 165.

[50] Butchvarov 1966:164, 166.

to the *Iliad* and the *Odyssey*, and therefore amounts to the overlap of Iliadness and Odysseyness. Inspecting the features shared by the Homeric poems shows that these traits compose portraits of epic form and content.

Epicness in form

The form that epic assumes consists in similarities between the *Iliad* and the *Odyssey* in scale, structure, and style. In scale, the compositions are extensive, each containing twenty-four books averaging somewhat fewer than 660 lines each in the *Iliad* and more than 500 lines each in the *Odyssey*. Yet the epics' extent is a matter not merely of length but additionally of depth. If "[e]verything is presented [in the poems] on a huge canvas[,] ... sketched in ... large outlines,"[51] these lines have been filled in with detailed designs rather than broad brush-strokes. The expanse of the epics' forests fails to overshadow the intricacy of the veins in their trees' leaves.

The extent of the epics is supported by their structure—an outgrowth of repetition, ring composition, and multiplication. About one-third of the lines in the *Iliad* appear elsewhere in the poem, and the same goes for the *Odyssey*. Additionally, the story line of each epic comes full circle. For instance, the *Iliad*'s first and last books both feature an angry Achilles speaking with his mother, divine Thetis, the sea nymph who intercedes for him with Zeus. Similarly, the *Odyssey* opens and closes with the goddess Athena descending from Mount Olympus to the island of Ithaca in order to aid Odysseus and his son Telemachus. Yet, as patly as the epics end, they delay their denouements, sustaining narrative tension through their twenty-second books' climaxes. What postpones the peaking of the epics' plots until the eleventh hour is the incessant interposition of episodes. In each poem, approximately twenty-two hundred lines separate the turning point from the climax, so there is a similar prolonging of the plot line between Odysseus' return to his palace and slaying of the suitors in the *Odyssey* as between Achilles' decision to avenge Patroclus and assailing of Hector in the *Iliad*.[52]

Thus, the structure of the Homeric epics is such that audiences wending their way through the woods of the *Iliad* and of the *Odyssey* retrace some steps and sidetrack while circumambulating. Beneath the strollers' feet, both paths parallel the styles of these poems, and thus are made of the same materials. The *Iliad* and the *Odyssey* exhibit like styles, relying on like types of poetic formulae and language.

51 Scott 1921:267.
52 Scott 1921:262–263, 257–258.

Epicness in content

The ground common to the epic forests that underlies their trees, as well as their paths, is their poetic tradition. The plot of this land on which the *Iliad* and the *Odyssey* stand yields four types of trees, four themes that constitute columns of epic content:

1. The hero's need to separate himself from his social surroundings
2. His social surroundings' destabilization by conflict
3. His ability to reorder his life
4. His mortal limits

To make a name for himself, an epic hero has to act exceptionally. Yet action in the epics is inextricable from a nexus of social relationships. The strong connections between warriors and their families and compatriots put recognizable faces on the society that would celebrate the successes of these fighters or deride their defeats, and provide a social context for the men's individual deeds.[53] A man who hopes to be a hero, however, can cement his local status only by isolating himself from others:

> Whether for wealth or reputation or by a code that demands leadership in adventure, a hero cannot tamely stay home. In the so-called shame-society and at a time before the protections of formal law, a man's standing with dependents and rivals turns on his will to demonstrate his power. Nothing will protect him if he fails to do so. But if he leaves home, he moves into a world the width and complexity of which only the gods fully know, yet which as a man of position he expects to master. The task will prove impossible on those assumptions. Great heroes will owe their fame to their self-fidelity in face of the fact. True to themselves, they will have moved out toward command and glory and will die when it becomes evident that safe return was not among the first conditions. On this view, the *Iliad* as much as the *Odyssey* concerns the relationship of home to the world. Both poems turn on the hard paradox that to stay home will, by a man's loss of wealth and reputation, undermine home and obscure its relation to the gods' wide world, yet to venture out will reveal enormity and danger and make return unlikely.[54]

[53] Dodds 1951:17–18; Crotty 1994:211.
[54] Finley 1978:42–43.

Yet venture out the Homeric heroes must, and enter the fights forged by their aspirations, for conflict creates opportunities for these men to prove their martial prowess. While the seizure of the Spartan queen Helen and its aftermath incite Achilles to lay down the lives of legions as well as his own on the Trojan battlefield, the encroachment of the suitors upon Odysseus' Ithacan estate spurs him to slaughter them after his arduous journey home.

However, even though the heroes ultimately mend rends in their societies' social fabrics by working to reunite Helen and Penelope with their husbands, there is more to the *Iliad* and the *Odyssey* than their third "theme of restored order."[55] The paradox in which the poems' heroes are placed as they exchange the ill-regarded security of home for the prestigious prospect of faraway success that necessarily remains unreachable has even larger implications to which classicist John H. Finley, Jr., has pointed. Once epic heroes leave home, they strive to prove themselves while discovering that they are less than divine.[56] Whitman develops this idea by describing these characters' condition as "the heroic paradox," the contradiction that they live as they attempt to emulate gods, in spite of confronting human constraints.[57] The route to which Achilles and Odysseus resort in order to escape this paradox is a path to poetic immortality. Although the men themselves cannot elude death, they can achieve *kléos*—and thereby live on in epic song.

Nevertheless, the Homeric heroes do not transcend their paradox, which actually is a prerequisite of their stories. Epics, as Doniger has discussed, are associated intimately with myths, narratives that "raise religious questions" and that "wrestle with insoluble paradoxes[—]as [anthropologist] Claude Lévi-Strauss noted long ago[—that] they inevitably fail to pin ... to the mat."[58] If, as Lévi-Strauss asserts, "the purpose of myth is to provide a logical model capable of overcoming a contradiction (an impossible achievement if, as it happens, the contradiction is real),"[59] and if the *Iliad* and the *Odyssey* address the heroic paradox, then it makes sense that these epics (like their counterparts in other cultures) feature, in Doniger's words, "the constant interaction of the two planes, the human and the divine,"[60] without allowing them to merge. By interacting with their anthropomorphic gods, Achilles and Odysseus become aware of the full measure of the power which they themselves may aspire to, if only imperfectly personify.

55 Finley 1978:194.
56 Finley 1978:211.
57 Whitman 1982:25, 22.
58 Doniger 1998:9, 2, 95.
59 Lévi-Strauss 1963:229.
60 Doniger 1998:9.

Although Olympus-like heights lie off-limits to Achilles and Odysseus, the *Iliad* and *Odyssey* occupy a privileged place atop their poetic tradition. Yet losing sight of the critical influences that have lifted them above other literary works leaves the Homeric poems aloft at an Archimedean point in the heavens, with these epics' connections to subsequent texts unwitnessed. Seeing such works as the *Iliad* and *Odyssey* as nearly unreachable benchmarks of the epic genre has two drawbacks, as classicist J. B. Hainsworth has observed. First, such single-minded sight blinds onlookers to later uses of the term "epic" in senses that may be separate from the poems that first bear its standard. Second, the spectators regard as deficient those works that differ from these Platonic forms of epics.[61]

These two problems threaten to cloud the surroundings of the Homeric poems in such a way that they seem likely to soar in mid-air, above not only other texts of the same tradition, but also similar texts of other traditions. Fortunately, however, the fresh zephyrs of two analyses keep clear the epics' rarified air, and account for their abstraction from works of their own and other cultures. One analysis, involving generic identity, has shown how the notion of epic has been built from the attributes of the *Iliad* and *Odyssey*, rather than from the attributes of later Greek texts, and thus indicates that this concept could be reconstructed from the characteristics of other apparently ur-works. The other analysis, which will make use of metaphor, will exhibit the reconstruction of the epic idea on the basis of two ancient Indian poems. Thus, I will turn to these works, the *Rāmāyaṇa* and the *Mahābhārata*, in Chapter 2.

61 Hainsworth 1991:3–4.

2

The Epic Metaphor of the *Rāmāyaṇa* and *Mahābhārata*

Ānandavardhana and Rājaśekhara's Expedient Influence

LIKE THE *ILIAD* AND *ODYSSEY*, the *Rāmāyaṇa* and *Mahābhārata* are now considered to be epics. Yet this label does not suit the Sanskrit poems as well as it does the Greek works, for Sanskrit, unlike Greek, has no etymon for the word "epic." Even so, the application of this term to the *Rāmāyaṇa* and the *Mahābhārata* by their twentieth-century interpreters recalls in one respect the assignment of other rubrics to these texts by their earlier exegetes: in both cases, literary critics each use a shorthand for this couplet of compositions that permits their comparison. What necessitates this shorthand are the varieties of ways in which the *Rāmāyaṇa* and the *Mahābhārata* each refer to themselves. Understanding the solution that their recent readers have posed to this problem of the poems' numerous self-portrayals—namely, pairing the poems as epics—requires awareness of similar strategies that these scholars' predecessors adopted, approaches that are rooted in the *Rāmāyaṇa*'s and the *Mahābhārata*'s respective self-representations.

Comprehending how the works have been compared relatively recently, then, calls for study of these self-depictions and of their adoption as categories by Sanskrit-speaking scholars seeking to explicate their sources. In this chapter, I will survey the *Rāmāyaṇa*'s and the *Mahābhārata*'s self-understandings, will show which of these informed medieval Indian interpretations of the poems, and will suggest why modern scholars eventually called them epics. This chapter's threefold focus, like that of Chapter 1, corresponds to what Sanskritist Sheldon Pollock presents as the "three ways of examining ... any ... question in the history of a literary culture[: w]e can listen (1) to the text itself, ... (2) to the tradition of listening to the text, [and] (3) to whatever we can hear in the world outside the text and the tradition."[1] Thus, I turn first to the texts themselves.[2]

1 Pollock 2003:81.

2 In my treatment of the Sanskrit poems, I begin with the *Rāmāyaṇa*, not just because the main events that it relates occur earlier in the Hindu cosmic time cycle than do those depicted by

The *Rāmāyaṇa*'s and the *Mahābhārata*'s Many Self-Designations

The *Rāmāyaṇa* and the *Mahābhārata* are each associated at once with one self-representation and with many self-representations: each poem refers to itself in an array of ways, but emphasizes a particular epithet by illustrating its enactment by the poem's putative composer.[3] The simultaneous plurality and singularity of these poems' self-representations recall the theology of the texts in which these self-designations appear. Both the *Rāmāyaṇa* and the *Mahābhārata* demonstrate what I call a "pointed polytheism," for they portray the acts and worship of numerous deities, but ultimately elevate the preserver god Viṣṇu above the rest.[4] The two texts also exhibit a "pointed poly-auto-onomatism," with each presenting a number of names for itself but implying that one of these is most apt.

The ranges of these poems' rubrics can be seen in Tables 1 and 2. Although a majority of each poem's designations are not adopted by the other (10 of 17 for the *Rāmāyaṇa* and 11 of 18 for the *Mahābhārata*), the pair share seven:

1. *carita* (adventures)
2. *ākhyāna* (tale)
3. *kathā* (narrative)
4. *kāvya* (poem)
5. *itihāsa* (account of the way things had been)
6. *purāṇa* (story of yore)
7. *saṃhitā* (collection)

---

the *Mahābhārata*, but also because the *Mahābhārata*, in the course of telling its own central story, takes these *Rāmāyaṇa* episodes as givens. While there is considerable controversy over the relative dating of these works, their compositions likely overlapped chronologically. For the purposes of this study, then, I assume that the *Rāmāyaṇa* and the *Mahābhārata* were contemporaneous, each composed by *brāhmaṇas* (priests) largely between 200 BCE and 200 CE.

3 While many people contributed to the *Rāmāyaṇa* and the *Mahābhārata* during the centuries over which they were composed, each poem ascribes itself to one author.

4 Religion scholar Nicholas Sutton (2000:146, 203) downplays the *Mahābhārata*'s polytheism by designating the poem's "predominant doctrinal perspective" as "epic monotheism" because it "postulates one Supreme Deity who creates and controls this world whilst remaining aloof and personally transcendent to its fluctuations." In my view, however, the phrase "pointed polytheism," in its suggestion that Viṣṇu plays the leading but not sole role in the universe, applies more readily than "epic monotheism" to the outlooks of the *Rāmāyaṇa* and the *Mahābhārata*—works in which divinities other than Viṣṇu (such as the destroyer god Śiva) figure prominently on occasion. Whereas a pointed polytheism (which assumes that Viṣṇu is paramount only most and not all of the time) can accommodate Śiva's sometime ascendancy quite easily, in this event epic monotheism (which assumes that a god must have all the power in the universe or none) must be reconstituted with Śiva rather than Viṣṇu at its center, as Sutton (2000:184–187, 191, 205, 242) himself finds.

Table 1: Terms That the *Rāmāyaṇa* Uses to Refer to Itself

Sanskrit term	English translation	(Number of) References in critical edition	(Number of) References in supplementary passages
carita	adventures	(6)	(24)
		1.1.77; 1.2.30; 1.4.1, 6, 26	1.29*; 1.44*; 1.152* 2; 1.153*; 1.154* 10, 14; 1.202*; 1.203* 38; 1.205*; 1.215* 10; 1.App. I.1.2, 47; 1.App. I.2.15
			6.3706* 3
		7.85.19	7.1327* 2; 7.1331*; 7.1527* 4; 7.1530* 7; 7.1533* 4; 7.1534* 6; 7.1543* 27, 29, 34; 7.App. I.9.23
ākhyāna	tale	(6)	(16)
		1.1.78; 1.4.11, 20, 25; 1.5.3	1.203* 21; 1.App. I.1.3, 17, 295, 297
			6.3703* 15; 6.3709* 1
		7.100.26	7.1522* 1, 9; 7.1524* 3; 7.1526*; 7.1527* 5; 7.1530* 10; 7.1540* 14, 18; 7.1542* 2
vṛtta	story	(3)	(3)
		1.2.31, 41; 1.3.1	1.195* 11
			6.3708* 4
			7.1336* 2
kathā	narrative	(3)	(12)
		1.2.34, 35, 36	1.4*; 1.5*; 1.13*; 1.203* 18; 1.App. I.1.300
			2.2335* 3
			6.App. I.76.8

Table 1 (*cont.*)

Sanskrit term	English translation	(Number of) References in critical edition	(Number of) References in supplementary passages
kathā (cont.)			7.1464* 2; 7.1467*; 7.1471* 3; 7.1473* 1; 7.1542* 6
kāvya	poem	(11)	(39)
		1.2.34, 40, 41; 1.3.29; 1.4.6, 8, 11, 13	1.151* 1; 1.152* 1; 1.195* 8; 1.197* 2; 1.200* 1; 1.203* 1, 9, 18, 20, 27, 32, 33; 1.206* 1, 4; 1.212* 1; 1.215* 5, 11; 1.219* 2; 1.App. I.1.283; 1.App. I.2.14
			6.3703* 10
		7.84.3; 7.85.17, 18	7.1326* 1, 2; 7.1329* 7; 7.1337* 3; 7.1516* 4; 7.1519* 4; 7.1520* 4; 7.1521* 2; 7.1527* 23; 7.1537* 14; 7.1540* 9; 7.1542* 13; 7.1543* 11, 23; 7.App. I.13.27, 32, 37, 55
geya	ballad	(2)	(4)
			1.217* 4; 1.218*
		7.84.13, 14	7.1338* 2; 7.1339*
vāṇī	composition	(1)	(0)
		7.84.16	---
gīta	song	(3)	(8)
			1.213* 1
		7.85.23; 7.86.1, 2	7.1337* 1, 7; 7.App. I.9.22, 27, 28, 33, 43
itivṛtta	account	(0)	(1)
		---	1.218*

Table 1 (*cont.*)

Sanskrit term	English translation	(Number of) References in critical edition	(Number of) References in supplementary passages
itihāsa	account of the way things had been	(0)	(2)
		---	1.App. I.1.4
			6.3709* 16
saṃbandha	text	(0)	(1)
		---	1.App. I.1.295
purāṇa	story of yore	(0)	(2)
		---	2.2335* 1
			6.3709* 13
ādikāvya	primary poem	(0)	(6)
		---	2.2335* 6
			6.3703* 2; 6.3704* 1
			7.1540* 1; 7.1541* 10; 7.App. I.13.31
saṃhitā	collection	(0)	(2)
		---	6.3709* 5
			7.1540* 16
purātana	hoary story	(0)	(1)
		---	7.1527* 34
likhita	writing	(0)	(1)
		---	7.1537* 1
pāṭhaka	reading	(0)	(1)
		---	7.1540* 20

Table 2: Terms That the *Mahābhārata* Uses to Refer to Itself

Sanskrit term	English translation	(Number of) References in critical edition	(Number of) References in supplementary passages
purāṇa	story of yore	(2)	(0)
		1.1.15; 1.56.15	---
ākhyāna	tale	(21)	(11)
		1.1.16; 1.2.29, 30, 235, 238, 239, 240, 241, 243; 1.53.27, 31, 32, 35; 1.56.1, 30, 32; 1.57.106; 1.93.46	1.20* 1, 5, 6; 1.75*; 1.485* 2; 1.App. I.1.1; 1.App. I.5.16, 21; 1.App. I.32.27
		12.331.2; 12.337.10	
		18.5.53	18.46*; 18.48* 1
itihāsa	account of the way things had been	(14)	(16)
		1.1.17, 24, 52; 1.2.31, 32, 33, 237; 1.54.23; 1.56.16, 18, 19	1.22* 4; 1.25*; 1.App. I.1.45; 1.App. I.32.31; 1.App. I.33.1, 11, 13; 1.App. I.39.13
		18.5.31, 39, 43	18.33* 1; 18.34*; 18.38* 6; 18.App. I.2.1, 5; 18.App. I.3.2, 19, 49
saṃhitā	collection	(3)	(2)
		1.1.19, 51	1.App. I.3.27
		18.5.46	18.56* 2
grantha	book	(2)	(1)
		1.1.48, 51	1.App. I.4.8
upaniṣad	esoteric instruction	(1)	(0)
		1.1.191	---

Table 2 (*cont.*)

Sanskrit term	English translation	(Number of) References in critical edition	(Number of) References in supplementary passages
veda	sacred source	(4)	(2)
		1.1.205; 1.56.17; 1.57.74	
		12.327.18	
			18.32* 1; 18.57*
āgama	scripture	(1)	(0)
		1.2.31	---
upākhyāna	anecdote	(1)	(0)
		1.2.236	---
kathā	narrative	(4)	(9)
		1.53.28, 33; 1.55.3; 1.56.2	1.21* 2, 4; 1.191*; 1.App. I.31.3, 22, 26; 1.App. I.33.7, 20
			18.60* 3
carita	adventures	(4)	(0)
		1.54.18; 1.56.1, 3	---
		18.5.25	
śāstra	treatise	(1)	(2)
		1.56.21	1.186*
			18.App. I.3.31
saṃdarbha	work	(1)	(0)
		18.5.41	---
adhyayana	teaching	(1)	(1)
			1.App. I.5.6
		18.5.45	

Table 2 (*cont.*)

Sanskrit term	English translation	(Number of) References in critical edition	(Number of) References in supplementary passages
sāvitrī	hymn	(1)	(0)
		18.5.51	---
saṃgraha	compilation	(0)	(1)
		---	1.26* 3
kāvya	poem	(0)	(4)
		---	1.187*; 1.App. I.1.13, 34, 35
prabandha	piece	(0)	(1)
		---	1.App. I.5.9

Of these seven labels, two—*kāvya* and *itihāsa*—receive special attention. Realized in the *Rāmāyaṇa*'s and the *Mahābhārata*'s respective depictions of their own makings by mythological men, these two terms are linked inextricably with the poems in whose plots they are featured. Their inextricability from these works accounts for their continued prominence as categories in medieval exegetes' interpretations of the poems.

The *Rāmāyaṇa* as a *kāvya*: An incipient composition of compassion

The *Rāmāyaṇa* opens somewhat startlingly by attributing its story not to the poem's avowed author, the ascetic Vālmīki, but to the celestial sage Nārada, who relates the narrative to Vālmīki (*Rāmāyaṇa* 1.1.1–76). Nārada's interaction with Vālmīki prior to the *Rāmāyaṇa*'s composition—like the dialogue between the creator god Brahmā and Vālmīki described below—may be seen as an instrument by which to infuse the *Rāmāyaṇa* with religious authority from the start.[5] From this perspective, these divinities' depictions would be considered "religious claims" that lend complete credence and prestige to the poem that Vālmīki composes, by associating it with superhuman beings. In doing so,

5 For instance, religion scholar Eric A. Huberman (now known as E. H. Rick Jarow) (1994:18) notes: "Nārada ... is known as the messenger of the gods. His appearance immediately indicates an authorized means of transmission which will validate whatever is to come."

"these claims create the appearance that their authorization [i.e. the authorization that the claims effect] comes from a realm beyond history, society, and politics, beyond the terrain in which interested and situated actors struggle over scarce resources [such as] ... the capacity to speak a consequential speech and to gain a respectful hearing."[6]

Yet, more saliently, Nārada's involvement clarifies the nature of Vālmīki's own contribution. Vālmīki recasts Nārada's rather terse narrative as a *kāvya*, a poem that expresses emotion. The account of how this *kāvya*, the *Rāmāyaṇa*, arises symbolizes its sensitivity to the sentiments that it seeks to convey.

The story of the poem's provenance goes like so:

> *sa muhūrtaṃ gate tasmin devalokaṃ munis tadā |*
> *jagāma tamasātīraṃ jāhnavyās tv avidūrataḥ || ...*
> *tasyābhyāśe tu mithunaṃ carantam anapāyinam |*
> *dadarśa bhagavāṃs tatra krauñcayoś cāruniḥsvanam ||*
> *tasmāt tu mithunād ekaṃ pumāṃsaṃ pāpaniścayaḥ |*
> *jaghāna vairanilayo niṣādas tasya paśyataḥ ||*
> *taṃ śoṇitaparītāṅgaṃ veṣṭamānaṃ mahītale |*
> *bhāryā tu nihataṃ dṛṣṭvā rurāva karuṇāṃ giram ||*
> *tathā tu taṃ dvijaṃ dṛṣtvā niṣādena nipātitam |*
> *ṛṣer dharmātmanas tasya kāruṇyaṃ samapadyata ||*
> *tataḥ karuṇaveditvād adharmo 'yam iti dvijaḥ |*
> *niśāmya rudatīṃ krauñcīm idaṃ vacanam abravīt ||*
> *mā niṣāda pratiṣṭhāṃ tvam agamaḥ śāśvatīḥ samāḥ |*
> *yat krauñcamithunād ekam avadhīḥ kāmamohitam ||*
> *tasyaivaṃ bruvataś cintā babhūva hṛdi vīkṣataḥ |*
> ***śokā**rtenāsya śakuneḥ kim idaṃ vyāhṛtaṃ mayā ||*
> *cintayan sa mahāprājñaś cakāra matimān matim |*
> *śiṣyaṃ caivābravīd vākyam idaṃ sa munipuṃgavaḥ ||*
> *pādabaddho 'kṣarasamas tantrīlayasamanvitaḥ |*
> ***śokā**rtasya pravṛtto me **śloko** bhavatu nānyathā || ...*
> *ājagāma tato brahmā lokakartā svayaṃ prabhuḥ |*
> *caturmukho mahātejā draṣṭuṃ taṃ munipuṃgavam || ...*
> *upaviṣṭe tadā tasmin sākṣāl lokapitāmahe |*
> *tadgatenaiva manasā vālmīkir dhyānam āsthitaḥ ||*
> *pāpātmanā kṛtaṃ kaṣṭaṃ vairagrahaṇabuddhinā |*
> *yas tādṛśaṃ cāruravaṃ krauñcaṃ hanyād akāraṇāt ||*
> ***śocann** eva muhuḥ krauñcīm upa **ślokam** imaṃ punaḥ |*

6 Lincoln 1994:112.

jagāv antargatamanā bhūtvā ***śoka****parāyaṇaḥ ||*
tam uvāca tato brahmā *prahasan* *munipuṃgavam |*
śloka *eva tvayā baddho nātra kāryā vicāraṇā ||*
macchandād eva te brahman pravṛtteyaṃ sarasvatī |
rāmasya caritaṃ sarvaṃ kuru tvam ṛṣisattama ||
dharmātmano guṇavato loke rāmasya dhīmataḥ |
vṛttaṃ kathaya dhīrasya yathā te nāradāc chrutam ||
rahasyaṃ ca prakāśaṃ ca yad vṛttaṃ tasya dhīmataḥ |
rāmasya sahasaumitre rākṣasānāṃ ca sarvaśaḥ ||
vaidehyāś caiva yad vṛttaṃ prakāśaṃ yadi vā rahaḥ |
tac cāpy aviditaṃ sarvaṃ viditaṃ te bhaviṣyati ||
na te vāg anṛtā kāvye kācid atra bhaviṣyati |
kuru rāmakathāṃ puṇyāṃ ***śloka****baddhāṃ* *manoramām* *||*
yāvat sthāsyanti girayaḥ saritaś ca mahītale |
tāvad rāmāyaṇakathā lokeṣu pracariṣyati ||
yāvad rāmasya ca kathā tvatkṛtā pracariṣyati |
tāvad ūrdhvam adhaś ca tvaṃ mallokeṣu nivatsyasi ||
ity uktvā bhagavān brahmā tatraivāntaradhīyata |
tataḥ saśiṣyo vālmīkir munir vismayam āyayau ||
tasya śiṣyās tataḥ sarve jaguḥ ***ślokam*** *imaṃ punaḥ |*
muhur muhuḥ *prīyamāṇāḥ* *prāhuś ca bhṛśavismitāḥ*[7] *||*
samākṣaraiś caturbhir yaḥ pādair gīto maharṣiṇā |
so 'nuvyāharaṇād bhūyaḥ ***śokaḥ śloka****tvam āgataḥ ||*
tasya buddhir iyaṃ jātā vālmīker bhāvitātmanaḥ |
kṛtsnaṃ rāmāyaṇaṃ kāvyam īdṛśaiḥ karavāṇy aham ||
udāravṛttārthapadair *manoramais* *tadāsya rāmasya cakāra kīrtimān |*
samākṣaraiḥ ***śloka****śatair yaśasvino yaśaskaraṃ kāvyam udāradhīr muniḥ ||*

Soon after [Nārada] went to the world of the gods, the ascetic
[Vālmīki]
went to the bank of the Tamasā River, not too far from the Ganges. ...
In that vicinity, the venerable one spied a couple of sweet-sounding
cranes,
who were unflagging in their motion and devotion.
But, as he looked on, an outcast hunter having evil designs
and brimming with hostility smote one of the two, the male.
When his mate saw him downed on the ground, with his contorting
body bathed in blood,

7 The compound *bhṛśavismitāḥ* appears incorrectly as *bhṛśavismatāḥ* in the main text, but correctly in the apparatus.

she cried out compassionately.
And, when the righteous sage saw the bird brought down by the hunter in this way,
compassion came over him.
Then, in the depth of his compassion, the priest thought, "This is unjust!"
As he heard the she-crane shrieking, he said these words:
"You never will have peace, outcast,
because you slew one of the two cranes when he was deluded by desire."
As [the sage] was saying this, and taking everything in, a thought occurred to him:
"What is this that I have said while in the throes of **sorrow** for this bird?"
Thinking it over, that smart man with the powerful intellect understood.
That man, who was the best ascetic of all, said these words to his student:
"Let what I created while in the throes of **sorrow**—a thing that is composed in quarters; that is regular in its number of syllables; and that can be accompanied by song, dance, and stringed instruments—
be known as **verse** and not otherwise." ...
Then lord Brahmā himself—the four-faced, exceedingly splendid creator of the cosmos—came
to see the best ascetic of all. ...
Yet, even with the grandfather of the universe sitting right in front of him at that time,
Vālmīki found his mind wandering back to the earlier events and contemplated them:
"That evil man whose mind had been seized by spite,
who causelessly could kill such a sweet-sounding crane, did wrong."
Sorrowing once more for the she-crane
once he had turned his thoughts inward, he sang that **verse** again while stuck in his **sorrow**[, this time to Brahmā].
Then Brahmā smiled and said to that man who was the best of all ascetics:
"What you have composed is a **verse**. Have no doubt about it.
On account of my desire alone, did you create this eloquent utterance, priest.

Author all the adventures of Rāma, you superlative sage!
Narrate to humankind the story of righteous, virtuous, intelligent, resolute Rāma
just as you have heard it from Nārada.
The public and private story of that intelligent man
Rāma (accompanied by Sumitrā's son [Lakṣmaṇa]), of the surrounding demons,
and of Videha's daughter [Sītā]—whether what happened is common knowledge or a secret—
will be made known to you in its entirety, even that of which you are unaware.
Nothing that you pronounce in this poem will be untrue.
Compose the noteworthy narrative about Rāma that consists of **verses** and that makes hearts happy!
The *Rāmāyaṇa* narrative will make the rounds among human beings
for as long as mountains and rivers remain ranging over the earth.
And you will live in my upper and lower worlds
for as long as the narrative about Rāma that you compose circulates."
After saying this, venerable Brahmā vanished from where he had been.
At this, the ascetic Vālmīki and his students marveled.
Then all his students intoned that **verse** once more.
Again and again, in their delight and extreme amazement, they declared:
"The **sorrow** that has been sung by the great sage into four equisyllabic quarters
has become, through its repeated repetition, **verse**!"
That thoughtful man Vālmīki came to this conclusion:
"Let me compose the whole *Rāmāyaṇa* poem in couplets of this kind."
Then the celebrated, consummately clever ascetic composed the renown-making poem about this renowned man Rāma—
with hundreds of heart-warming, equisyllabic **verses** having elevated words, meanings, and meters.

Rāmāyaṇa 1.2.3, 9–17, 22, 26–41 (emphases mine)

According to this account, the *Rāmāyaṇa kāvya* comes from the critical conversion of Vālmīki's sorrow (*śoka*) into verse (*śloka*).[8] To stress this transformation,

8 Like Sanskritist G. H. Bhatt before them (Bhatt and Shah 1960–1975, critical notes to vol. 1:1.2.17n), Sanskritists Robert P. Goldman and Sally J. Sutherland Goldman (1984–2009,

the poem juxtaposes these two similar-sounding terms (which have been bold-faced in the passage above) at three points: when Vālmīki identifies as verse his poetic outcry over the crane killing, when the sage's persisting sorrow compels him to sing his verse to Brahmā, and when Vālmīki's disciples declare that his sorrow has become verse (*Rāmāyaṇa* 1.2.17, 28, 39).

The poetic process continues even after Vālmīki voices his verse, which (as the underlined words in the above passage indicate) induces delight in all three of his audiences: Brahmā, the sage's students, and all those who hear the couplet in the context of the entire *Rāmāyaṇa* (*Rāmāyaṇa* 1.2.29, 38, 34, 41). Part of the pleasure that Vālmīki's poetry provides indubitably issues from its musical aspects. Like the first verse of this maestro's making, the *Rāmāyaṇa* can be "accompanied by song, dance, and stringed instruments" (*tantrīlayasamanvitam*) (*Rāmāyaṇa* 1.2.17b, 1.4.7d). Additionally, this poem arising from the dying of a bird said twice to have been singing sweetly[9] is said itself to be "sweet when recited and when sung" (*pāṭhye geye ca madhuraṃ*) (*Rāmāyaṇa* 1.2.9, 27; 1.4.7a).

Yet the *Rāmāyaṇa* also is enjoyable insofar as it intriguingly reenacts emotional experiences, and this quality of the *kāvya* accords with its truthfulness and memorability. The veracity of Vālmīki's work inheres not only in its articulation of everything that has happened (and that will happen) to its hero, Rāma (*Rāmāyaṇa* 1.2.34, 30–33; 1.1.76; 1.3.29; 1.4.2), but also in its vivid evocation of the sentiments that the events of his story elicit among those who live through them. Furthermore, the affective profundity of the poem makes it more memorable to the audiences pleasuring in the expanse of its narrative, and thereby ensures its reverberation among the mountain peaks and river creeks that are its contemporaries (*Rāmāyaṇa* 1.2.35).

---

vol. 1:1.2.17n) suggest that, in this passage, *śloka* has its specific sense as a couplet composed in the *anuṣṭubh* meter. The Goldmans note, as does Bhatt, that the paradigmatic verse of Vālmīki's curse (*Rāmāyaṇa* 1.2.14) is in this meter, and do not indicate in their apparatus any shift in *śloka*'s signification. I, however—building on a suggestion made by Sanskritist Barbara Stoler Miller (1973:167)—think that, in this passage, *śloka* is used in its more general sense as any unit of poetry. The passage characterizes *śloka* as a verse form comprising four quarters (or hemistichs) having the same number of syllables (*Rāmāyaṇa* 1.2.39), but nowhere names the *anuṣṭubh* meter nor mentions its characteristic eight-syllable quarter. Moreover, the passage acknowledges in two ways the *Rāmāyaṇa*'s reliance on meters other than the *anuṣṭubh*, the poem's prevailing, but not sole, meter. (For an overview of the *Rāmāyaṇa*'s metrical make-up, see Brockington 1998:373–377.) First, the passage states that the poem's "hundreds of ... verses hav[e] elevated words, meanings, and meters" (*udāravṛttārthapadair ... | ... ślokaśatair ...*) (*Rāmāyaṇa* 1.2.41). (By contrast, Robert P. Goldman renders *udāravṛttārthapadair* here as "words noble in sound and meaning," and thus does not seem to consider as *śloka*s verse forms following non-*anuṣṭubh* meters.) Second, this verse that notes the *Rāmāyaṇa*'s use of more than one meter is itself in the *jagatī* meter (with twelve-syllable quarters) rather than in the *anuṣṭubh*!

9 I owe this observation to Doniger (personal communication, August 4, 2006).

The *Rāmāyaṇa* pairs with its endurance its exemplarity. Implicit in the *Rāmāyaṇa*'s self-description as a "divine primary poem" (*divyaṃ ... ādikāvyaṃ*) is the idea that its god-given durability enables it to epitomize poetry for posterity (*Rāmāyaṇa* 6.3704* 1). As the *ādikāvya* (primary poem), the *Rāmāyaṇa* is the "foremost font for poets" (*paraṃ kavīnām ādhāraṃ*) (*Rāmāyaṇa* 2.2335* 6, 6.3703* 2, 6.3704* 1, 7.1540* 1, 7.1541* 10, 7.App. I.13.31, 1.4.20c). And its author is admired accordingly as the "principal poet" (*prathamakavir*) and the "best of the best poets" (*kavivarapravareṇa*) (*Rāmāyaṇa* 1.10*, 1.11*).

Appreciating Vālmīki's virtuosity requires recognizing the affective resources with which the *Rāmāyaṇa* receptacle is replete. Among its most important contents is the seed of an affective aesthetics that eventually was brought to fruition by belletrists whose contributions I will characterize later in this chapter. At the core of this aesthetics is a concept called *rasa* (essence), which indicates the type of emotion that a piece of poetry arouses. The *Rāmāyaṇa*, by its own account, is "endowed with the humorous, erotic, compassionate, irascible, heroic, fearsome, abhorrent, and additional essences" (*hāsyaśṛṅgārakāruṇyaraudravīrabhayānakaiḥ / bībhatsādirasair yuktaṃ ...*); and one of the work's supplementary passages enumerates as these additional essences the "amazing" (*adbhuta*) and the "peaceful" (*śānta*) (*Rāmāyaṇa* 1.4.8, 1.203* 16).

In addition to listing these literary cues to sentiments, the *kāvya* alludes to the *rasa*s in the anecdote about its own composition. Here the copulating cranes represent the erotic (*śṛṅgāra*) essence; the hostile hunter, the fearsome (*bhayānaka*); the he-crane's broken, bloody body, the abhorrent (*bībhatsa*); the crying she-crane and sympathetic sage, the compassionate (*kāruṇya*); the angry ascetic, the irascible (*raudra*); the tranquillity taken from the hunter, the peaceful (*śānta*); Brahmā's beaming, the humorous (*hāsya*); Rāma's resolve, the heroic (*vīra*); and the deity's disappearance, the amazing (*adbhuta*) (*Rāmāyaṇa* 1.2.9, 14, 10, 27, 11, 11–13, 13–14, 14, 29, 31, 37, 38).

The *Rāmāyaṇa*, for all of its efforts to encompass a range of *rasa*s in its creation scene, stresses the compassionate essence most strongly. The compassion that Vālmīki feels when he witnesses the she-crane's show of compassion for her misfortunate mate is what produces his poetry, and its emotional immediacy is underscored by the *Rāmāyaṇa*'s reenactment of its own origin in affect. The emotion of compassion also is key to the portrayal by the *Rāmāyaṇa* of the affective effect that this *kāvya* seeks to have on its audience.

In order to have this effect in the first place, the *Rāmāyaṇa kāvya* needs to be performed. The performance of the *Rāmāyaṇa* within the *Rāmāyaṇa* itself is made possible by the compassion that Vālmīki evinces on another occasion. The sage kindly takes Sītā in after her husband—Rāma, the king of Ayodhyā—banishes her to the forest so that his subjects no longer will censure him for reaccepting her after the demon Rāvaṇa has kidnapped, confined, and thus come into contact with her (*Rāmāyaṇa* 7.48, 7.44.15–17, 7.42.16–20). When Sītā, who has been completely faithful to Rāma, moves to Vālmīki's hermitage, she already is pregnant with their twin sons (*Rāmāyaṇa* 7.41.20–26).

The names that the twins receive from Vālmīki signal the role that they will play in preserving his great poem. Vālmīki names the elder twin "Kuśa" and the younger "Lava" (*Rāmāyaṇa* 7.58.5–6), and teaches them to recite his *Rāmāyaṇa* in the manner of the wandering poem-performers of classical Indian society who were known as *kuśīlavas*.[10] By the time that the boys are twelve years old (*Rāmāyaṇa* 7.56.16–17; 7.57.1–2; 7.58.1; 7.63.1, 5–7; 7.82.1–3; 7.83.6; 7.84.1–3), they actually recite the *Rāmāyaṇa* to their father during a ritual that he is sponsoring to consolidate his royal power. As Rāma hears the story of his past, present, and future being recounted in unison by his identical twin sons (who look just like him), he learns not only who they are to him but also that he—a human manifestation of Viṣṇu—has been born on earth to save the universe from Rāvaṇa and will be united in heaven with Lakṣmī (who also is known as Śrī), Viṣṇu's divine wife who has appeared on earth as Rāma's queen, Sītā (*Rāmāyaṇa* 7.86.2, 7.88.4, 6.105.25–26, 7.99.6).[11]

Thus, the *Rāmāyaṇa* not only originates in, but also succeeds aesthetically as a consequence of, Vālmīki's compassion. The compassion that Vālmīki shows to Sītā and her sons allows him to create the ideal conditions for the performance of his *kāvya*. On Vālmīki's command, Kuśa and Lava recite the *Rāmāyaṇa* to the person most likely to respond emotionally to this *kāvya*. The *Rāmāyaṇa* thus showcases the immediacy and importance that a poem can have for its audience and exalts itself as an exemplar for *kāvyas* to come, compositions that can be made from the same metrical material as the *Rāmāyaṇa*, namely, the verse Vālmīki invented from his own outpouring of feeling. The poem, in keeping with its prototypical role, also portrays itself as having power over people other than its protagonist. Some sages initially listening to the *Rāmāyaṇa* during a rehearsal of it before Rāma's ritual declare: "Even though this arose a long time ago, it seems like something we can see before us" (*ciranirvṛttam apy etat pratyakṣam iva darṣitam*) (*Rāmāyaṇa* 1.4.16cd). So begins the continuing construal of the *Rāmāyaṇa* as an emotion-evoking poem that is as true to life as Sītā is to Rāma, a work whose audiences today can second what the aforementioned

10 The twin princes' names not only are bardic, but also refer to the handful of sacred *kuśa* grass and the portion (*lava*) plucked off from it over which Vālmīki pronounced protective incantations and with which both newborns were cleaned (*Rāmāyaṇa* 7.58.4–6, 8).

11 These passages amplify the more measured assertion that Rāma, at birth, incarnates only "half of Viṣṇu" (*viṣṇor ardhaṃ*). Still, he has been "endowed with divinity's distinctive indicators" (*divyalakṣaṇasaṃyutam*) (*Rāmāyaṇa* 1.17.6b).

sages hearing the *Rāmāyaṇa* for the first time had to say. But much different from this poem's self-portrayal as a nascent narrative is the *Mahābhārata*'s self-image as a story far removed from its first telling.

The *Mahābhārata* as an *itihāsa*: An old eyewitness account of the way things had been

From its outset, the *Mahābhārata* depicts itself as a tale doubly distanced from its author. Before starting the story's third telling, the charioteer-bard (or *sūta*) Ugraśravas explains how he himself heard say of it:

> *janamejayasya rājarṣeḥ sarpasattre mahātmanaḥ |*
> *samīpe pārthivendrasya samyak pārikṣitasya ca ||*
> *kṛṣṇadvaipāyana**proktāḥ** supuṇyā vividhāḥ **kathāḥ** |*
> ***kathitāś cāpi** vidhivad yā vaiśaṃpāyanena vai ||*
> *śrutvāhaṃ tā vicitrārthā mahābhāratasaṃśritāḥ |*
>
> It was at the snake sacrifice of the magnanimous royal sage Janamejaya,
> in the presence of this king of kings who was Parikṣit's son,
> that I heard the various, highly auspicious, multivalent **narratives**
> belonging to the *Mahābhārata*—which were **articulated originally**
> by Kṛṣṇadvaipāyana—
> **related again** by Vaiśaṃpāyana, in just the way in which they had
> occurred.
>
> *Mahābhārata* 1.1.8–10ab (emphases mine)

Ugraśravas also elaborates on the *Mahābhārata*'s second transmission, by Vaiśaṃpāyana:

> *tapasā brahmacaryeṇa **vyasya vedaṃ sanātanam** |*
> ***itihāsam** imaṃ cakre puṇyaṃ satyavatīsutaḥ ||*
> *parāśarātmajo vidvān brahmarṣiḥ saṃśitavrataḥ |*
> *mātur niyogād dharmātmā gāṅgeyasya ca dhimataḥ ||*
> *kṣetre vicitravīryasya kṛṣṇadvaipāyanaḥ **purā** |*
> *trīn agnīn iva **kauravyāñ** janayāmāsa vīryavān ||*
> *utpādya dhṛtarāṣṭraṃ ca pāṇḍuṃ viduram eva ca |*
> *jagāma tapase dhīmān punar evāśramaṃ prati ||*
> ***teṣu jāteṣu vṛddheṣu gateṣu paramāṃ gatim** |*
> *abravīd bhārataṃ loke mānuṣe 'smin mahān ṛṣiḥ ||*
> *janamejayena pṛṣṭaḥ san brāhmaṇaiś ca sahasraśaḥ |*
> *śaśāsa śiṣyam āsīnaṃ vaiśaṃpāyanam antike ||*

sa sadasyaiḥ sahāsīnaḥ śrāvayāmāsa bhāratam |
karmāntareṣu yajñasya codyamānaḥ punaḥ punaḥ ||
vistaraṃ kuruvaṃśasya gāndhāryā dharmaśīlatām |
kṣattuḥ prajñāṃ dhṛtiṃ kuntyāḥ samyag dvaipāyano 'bravīt ||
vāsudevasya māhātmyaṃ ***pāṇḍavānāṃ*** *ca* ***satyatām*** *|*
durvṛttaṃ dhārtarāṣṭrāṇām *uktavān bhagavān ṛṣiḥ ||*

After he had arranged the everlasting Veda on the strength of his austerities and study,
Satyavatī's son composed this auspicious **account of the way things had been**.
In olden days—at the mandate of his mother and Gaṅgā's intelligent son [Bhīṣma]—righteous,
virile Kṛṣṇadvaipāyana (Parāśara's son), a learned priestly sage who fulfilled his vows,
fathered in Vicitravīrya's field
the next generation of Kurus, who were like the three fires of divine Agni.
After begetting Dhṛtarāṣṭra, Pāṇḍu, and Vidura,
the intelligent man went back again to his ashram to resume his austerities.
Once these three had been born, had aged, and had departed for their final destination,
the great sage uttered the *Bhārata* in the human world.
When asked to do so by Janamejaya and thousands of priests,
he instructed his student sitting nearby, Vaiśaṃpāyana.
As that [student] sat with the sacrificial priests, he recounted the *Bhārata* to them
at their unceasing urging, in the interstices of the sacrifice.
Dvaipāyana told thoroughly of the Kuru dynasty's intricacies, of Gāndhārī's righteousness,
of the maid's son [Vidura]'s sagacity, of Kuntī's constancy.
The venerable sage spoke of Vasudeva's son [Kṛṣṇa]'s magnitude,
of Pāṇḍu's sons' veracity,
of Dhṛtarāṣṭra's sons' maleficence.

Mahābhārata 1.1.52–60 (emphases mine)

When Ugraśravas' tale later turns back on itself, the scene of its second telling comes into still sharper focus:

tatas taṃ satkṛtaṃ sarvaiḥ sadasyair janamejayaḥ |
idaṃ paścād dvijaśreṣṭhaṃ paryapṛcchat kṛtāñjaliḥ ||
kurūṇāṃ pāṇḍavānāṃ *ca bhavān pratyakṣadarśivān* |
teṣāṃ caritam icchāmi kathyamānaṃ tvayā dvija ||
kathaṃ samabhavad bhedas teṣām akliṣṭakarmaṇām |
tac ca yuddhaṃ kathaṃ vṛttaṃ bhūtāntakaraṇaṃ mahat ||
pitāmahānāṃ *sarveṣāṃ daivenāviṣṭacetasām* |
kārtsnyenaitat samācakṣva bhagavan kuśalo hy asi ||
tasya tad vacanaṃ śrutvā kṛṣṇadvaipāyanas tadā |
śaśāsa śiṣyam āsīnaṃ vaiśaṃpāyanam antike ||
kurūṇāṃ pāṇḍavānāṃ ca yathā bhedo 'bhavat ***purā*** |
tad asmai sarvam ācakṣva yan mattaḥ śrutavān asi ||
guror vacanam ājñāya sa tu viprarṣabhas tadā |
ācacakṣe tataḥ sarvam ***itihāsaṃ purātanam*** ||
tasmai rājñe sadasyebhyaḥ kṣatriyebhyaś ca sarvaśaḥ |
bhedaṃ rājyavināśaṃ ca kurupāṇḍavayos tadā ||

Then Janamejaya saluted that preeminent priest, whose honors had been done by all the sacrificial priests,
and requested this of him afterward:
“Sir, you have witnessed with your own eyes **what Dhṛtarāṣṭra’s sons and Pāṇḍu’s sons did**.
I would like you to narrate their adventures, priest.
How did the rift among those men of effortless action arise,
and how did that great war that ended the lives of so many beings break out
among all my **forefathers**, whose powers of reason were possessed by fate?
Report this in its entirety, venerable one, for you are the proper person to do so.”
Upon hearing that man’s words, Kṛṣṇadvaipāyana
instructed his student sitting nearby, Vaiśaṃpāyana:
“Report to this man all that you have heard from me—
how **in olden days** there was a rift between Dhṛtarāṣṭra’s sons and Pāṇḍu’s sons.”
Heeding his teacher’s words, that man, a superlative sage himself, then
related to that king, the sacrificial priests, and the surrounding warriors
the entire **ancient account of the way things had been**—

and thus the kingdom-wrecking rift between Dhṛtarāṣṭra's sons and Pāṇḍu's sons.

Mahābhārata 1.54.17–24 (emphases mine)

The double thrust of the three preceding excerpts is signified by the two main morphemes of the *Mahābhārata*'s most important self-appellation: *itihāsa*. The meaning of this term emerges from its etymology, which—like some academic endeavors—is begun best at the end of the term. The word's third part, *āsa*, is the third-person singular form of the perfect tense of the verb *as* (to be). This form may be translated as "it was," given that, in the Sanskrit used at the time of the *Mahābhārata*, the perfect is a past tense tantamount to the imperfect.[12] The second segment of *itihāsa*, *ha*, is a particle that emphasizes whatever precedes it, which in this case is the particle *iti*—an equivalent of a closing quotation mark that is used here in its adverbial sense as "thus." Literally, these pieces compose the phrase "it was just as said" or "it was just thus," but my translation of them—a reworking of their recent rendering by Pollock as "'narrative of the way things were'"[13]—is "account of the way things had been." This translation tallies with Pollock's in acknowledging that the term *itihāsa* is applied to a text that is told (i.e. an "account" or "narrative") and that treats numerous entities (or "things"). But, where Pollock employs "were," the imperfect tense of the verb "to be," I use the pluperfect "had been," which conveys the fact that the events unfolding in the *itihāsa* already had elapsed by the time at which the text was told. Still, even events that follow the *itihāsa*'s telling are included in this text, for its author already knows how these events will turn out, and thereby has hindsight of them.

In the three aforementioned extracts (as the boldfaced terms evidence), Ugraśravas showcases in two steps the temporal distance between his audience and the incidents addressed in the *Mahābhārata itihāsa*. First, he observes the long interval between these incidents and their initial incorporation into the *itihāsa*. Two of the text's turning points—Kṛṣṇadvaipāyana's fathering of Dhṛtarāṣṭra, Pāṇḍu, and Vidura for Vicitravīrya[14] and the break between Dhṛtarāṣṭra's sons and Pāṇḍu's sons—are said to have occurred "in olden days"

12 Whitney 1889:821b.

13 Pollock 2003:44.

14 Kṛṣṇadvaipāyana is the unmarried, ascetic maternal half-brother of Vicitravīrya, a married monarch who dies before he can beget an heir. Kṛṣṇadvaipāyana, at the "mandate" (*niyogād*) of their mother and of Vicitravīrya's paternal half-brother Bhīṣma (who earlier had vowed to remain celibate), impregnates both of Vicitravīrya's widowed queens as well as a servant woman, and thus engenders Dhṛtarāṣṭra, Pāṇḍu, and Vidura (*Mahābhārata* 1.1.53, 1.99–100). Here, then, the word *niyogād*, in addition to denoting an injunction, refers to this particular practice of intercourse between in-laws for the purpose of preserving a patriline.

(*purā*) (*Mahābhārata* 1.1.54, 1.54.22). Moreover, Kṛṣṇadvaipāyana composes the *Mahābhārata* only after the three Kuru scions whom he himself sired have died (*Mahābhārata* 1.1.53–56). Second, Ugraśravas reveals that much time has passed since the *Mahābhārata*'s first telling. The "narratives" (*kathāḥ*) constituting this "ancient account of the way things had been" (*itihāsaṃ purātanam*) were "articulated originally" (*proktāḥ*) by Kṛṣṇadvaipāyana "after he had arranged the everlasting Veda" (*vyasya vedaṃ sanātanam*), the earliest corpus of sacred texts in the Hindu tradition, and were "related again" (*kathitāś cāpi*) by Vaiśaṃpāyana to Ugraśravas and everyone else who attended Janamejaya's snake sacrifice (*Mahābhārata* 1.1.9; 1.54.23d; 1.1.9, 52b, 9). The *itihāsa*'s aging process also is embodied by the lengthening of the line of kings whom the text commends. Janamejaya, the ruler who asks Kṛṣṇadvaipāyana to narrate his composition anew (a request that the sage grants only in part, because he has his student Vaiśaṃpāyana tell the tale), is the author's great-great-great-grandson, the grandson of his great-grandson. The "'forefathers'" (*pitāmahānāṃ*) about whom Janamejaya wishes to hear are actually his ancestors in his great-grandfather's generation, namely, the sons of Dhṛtarāṣṭra and of Pāṇḍu, who is Janamejaya's great-great-grandfather (*Mahābhārata* 1.54.20).

In the continuation of the Kuru lineage, then, Ugraśravas finds an emblem for the extended making of the *Mahābhārata* itself. He traces first the transformation of action into text that is represented by the aging of Kṛṣṇadvaipāyana's biological children Dhṛtarāṣṭra, Pāṇḍu, and Vidura: while the births of these boys belong to the lore of yore that eventually will wend its way into an *itihāsa*, the deaths of these characters after they have grown up usher in the creation of the actual *itihāsa* that immortalizes them poetically. Ugraśravas then follows the shift from first- to secondhand story that is signaled by the different relationships that Pāṇḍu's sons have with the men who memorialize them. When Kṛṣṇadvaipāyana describes in his *itihāsa* "Pāṇḍu's sons' veracity" (*pāṇḍavānāṃ ... satyatām*) (*Mahābhārata* 1.1.60), the sage speaks of grandsons whom he guided once they grew up,[15] who at the time of the *Mahābhārata*'s composition already have superseded their father's generation at court. But, when Janamejaya calls on Kṛṣṇadvaipāyana to tell him "'what ... Pāṇḍu's sons did'" (*pāṇḍavānāṃ*) (*Mahābhārata* 1.54.18), the king commands the reperformance of an *itihāsa* about the great-grandfather and great-granduncles whom he never knew personally.

The *Mahābhārata* also uses three other procedures to place itself in a long-gone past. First, the poem specifies that Kṛṣṇadvaipāyana completed its composition in three years (*Mahābhārata* 1.56.32, 1.App. I.5.8–9, 1.App. I.32.42–43, 1.App. I.33.3–4,

[15] On Kṛṣṇadvaipāyana Vyāsa's interventions in the Pāṇḍavas' lives, see Hiltebeitel 2001:48–54, 59, 62–83, 85–91.

18.37*, 18.5.41, 18.App. I.3.1–2), and thus demarcates temporally its own indeterminacy and implies itself to have been a fixed text for some time. Second, the work suggests that it is the last segment of the first Hindu sacred text. The *Mahābhārata*, immediately after explaining that Kṛṣṇadvaipāyana also is known as Vyāsa (the Divider) because he "divided the Vedas" (*vivyāsa vedān*) into four parts, names itself as the "fifth" (*mahābhāratapañcamān*) of the Vedas that Vyāsa taught his students (*Mahābhārata* 1.57.73, 74b).[16] Third, Vyāsa is able to pass down to his pupils the entire *Mahābhārata* as a Veda, even before the events that he will record in the poem have finished unfolding (*Mahābhārata* 12.327.18). Thus, even before it comes into being, the *Mahābhārata* manages already to be complete. Yet the text prevents its precomposition completion from being a paradox, by emphasizing Vyāsa's prescience.

If the *āsa* in *itihāsa* stands for the twofold temporal remoteness that such a text has from the incidents that it treats and from the times at which it is retold, the *iti* represents the perceptual proximity that the author of the text has to the ancient occurrences that he recounts in it. What this cognitive nearness entails is evinced by the underlined terms in Ugraśravas' triad of descriptions. Vyāsa is able to tell "thoroughly" (*samyag*) and "'in its entirety'" (*kārtsnyena*) his "account of the way things had been" (*itihāsam*) because he has "'witnessed [these things] with [his] own eyes'" (*pratyakṣadarśivān*) (*Mahābhārata* 1.1.59, 1.54.20, 1.1.52, 1.54.18). And, by virtue of the vividness with which Vyāsa has imparted his *itihāsa* to him, Vaiśaṃpāyana can retell "'all [the narratival episodes about] which [he] ha[s] heard'" (*tad ... sarvam ... yan ... śrutavān*) from his instructor, "in just the way in which they ha[ve] occurred" (*vidhivad*) (*Mahābhārata* 1.54.22, 1.1.9).

Vyāsa can make his *Mahābhārata* so lifelike because he has divine vision (*divyaṃ cakṣus*) (*Mahābhārata* 3.8.22; 14.61.9; 18.5.7, 33; 18.31*). As a result, he has extrasensory awareness (*atīndriyajñāna*) that extends over time and space: in addition to knowing the past, present, and future (*bhūtabhavyabhaviṣyavid*)—his foreknowledge presumably being what enables him to hand down the *Mahābhārata* prior to the occurrence of all the acts that the poem depicts—he is capable of hearing and seeing things from afar that ordinarily would be beyond his ken (*dūraśravaṇadarśana*) (*Mahābhārata* 1.100.8, 6.2.2d, 15.37.16b). Thus cognizant of everything (*sarvajña*), Vyāsa attributes his omniscience to the grace of the god Nārāyaṇa, who identifies himself with Viṣṇu (*Mahābhārata* 18.5.8, 32; 12.327.21–23; 12.328.35, 38).[17]

16 For further discussion of the *Mahābhārata* as a fifth Veda, refer to Fitzgerald 1991:150–170.

17 The relationship between Vyāsa and Nārāyaṇa has been studied by historian of religions Bruce M. Sullivan (1990:69–80), Sutton (2000:ix, 28, 164), and historian of religions Alf Hiltebeitel (2001:34, 89).

Possessing such exceptional powers of perception renders Vyāsa the ultimate reliable witness. With everything within his cognitive reach, he sees reality (*tattvadarśin*) and utters the truth (*satyavādin*) (*Mahābhārata* 1.2.168, 211, 219, 231; 1.99.15; 18.5.31). Therefore, the *itihāsa* that he articulates also is veridical; and the circumstances of its second and third tellings—during which Vaiśaṃpāyana and Ugraśravas each voice Vyāsa's "complete cognition" (*mataṃ kṛtsnaṃ*) (*Mahābhārata* 1.55.2, 1.56.12, 1.1.23)—suggest that the text retains its veracity because the text's subsequent recitations remain true to those that precede them.

In line with its self-portrayal as an *itihāsa* that is old and faithful, the *Mahābhārata* poses itself as an enduring object whose aesthetic worth will influence imitators rather than inspire innovators. Poets themselves preserve the *Mahābhārata* on account of its excellences:

> *ācakhyuḥ kavayaḥ kecit saṃpraty ācakṣate pare |*
> *ākhyāsyanti tathaivānye itihāsam imaṃ bhuvi ||*
> *idaṃ tu triṣu lokeṣu mahaj jñānaṃ pratiṣṭhitam |*
> *vistaraiś ca samāsaiś ca dhāryate yad dvijātibhiḥ ||*
> *alaṃkṛtaṃ śubhaiḥ śabdaiḥ samayair divyamānuṣaiḥ |*
> *chandovṛttaiś ca vividhair anvitaṃ viduṣāṃ priyam ||*

> Some poets have narrated on earth this account of the way things
> had been, others are recounting it now,
> and others still will narrate it.
> This great knowledge placed in the three worlds—
> which is kept by priests in its full and its brief forms,
> and which is ornamented with elegant words and divine and human
> devices
> and is endowed with assorted meters—is beloved by the learned.
>
> *Mahābhārata* 1.1.24–26

In fact, the *Mahābhārata* asserts itself as the basis of all intellectual efforts:

> *yo vidyāc caturo vedān sāṅgopaniṣadān dvijaḥ |*
> *na cākhyānam idaṃ vidyān naiva sa syād vicakṣaṇaḥ ||*
> *śrutvā tv idam upākhyānaṃ śrāvyam anyan na rocate |*
> *puṃskokilarutaṃ śrutvā rūkṣā dhvāṅkṣasya vāg iva ||*
> *itihāsottamād asmāj jāyante kavibuddhayaḥ |*
> *pañcabhya iva bhūtebhyo lokasaṃvidhayas trayaḥ ||*
> *asyākhyānasya viṣaye purāṇaṃ vartate dvijāḥ |*

antarikṣasya viṣaye prajā iva caturvidhāḥ ||
kriyāguṇānāṃ sarveṣām idam ākhyānam āśrayaḥ |
indriyāṇāṃ samastānāṃ citrā iva manaḥkriyāḥ ||
anāśrityaitad ākhyānaṃ kathā bhuvi na vidyate |
āhāram anapāśritya śarīrasyeva dhāraṇam ||
idaṃ sarvaiḥ kavivarair ākhyānam upajīvyate |
udayaprepsubhir bhṛtyair abhijāta iveśvaraḥ ||

A priest who knows the four Vedas along with their Aṅgas
 [Auxiliaries] and Upaniṣads
but does not know this tale, is not at all learned.
After hearing this anecdote deserving to be heard, a person takes
 pleasure in no other,
just as, after the song of a he-cuckoo is heard, the caw of a crow
 seems raucous.
The ideas of poets arise from this optimal account of the way things
 had been,
just as the three worlds are structured from the five elements.
Stories of yore traverse the sphere of this tale, priests,
just as the four kinds of creatures traverse the sphere of space.
This tale is the seat of all accomplishments and merits,
just as sundry mental acts are the seat of all the senses.
On earth, no narrative exists that does not depend on this tale,
just as no body survives that does not fare on food.
This tale sustains all the princes among poets,
just as a nobly born lord sustains the lackeys who aim to advance.

Mahābhārata 1.2.235–241

Although this *itihāsa* allows that other poems will appear after it, it declares that they will not deviate far from the path that it has broken. The poets whom the *Mahābhārata* precedes and who draw material from its many narratives thus cannot create anything altogether new. That the *itihāsa* takes pains to minimize the inventiveness of its successors, so as to silence any suggestion of having been excelled, is attested by the following verse, which has been inserted into most of the northern-recension manuscripts contributing to the first volume of the *Mahābhārata*'s critical edition, after the selection that I just have cited:

asya kāvyasya kavayo na samarthā viśeṣaṇe |
sādhor iva gṛhasthasya śeṣās traya ivāśramāḥ ||

> Poets are incapable of surpassing this poem,
> just as the three other stages of life are incapable of surpassing that
> of a truly honorable householder.
>
> *Mahābhārata* 1.187*[18]

If Vyāsa's successors indeed derive their narratives from his, these poets are highly unlikely to outdo him in the area of authoring immense *itihāsas*. These poets, to achieve eminence in their own rights, need to play on another field.

The main models for the efforts of Vālmīki's and Vyāsa's poetic heirs, the *Rāmāyaṇa* and the *Mahābhārata*—true to their respective self-representations as a *kāvya* and an *itihāsa*—set starkly different examples. Whereas the *Rāmāyaṇa* provides prospective poets with whiffs of the essences that these artists can use as ingredients in delicacies that are decidedly their own, the *Mahābhārata* offers itself to these authors as a time-tested recipe for a story that surely will sustain these scholars as well as it has maintained their ancestors. The contrast between this *kāvya* and this *itihāsa* has far-reaching repercussions, shaping the ways in which subsequent intellectuals categorize and compare these texts. Two of the *Rāmāyaṇa* and *Mahābhārata*'s earliest and most influential classifications have been offered by the medieval Indian thinkers Ānandavardhana (ca. the ninth century CE) and Rājaśekhara (ca. 880–920 CE), in their respective treatises on poetry.

Ānandavardhana and Rājaśekhara: Interpreters Unifying the *Rāmāyaṇa* and *Mahābhārata* as *Kāvya*s and as *Itihāsa*s

Ānandavardhana and Rājaśekhara each make the move of applying the same term to the *Mahābhārata* as to the *Rāmāyaṇa*. But, whereas Ānandavardhana adopts *kāvya* as his term for these poems, Rājaśekhara uses *itihāsa*. Ānandavardhana's and Rājaśekhara's word choices reflect the roles in which these critics cast these works. Ānandavardhana characterizes the *Rāmāyaṇa* and *Mahābhārata*—like the later poems that he and his peers compose—as *kāvyas* that continue to invite interpretation on the basis of the *rasas* with which they are imbued. Rājaśekhara, however, considers the *Rāmāyaṇa* and *Mahābhārata* to be *itihāsas*, ancient sources of stories that he and his contemporaries rework in their *rasa*-containing *kāvyas* centuries afterward.

[18] Three variants of this verse occur at 1.App. I.1.35–36, 1.App. I.5.18–19, and 18.App. I.3.31–32.

The *Rāmāyaṇa* and *Mahābhārata* in Ānandavardhana's view: Poems suggestive of single essences

Although Ānandavardhana, in his *Dhvanyāloka* (*Illumination of Poetic Suggestion*), does not explicitly label the *Rāmāyaṇa* and *Mahābhārata* as *kāvyas*, he implies in two ways that the works are such. First, he calls their composers poets: Vālmīki, the *ādikavi* (primary poet); Vyāsa, a *kavivedhas* (poet-creator); and both, *kavīśvaras* (master poets) (*Dhvanyāloka*[19] 1.5; comments on 1.5, 2.1, 4.7, 4.5, 3.18–19). Second, Ānandavardhana ascribes to the *Rāmāyaṇa* and *Mahābhārata* what he considers to be characteristic of the best kind of *kāvyas*.

In his eyes, the *Rāmāyaṇa* and *Mahābhārata* are distinguished by their *dhvani* (poetic suggestion), the linchpin of his poetics: "[T]he nature of this poetic suggestion—which is the pith of the poems of all the best poets, and which is exceedingly delightful—has not been brought to light before, even by the more subtle minds of ancient exponents of definitions of poetry. Yet its operation in regard to the *Rāmāyaṇa*, *Mahābhārata*, etc., is recognized everywhere by discerning critics. It is elucidated here, in order that happiness may be housed in their hearts" (*tasya ... dhvaneḥ svarūpaṃ sakalasatkavikāvyopaniṣadbhūtam atiramaṇīyam aṇīyasībhir api cirantanakāvyalakṣaṇavidhāyināṃ buddhibhir anunmīlitapūrvam, atha ca rāmāyaṇamahābhārataprabhṛtini lakṣye sarvatra prasiddhavyavahāraṃ lakṣayatāṃ sahṛdayānām ānando manasi labhatāṃ pratiṣṭhām iti prakāśyate |*) (*Dhvanyāloka*, comment on 1.1).[20] Ānandavardhana opens his discussion by defining *dhvani*:

> *yatrārthaḥ śabdo vā tam artham upasarjanīkṛtasvārthau |*
> *vyaṅktaḥ kāvyaviśeṣaḥ sa dhvanir iti sūribhiḥ kathitaḥ ||*

> The erudite term as "poetic suggestion" that property of poetry
> where a usual meaning that itself was subordinated to another one, or a word whose usual meaning was subordinated to another meaning,
> has alluded to that other meaning.
>
> *Dhvanyāloka* 1.13

[19] All translations of passages from this work are my own.

[20] Following in the footsteps of Ānandavardhana's turn-of-the-eleventh-century commentator Abhinavagupta, Sanskritist Daniel H. H. Ingalls (Ingalls, Masson, and Patwardhan 1990:1.1e An2) observes: "Abhinava's remark on the word *ānanda* should be accepted. The author is here playing on the proper name. The effect of his book will be to give firm footing in the hearts of sensitive readers not only to the bliss of understanding *dhvani* but to the fame of Ānandavardhana." Thus, the phrase *ānando manasi labhatāṃ pratiṣṭhām* literally means either "may happiness obtain a house in the heart" or "may Ānanda find fame in the heart." Thanks to Sanskrit's multivocality, self-promotion may be modest and shameless simultaneously!

Then Ānandavardhana clarifies this definition: "Poetic suggestion occurs where a meaning distinct from the expressed one, is shown—by the expressed meaning and by the word that expresses it—to be the main point, it being the case that the suggested meaning is paramount" (*vācyavyatiriktasyārthasya vācyavācakābhyāṃ tātparyeṇa prakāśanaṃ yatra vyaṅgyaprādhānye sa dhvaniḥ* |) (*Dhvanyāloka*, comment on 1.13). Subsequently, to align his idea of *dhvani* with earlier aesthetics, Ānandavardhana has it subsume the concept of *rasa*:

> *vācyavācakacārutvahetūnāṃ vividhātmanām* |
> *rasādiparatā yatra sa dhvaner viṣayo mataḥ* ||
>
> The sphere of poetic suggestion is thought to be wherever the many
> expressed meanings, words that express them, and things that
> make pretty these meanings and words
> subserve the essences, etc.
>
> *Dhvanyāloka* 2.4

Although Ānandavardhana enriches the *rasa* notion, he maintains many of the elements advanced in its earliest extant exposition, which appears in ancient thinker Bharata's *Nāṭyaśāstra* (*Treatise on the Dramatic Arts*) (a work composed collectively ca. 100 BCE–200 CE).

Like a garrulous guide whose tour is taken over by a terse one, Bharata indicates in his elaborate *rasa* theory what Ānandavardhana abbreviates as "essences, etc." Bharata begins by enumerating the *rasas*:

> *śṛṅgārahāsyakaruṇā raudravīrabhayānakāḥ* |
> *bībhatsādbhutasaṃjñau cety aṣṭau nāṭye rasāḥ smṛtāḥ* ||
>
> Eight essences are evoked by the dramatic arts: the erotic, the
> humorous, and the compassionate; the irascible, the heroic,
> and the fearsome;
> and the two termed the abhorrent and the amazing.
>
> *Nāṭyaśāstra* 6.15

Associated with the *rasas* in his system are several types of states, or *bhāvas*, one type of which is specified in the following verse:

> *ratir hāsaś ca śokaś ca krodhotsāhau bhayaṃ tathā* |
> *jugupsā vismayaś ceti sthāyibhāvāḥ prakīrtitāḥ* ||

passion and amusement, sorrow, ire and mettle, fear,
and abhorrence and amazement are known as the steady states.

Nāṭyaśāstra 6.17

These steady states, upon interacting with other sorts of states, actually turn into the essences, as Bharata's gustatory imagery illustrates:

tatra vibhāvānubhāvavyabhicārisaṃyogād rasaniṣpattiḥ |
ko dṛṣṭāntaḥ | atrāha—yathā hi nānāvyañjanauṣadhidravyasaṃyogād rasaniṣpattiḥ tathā nānābhāvopagamād rasaniṣpattiḥ | yathā hi—guḍādibhir dravyair[21] *vyañjanair auṣadhibhiś ca ṣāḍavādayo rasā nirvartyante tathā nānābhāvopagatā api sthāyino bhāvā rasatvam āpnuvantīti | atrāha—rasa iti kaḥ padārthaḥ | ucyate—āsvādyatvāt | katham āsvādyate rasaḥ | yathā hi nānāvyañjanasaṃskṛtam annaṃ bhuñjānā rasān āsvādayanti sumanasaḥ puruṣā harṣādīṃś cādhigacchanti tathā nānābhāvābhinayavyañjitān vāgaṅgasattvopetān sthāyibhāvān āsvādayanti sumanasaḥ prekṣakāḥ harṣādīṃś cādhigacchanti | tasmān nāṭyarasā ity abhivyākhyātāḥ |*

In that regard, essences arise from the combination of states that elicit others, of the outward signs of states, and of transitory states.

What is an example of this? On this topic, someone has said: "Just as flavors arise from the combination of sundry spices, herbs, and ingredients, so too arise essences from the intermingling of sundry states. Just as the flavors of sweets and other foods are made with things like molasses, with spices, with herbs, and with other ingredients, so too the steady states—as soon as they have intermingled with the sundry other states—become essences."

On this topic, someone else has said: "What is the sense of the word 'essence'?"

This is what is said in response: "It derives from its ability to be savored."

"How is an essence savored?"

"Just as satisfied people savor flavors while eating food cooked with sundry spices and are pleased and so forth, so too satisfied spectators savor the steady states—which involve speech, body, and character and are shown by the acting out of the sundry other states—and are

21 The phrase *guḍādibhir dravyair* is misprinted in Nagar 1981–1984 as *guṇādibhir drar* (the phrase appears correctly in Krishnamoorthy 1992).

> pleased and so forth. It is to this [process] that the 'essences of the dramatic arts' owe their name."
>
> *Nāṭyaśāstra*, section after 6.31

And Ānandavardhana borrows from Bharata the system of states for which "essences, etc." serves as a shorthand.

Even after Ānandavardhana transplants *rasas* from the field of dramatics to the plot of poetics, these essences flourish further. Interweaving them into his theoretical framework, like prize tea roses on a trellis, he highlights *rasas* (along with the *bhāvas* on which they are based) accordingly:

> *mukhyā vyāpāraviṣayāḥ sukavīnāṃ rasādayaḥ |*
> *teṣāṃ nibandhane bhāvyaṃ taiḥ sadaivāpramādibhiḥ ||*
>
> The foremost objects of praiseworthy poets' efforts are the essences, etc.
> They should be prepared by those who always are attentive.
>
> *Dhvanyāloka*, comment on 3.18–19

More specifically, such authors are to assemble words and meanings in a way that encourages the essences and states to be evident (*Dhvanyāloka*, comment on 3.32).

Ānandavardhana esteems "the essences, etc." so highly because they permit poets to keep making original art out of long-extant life: "Because the essences, etc., are employed, this path of poetry—despite having been measured off when trod in many ways by a thousand or countless poets of old—goes on infinitely. For the essences, states, etc., are boundless because they each are associated with states that elicit others, outward signs of states, and transitory states. And indeed—by the very act of considering each sort of these [essences, states, etc.]—praiseworthy poets, by dint of their desire, can cause a worldly incident that they are treating to seem just one way, even though it is otherwise" (*yasya rasāder āśrayād ayaṃ kāvyamārgaḥ purātanaiḥ kavibhiḥ sahasrasaṃkhyair asaṃkhyair vā bahuprakāraṃ kṣuṇṇatvānmito 'py anantatām eti | rasabhāvādīnāṃ hi pratyekaṃ vibhāvānubhāvavyabhicārisamāśrayād aparimitatvam | teṣāṃ caikaikaprabhedāpekṣayāpi tāvaj jagadvṛttam upanibadhyamānaṃ sukavibhis tadicchāvaśād anyathā sthitam apy anyathaiva vivartate |*) (*Dhvanyāloka*, comment on 4.3). The presence of *rasas* and *bhāvas* thus presents poets with an endless array of narrative possibilities.

Yet the infinitude of these options is not overwhelming, as Ānandavardhana urges poets to take on only one particularly productive task: "And, in a major work, treating only one essence makes the work more likely to have unique content and abounding beauty" (*prabandhe cāṅgī rasa eka evopanibadhyamāno 'rthaviśeṣalābhaṃ chāyātiśayaṃ ca puṣṇāti |*) (*Dhvanyāloka*, comment on 4.5). In addition to improving poems aesthetically, concentrating on a single *rasa* licenses poets to create compositions that contrast starkly with earlier kinds of accounts: "A poet composing a poem should be devoted to its essence with his whole soul. That being the case, if he perceives in an account a situation that does not suit the essence, he should excise that altogether and construct on his own another narrative that does suit the essence. For a poet need not maintain a mere account, because that is brought about only by an account of the way things had been" (*kavinā kāvyam upanibadhnatā sarvātmanā rasaparatantreṇa bhavitavyam | tatretivṛtte yadi rasānanuguṇāṃ sthitiṃ paśyet tāṃ bhaṅktvāpi svatantratayā rasānuguṇaṃ kathāntaram utpādayet | na hi kaver itivṛttamātranirvahaṇena kiñcit prayojanam, itihāsād eva tatsiddheḥ |*) (*Dhvanyāloka*, comment on 3.13–14). Thus, rather than preserve in an *itihāsa* an account of past events, a poet composes a *kāvya* to convey a certain *rasa*. As a container of a narrative newly conceived for this particular purpose, a poem—from Ānandavardhana's perspective—is clearly distinct from an account that asserts itself as evidence of an earlier time.

There are nine *rasas* from which poets may select. The first eight essences to appear in the *Dhvanyāloka* are those studied by Bharata (*Dhvanyāloka*, comment on 1.5; 2.7; 2.9; 3.4; comments on 3.6, 3.9, 3.23):

1. the compassionate
2. the erotic
3. the irascible
4. the abhorrent
5. the amazing
6. the heroic
7. the humorous
8. the fearsome

To this octet, Ānandavardhana adds the peaceful (*Dhvanyāloka*, comment on 3.23).[22] As Ānandavardhana exemplifies the evocation of the first and the last of

[22] Ānandavardhana, however, was not the first scholar to study the *śānta rasa*. That distinction probably belongs to *Nāṭyaśāstra* commentator Udbhaṭa, who—in spite of only naming this essence as the ninth in verse 6.14 of his *Kāvyālaṃkārasārasaṃgraha* (*Compilation of the Greatest Ornaments of Poetry*) (ca. 750 CE)—"must have dealt with [the *śānta rasa*] at greater length, perhaps refuting the opposition to it also, in his now lost commentary on the *Nāṭya-śāstra*" (Raghavan 1967:47). The exposition of the peaceful essence after the others bears out G. H. Bhatt's belief that the reading of *Rāmāyaṇa* 1.4.8 that comprises the *śānta rasa* (namely, the variant in most of the northern manuscripts) results from an interpolation (Bhatt and Shah 1960–1975, critical notes to vol. 1:1.4.8n). Indeed, Bhatt's assertion about this verse accords with his broader observation that

the *rasas* in his series, he shows his audience the variety of affects that effects this *rasa* range.

At one pole, he places the foremost source of the *karuṇa rasa*: "[I]n the *Rāmāyaṇa*, the primary poet himself has interwoven the compassionate essence, affirming to this effect, 'Sorrow has become verse!' And he has developed that very [essence] simply by ending his work with Rāma's permanent separation from Sītā" (*rāmāyaṇe ... karuṇo rasaḥ svayam ādikavinā sūtritaḥ 'śokaḥ ślokatvam āgataḥ' ity evaṃ vādinā | nirvyūḍhaś ca sa eva sītātyantaviyogaparyantam eva svaprabandham uparacayatā |*) (*Rāmāyaṇa* 1.2.39d, quoted in *Dhvanyāloka*, comment on 4.5). The unbridgeable rift between King Rāma and his queen, Sītā, that results from her live interment crowns the *Rāmāyaṇa*'s *karuṇa rasa* by consummating in the poem the sorrow that Ānandavardhana identifies as the compassionate essence's steady state (*Rāmāyaṇa* 7.89.1; *Dhvanyāloka*, comment on 1.5). So as to connect more closely the sorrow concluding the *Rāmāyaṇa* to the sorrow producing the poem, Ānandavardhana interchanges the genders of the crane couple in Vālmīki's view. In stating, then, that the sage's *śoka* that was turned into *śloka* was "generated by the cry of the he-crane distressed by his separation from his mate lying close by" (*sannihitasahacarīvirahakātarakrauñcākrāndajanitaḥ*) (*Dhvanyāloka*, comment on 1.5), Ānandavardhana implicitly parallels the grieving crane and king.[23] In doing so, the critic nudges into an even brighter spotlight in the *Dhvanyāloka* the *karuṇa rasa* that the *Rāmāyaṇa* itself foregrounds.[24]

---

the southern recension of the *Rāmāyaṇa* "has generally preserved the text ... in an original or older form" (Bhatt and Shah 1960–1975, introduction to vol. 1:XXXII). Yet, even the southern manuscripts' version of verse 1.4.8 probably postdates the remainder of the *Rāmāyaṇa*'s first volume, for Bhatt also adduces evidence that suggests that this volume once started with its fifth chapter (Bhatt and Shah 1960–1975, introduction to vol. 1:XXXI). Moreover, the *rasa* list that certain southern manuscripts present and that the critical edition adopts (*hāsyaśṛṅgāra-kāruṇyaraudravīrabhayānakaiḥ | bībhatsādirasair ...* [with the essences beginning with the humorous, the erotic, the compassionate, the irascible, the heroic, the fearsome, and the abhorrent]) does not preclude the possibility that the producers of these manuscripts were aware of the peaceful essence. These manuscript authors do not specify that the essences number only eight, and the authors' use of the term *ādi* (beginning) implies that they just have started to describe the set of essences and have omitted more than one (perhaps the amazing and the peaceful, as most of the northern manuscripts make explicit).

23 Vaudeville 1961:124; Masson 1969:210–215. Sanskritists Charlotte Vaudeville and Jeffrey Masson, like pandit Paṭṭābhirāma Śāstrī (1940:88n1) before them, assume that the "separation" to which Ānandavardhana refers here is that arising from the abduction of Sītā by Rāvaṇa (*Rāmāyaṇa* 3.47.22). However, on the basis of Ānandavardhana's subsequent specification of the "permanent separation" in his comment on *Dhvanyāloka* 4.5, I conclude that his comment on *Dhvanyāloka* 1.5 alludes to Sītā's entry into the earth toward the end of the *Rāmāyaṇa*.

24 Despite these sources' concentration on the compassionate essence, Sanskritist B. N. Bhatt (1986:57–60) locates all the essences in the *Rāmāyaṇa* narrative. Yet Bhatt's analysis, in emphasizing the peaceful essence as the end to which all the others lead, is less like the *Rāmāyaṇa*'s *rasa*

At the other pole, Ānandavardhana positions the quintessential cache of the *śānta rasa*: "The main point of the *Mahābhārata* appears very plainly indeed to involve the intention that the peaceful essence, which is attended by other essences that are its subordinates, is the principal one; and that the human aim defined as the transcendence of transmigration, which is attended by other aims that are its subordinates, is the principal one" (*śānto raso rasāntaraiḥ, mokṣalakṣaṇaḥ puruṣārthaḥ puruṣārthāntaraiḥ tadupasarjanatvenānugamyamāno 'ṅgitvena vivakṣāviṣaya iti mahābhāratatātparyaṃ suvyaktam evāvabhāsate* |) (*Dhvanyāloka*, comment on 4.5). According to Ānandavardhana, the twofold significance of the *Mahābhārata* stems from its double identity as a poem (*kāvya*) and a treatise (*śāstra*): "It is well established that the *Mahābhārata*, in its capacity as a treatise, is intended to have as its principal human aim the single highest human aim, which is defined only as the transcendence of transmigration; and that [the text], in its capacity as a poem, is intended to have as its principal essence the peaceful essence, which is defined as the development of happiness ensuing from the ending of desire" (*mokṣalakṣaṇa evaikaḥ paraḥ puruṣārthaḥ śāstranayena, kāvyanayena ca tṛṣṇākṣayasukhaparipoṣalakṣaṇaḥ śānto raso mahābhāratasyāṅgitvena vivakṣita iti supratipāditam* |) (*Dhvanyāloka*, comment on 4.5). But the specific type of *śāstra* as which Ānandavardhana sees the *Mahābhārata* is shaped by his notion of poetry, for he modifies the *Mahābhārata*'s own śāstric self-image to highlight what he regards as the work's most prominent poetic feature. While the *Mahābhārata* portrays itself as a triad of treatises that each address a human aim—as an *arthaśāstra* (treatise on acquisition) and a *dharmaśāstra* (treatise on righteousness), as well as a *mokṣaśāstra* (treatise on the transcendence of transmigration) (*Mahābhārata* 1.56.21)—Ānandavardhana attends only to this last limning. By depicting the poem's primary purpose as release from the round of rebirth, he casts into relief the *śānta rasa* that pervades the poem.

With its quintessence of quietude, whose steady state is the aforementioned "happiness" accompanying desire's end,[25] the *Mahābhārata* makes an affective and effective model that Ānandavardhana is able to oppose to a similarly evocative, but antithetically oriented, *Rāmāyaṇa*. Running counter to the *Rāmāyaṇa*'s *karuṇa rasa*—the consequence of sorrow at someone else's plight and an expression of outward-looking empathy[26]—is the *Mahābhārata*'s *śānta rasa*, the result

statement than like Abhinavagupta's revision of Ānandavardhana's *rasa* theory (for details, see Masson and Patwardhan 1969:139–142).

25 As Masson and pandit M. V. Patwardhan (1969:98n1) have shown, Abhinavagupta's gloss on Ānandavardhana's explanation of *Dhvanyāloka* 3.26 indicates that *tṛṣṇākṣayasukha* is the *sthāyibhāva* of the *śānta rasa*.

26 For further discussion of Vālmīki's empathetic response, see Masson 1969.

of a contentment attained by turning inward, away from external objects that arouse emotions. Ānandavardhana, by situating this pair of poems at opposite ends of his essence spectrum, illustrates the extent of its applicability.

Thus, he advances the *Rāmāyaṇa* and *Mahābhārata* as primers on his poetics. Although he clearly considers these works to be *kāvya*s, they serve in his system as *śāstras*, object lessons for future pliers of his poetic craft. In Pollock's terms, Ānandavardhana here appropriates products of poetic "practice" (i.e. the *Rāmāyaṇa* and *Mahābhārata*) expressly for the purpose of expounding his "theory" of poetic suggestion.[27] Furthermore, Ānandavardhana's emphasis on the instructive value of these two texts for poets prefigures Rājaśekhara's rendering of both works as *śāstra*s that have left a poetic legacy to *kavi*s such as himself.

The *Rāmāyaṇa* and *Mahābhārata* from Rājaśekhara's perspective: Pathbreaking poetic accounts of the way things had been

Rājaśekhara begins his *Kāvyamīmāṃsā* (*Inquiry into Poetry*) by advising other poets to become versed in the *śāstras* (*Kāvyamīmāṃsā*, 8–9). The reason for his advice is clarified by his modern commentator Madhusudan Sharma, who reveals that Rājaśekhara encourages his counterparts to consult treatises because these texts already have addressed the same topics that these scholars seek to treat in their poems (*Kāvyamīmāṃsā*, 9n).

Moreover, Rājaśekhara admits as *śāstra*s the *Rāmāyaṇa* and *Mahābhārata*. Specifically, he distinguishes *śāstra*s that are human-made (*pauruṣeya*) from those that are not (*apauruṣeya*); he divides the human-made ones into four groups—stories of yore (*purāṇa*s), metaphysical speculations (*ānvīkṣikī*s), Vedic explications (*mīmāṃsā*s), and legal texts (*smṛtitantra*s); he includes *itihāsa*s among those stories of yore;[28] and he subdivides these accounts of the way things had been, according to whether they are about the action of the greatest (*parakriyā*) or about a bygone age (*purākalpa*) (*Kāvyamīmāṃsā*, 9, 14–15).[29] Rājaśekhara regards the first sort of *itihāsa* as having a single hero, but sees the second sort as having

27 Pollock 1985:504.

28 Classifying *itihāsa*s as *purāṇa*s here, however, does not prevent Rājaśekhara from paralleling these types of literature. Through this combination of subsumption and juxtaposition, he suggests that the *itihāsa* and *purāṇa* categories overlap to a limited degree.

29 Sharma reads *parakriyā* (action of the greatest) (*Kāvyamīmāṃsā*, 15) where pandits C. D. Dalal and R. Anantakrishna Shastry (1916:3) read *parikriyā* (exercise). While Sharma's reading is consistent with the subsequent description of the *Rāmāyaṇa*, Dalal and Shastry's is not particularly so. Thus, Sanskritist Sadhana Parashar (2000:23–24), in her recent translation of Dalal and Shastry's text, emends it so that it reads *parakriyā* rather than *parikriyā*.

many heroes; and he adduces as instances of these two types the *Rāmāyaṇa* and the *Mahābhārata*, respectively (*Kāvyamīmāṃsā*, 16).

Later in his work, Rājaśekhara details the narrative resources that *itihāsas* and other *śāstras* provide to poets:

> *atrāhuḥ—"śrutīnāṃ sāṅgaśākhānām itihāsapurāṇayoḥ |*
> *arthagranthaḥ kathābhyāsaḥ kavitvasyaikam auṣadham ||*
> *itihāsapurāṇābhyāṃ cakṣurbhyām iva satkaviḥ |*
> *vivekāñjanaśuddhābhyāṃ sūkṣmam apy artham īkṣate ||*
> *vedārthasya nibandhena ślāghyante kavayo yathā |*
> *smṛtīnām itihāsasya purāṇasya tathā tathā ||"*
>
> In this regard, people have said:
> "The supreme remedy of poetic expertise is the stringing together of subjects and the regular study of narratives
> from the Vedas and their supplements and recensions and from the accounts of the way things had been and the stories of yore.
> The best poet sees even subtle subject matter by means both of the accounts of the way things had been and of the stories of yore, as if with a pair of eyes
> purified by the salve of discernment.
> Just as poets are commended because their compositions treat the subject matter of the Vedas,
> so too are commended poets whose compositions treat the subject matter of the law codes, of the accounts of the way things had been, and of the stories of yore."
>
> *Kāvyamīmāṃsā*, 114

More precisely, Rājaśekhara produces this passage to prove to his peer poets that they will gain as much acclaim by drawing story material from the stores of such human-made *śāstras* as *itihāsas*, *purāṇas*, and *smṛtis* (law codes) as by tapping topics from *śāstras* of divine origin, like the Vedas and their various parts.

Rājaśekhara not only promotes the *pauruṣeya śāstras* as sources for poets, but also prescribes a particular way in which they should study these texts:

> *atrāha sma—*
> *"bahv api svecchayā kāmaṃ prakīrṇam abhidhīyate |*
> *anujjhitārthasambandhaḥ prabandho durudāharaḥ ||*
> *rītiṃ vicintya vigaṇayya guṇān vigāhya*
> *śabdārthasārtham anusṛtya ca sūktimudrāḥ |*
> *kāryo nibandhaviṣaye viduṣā prayatnaḥ*

ke potayantrarahitā jaladhau plavante ||
līḍhābhidhopaniṣadāṃ savidhe budhānām
abhyasyataḥ pratidinaṃ bahudṛśvano 'pi |
kiñcit kadācana kathañcana sūktipākād
vāktattvam unmiṣati kasyacid eva puṃsaḥ ||"

On this issue, someone has said:

"Although it certainly is the case that a hodgepodge is expounded ad nauseam as one desires,
a composition connected with a topic that is treated steadfastly (rather than being abandoned for something else) is difficult to compose.
Once he has thought about style, has considered other qualities, has examined a multitude of words and meanings, and has turned phrases well and has worded things right,
a scholar should strive in the area of composition. Who crosses the ocean, without the support of a ship?
Only for some man who also is very observant as he practices every day, in the presence of smart people who have absorbed the secret of words' conventional meanings,
does a bit of rarefied language open out at a certain time—with great difficulty—from the finishing of well-turned phrases."

Kāvyamīmāṃsā, 173

Arguing here that—to adopt Archaic Greek lyric poet Archilochus' terms—being a hedgehog expert in one field (i.e. a poet who devotes his composition to a single topic) is harder than being a fox somewhat familiar with many (i.e. a poet whose work ranges readily from topic to topic), Rājaśekhara recommends that authors attempting to address a certain subject become acquainted with the various verbal elements that are available for its exposition, and that these poets compose under the supervision of their successful predecessors.

Yet these adepts are not the only role models for poets, whose intellectual ancestry Rājaśekhara traces to the authors of the two *itihāsa*s most important to him:

valmīkajanmā sa kaviḥ purāṇaḥ kavīśvaraḥ satyavatīsutaś ca |
yasya praṇetā tad ihānavadyaṃ sārasvataṃ vartma na kasya vandyam? ||

Who would not worship that flawless avenue of eloquence here that was created by

that primeval poet who had emerged from an anthill and by the
master poet who was Satyavatī's son?

Kāvyamīmāṃsā, 91

Rājaśekhara refers here to Vālmīki and Vyāsa, respectively. But, unlike Ānandavardhana, who calls both composers *kavīśvaras* (master poets) (*Dhvanyāloka*, comment on 3.18–19), Rājaśekhara reserves this title for Vyāsa and labels Vālmīki the "primeval poet" (*kaviḥ purāṇaḥ*). The sages' distinct designations reflect the different roles that these authors play in Rājaśekhara's model of poetic production. His representation also clarifies why the road originated by the two ascetics—an "avenue of eloquence" (*sārasvataṃ vartma*)—relates to Sarasvatī, the goddess of knowledge who is Brahmā's wife.

The story that Rājaśekhara relates about how poetry came to be composed by people begins with the rather remarkable birth of Sarasvatī's son Kāvyapuruṣa (Poetry Personified):

purā putrīyantī sarasvatī tuṣāragirau tapasyāmāsa | prītena manasā tāṃ viriñcaḥ provāca putraṃ te sṛjāmi | athaiṣā kāvyapuruṣaṃ suṣuve | so 'bhyutthāya sapādopagrahaṃ chandasvatīṃ vācam udacīcarat |

"yadetadvāṅmayaṃ viśvam arthamūrttyā vivarttate |
so 'smi kāvyapumān amba pādau vandeya tāvakau ||"

tām āmnāyadṛṣṭacarīm upalabhya bhāṣāviṣaye chandomudrāṃ devī sasammadam aṅkaparyaṅkenādāya tam udalāpayat | "vatsa! sacchandaskāyā giraḥ praṇetaḥ! vāṅmayamātaram api mātaraṃ māṃ vijayase | praśasyatamaṃ cedam udāharanti yad uta 'putrāt parājayo dvitīyaṃ putrajanma' iti | tvattaḥ pūrve hi vidvāṃso[30] *gadyaṃ dadṛśur na padyam | tvadupajñam athātaḥ chandasvad vacaḥ pravartsyati | aho ślāghanīyo 'si | śabdārthau te śarīraṃ, saṃskṛtaṃ mukhaṃ, prākṛtaṃ bāhuḥ, jaghanam apabhraṃśaḥ, paiśācaṃ pādau, uro miśram | samaḥ prasanno madhura udāra ojasvī cāsi | ukticaṇaṃ te vaco, rasa ātmā, romāṇi chandāṃsi, praśnottarapravahlikādikaṃ ca vākkeliḥ, anuprāsopamādayaś ca tvām alaṅkurvanti |"*

In olden days, Sarasvatī performed austerities in the snowy Himālaya Mountains because she wanted to bear a son. Pleased by her behavior, Brahmā proclaimed to her, "I will sire a son for you." She then gave birth to Poetry Personified. He got up to greet her, grasped her feet, and came out with a metrical utterance:

30 Although misprinted as *rvidvāṃso* in the *Kāvyamīmāṃsā*'s main text, the word *vidvāṃso* appears correctly in Sharma's commentary (*Kāvyamīmāṃsā*, 25, 25n).

"I am that Poetry Personified, because of whom all this eloquence
takes shape.
Mother, let me worship at your feet."

Upon hearing that statement that had been seen before in the Vedas and whose language was marked by its metrical composition, the goddess picked up [the baby], put him on her lap, and happily cried this out to him: "Darling! Producer of metrically shaped speech! You surpass me, your mother, even though I am the mother of eloquence. But this is most admirable. That is, they say, 'Being outdone by a son is tantamount to the birth of a second son.' For the scholars who preceded you, were acquainted with prose, not poetry. Henceforth, versified speech will arise as your invention. How praiseworthy you are. Word and meaning are your body; Sanskrit, your mouth; Prakrit, your arm; Apabhraṃśa, your haunches; Paiśācī, your feet; and Miśra languages, your chest. You are whole, clear, mellifluous, lofty, and powerful. Famously expressive words are your speech; essence, your soul; metrical compositions, your bodily hair; and conundrums, etc., consisting of questions and answers, your repartee. Moreover, alliteration, similes, and so forth, ornament you."

Kāvyamīmāṃsā, 24–26

After praising her son, Sarasvatī asks him to conceal his precocity and to act like an infant, and she lays him on the surface of a boulder so that she can go bathe in the heavenly Ganges. In Sarasvatī's absence, Uśanas (a.k.a. Śukra), son of the celestial sage Bhṛgu, happens upon the lone child and takes him to his ashram (*Kāvyamīmāṃsā*, 27–28).

Consequently, Kāvyapuruṣa no longer is lying upon the boulder by the time Sarasvatī comes back to it. Fortunately, though, for her (and for future poets and their publics), a familiar figure helps her find the infant:

tataś ca vinivṛttā vāgdevī tatra putram apaśyantī madhyehṛdayaṃ cakranda / prasaṅgāgataś ca vālmīkir munivṛṣā sapraśrayaṃ tam udantam udāhṛtya bhagavatyai bhṛgusūter āśramapadam adarśayat / sāpi prasnutapayodharā putrāyāṅkapālīṃ dadānā śirasi ca cumbantī svastimatā cetasā prācetasāyā'pi maharṣaye nibhṛtaṃ sacchandāṃsi vacāṃsi prāyacchat / anupreṣitaś ca sa tayā niṣādanihatasahacarīkaṃ krauñcayuvānaṃ karuṇakreṅkārayā girā, krandantam udīkṣya śokavān ślokam ujjagāda /

"mā niṣāda! pratiṣṭhāṃ tvam agamaḥ śāśvatīḥ samāḥ /
yat krauñcamithunād ekam avadhīḥ kāmamohitam //"

tato divyadṛṣṭir devī tasmā api ślokāya varam adāt, yad utānyad anadhīyānoyaḥ prathamam enam adhyeṣyate sa sārasvataḥ kaviḥ saṃpatsyata iti | sa tu mahāmuniḥ pravṛttavacano rāmāyaṇam itihāsaṃ samadṛbhat; dvaipāyanas tu ślokaprathamādhyāyī tatprabhāvena śatasāhasrīṃ saṃhitāṃ bhāratam |

And then, as soon as she had returned, the speech goddess, not seeing her son there, burst out crying from the core of her heart. But Vālmīki, the best of the ascetics, chanced to come by and courteously gave the goddess the news and showed her the road to the ashram of Bhṛgu's son. She, in turn—with her cloudlike breasts raining milk as she scooped her son onto her lap and kissed his head—quietly made the goodhearted gesture of granting to the great sage himself, Pracetas' son, the gift of metrical speech. And, after she had dismissed him, he saw a he-crane whose mate had been killed by an outcast hunter and who was crying out "Kreng! Kreng!" in his compassion. The sorrowful sage then cried out this couplet:

"You never will have peace, outcast,
because you slew one of the two cranes when she was deluded by desire."

Then the goddess, who had seen with her divine vision what had gone on, blessed that very verse, saying in addition, "Anyone—even a nonscholar—who studies this [verse] first will become an eloquent poet." And that great ascetic from whom poetic speech had sprung composed the *Rāmāyaṇa*, an account of the way things had been, while Dvaipāyana—by dint of starting his study with [Vālmīki's] verse—composed the *Mahābhārata*, a collection of one hundred thousand couplets.

Kāvyamīmāṃsā, 29–31

This narrative is notable because it illustrates how Rājaśekhara incorporates an earlier idea into his own conception of poetic creativity. He seems to tell the story to prompt other poets to avail themselves of *rasa* resources while bringing new works into being.

Although poetic essence is only one of Kāvyapuruṣa's components, Rājaśekhara signals the significance of it by equating it with the infant's *ātman*. Translated most often as "soul" or "self," the *ātman* is that part of a person that persists after death, either to unite with Brahman (the reality instantiated by the universe) or to reenter the round of rebirth. Associated in either event with endurance and infinitude, the *ātman* is an apt equivalent for Rājaśekhara to employ to elevate essence above all other poetic elements. Indeed, he relates only *rasa* to the perpetuation of poetry, by predicating the production of poetry on the appreciation of essence.

He cites as the primary exemplar of a poem deserving admiration for its *rasa* Vālmīki's verse à la Ānandavardhana. This couplet, which expresses the compassion that its author feels after watching a widowered crane experience the same emotion, affords a similar eloquence to anyone attending properly to it. The first follower in Vālmīki's footsteps, according to Rājaśekhara, is Vyāsa.

Presumably, the articulateness that Vyāsa acquires by studying the *Rāmāyaṇa* stanza allows him to generate *rasa* in his own work. Yet, Rājaśekhara, departing from Ānandavardhana, does not depict Vyāsa as such. Rather, Rājaśekhara retains the sage in his student role so that Vālmīki can remain at the center of this story. The different positions of the two composers are reflected by their aforementioned epithets (*Kāvyamīmāṃsā*, 91). As the "primeval poet" (*kaviḥ purāṇaḥ*), Vālmīki is given the gift of poetry by a goddess and is responsible for passing poetry down to posterity. In contrast, Vyāsa the "master poet" (or, more literally, "master among poets") (*kavīśvaraḥ*) is the model student whose diligence has returned the dividend of poetic expertise. Accordingly, Rājaśekhara distinguishes in his narrative the works of ur-poet Vālmīki and newer poet Vyāsa, by terming only the *Rāmāyaṇa* an *itihāsa*. Rājaśekhara also implies that those who study such an account of the way things had been can compose their own collections of couplets, even if authoring an *itihāsa* is beyond these composers' capabilities. Yet he simultaneously suggests the immense accomplishments of which these poets are capable, by offering as their role model the author of the longest couplet "collection" (*saṃhitāṃ*) ever, which itself has Vedic aspirations. Indeed, the word *saṃhitā* can refer particularly to a collection of Vedic hymns.

But, given that Rājaśekhara has referred earlier to the *Mahābhārata* as an *itihāsa* and later will state that poets treating topics from any *itihāsa* are praiseworthy (*Kāvyamīmāṃsā*, 15–16, 114), why does he focus his audience's attention here on Vālmīki's activity? In my view, Rājaśekhara spotlights Vālmīki to elucidate the symbolic valence of his interaction with Sarasvatī. Because the goddess and the ascetic's meeting has a latent meaning that proceeds from the meeting's patent meaning, I will look initially at the latter.

The overt reason why the ascetic and the goddess encounter each other is so that this deity known for "possessing speech" (*sarasvatī*) can cause the sage to compose poetry. He can invent simply because she enables him, as well as his poetic heirs, to view something new:

> *tadāhuḥ—suptasyāpi mahākaveḥ śabdārthau sarasvatī darśayati taditarasya tatra jāgrato 'py andhaṃ cakṣuḥ | anyadṛṣṭacare hy arthe mahākavayo*[31] *jātyandhās tadviparīte tu divyadṛśaḥ | na tat tryakṣaḥ sahasrākṣo vā yac carmacakṣuṣo 'pi kavayaḥ paśyanti | matidarpaṇe kavīnāṃ viśvaṃ pratiphalati | kathaṃ nu vayaṃ dṛśyāmaha iti mahātmanām ahampūrvikayaiva śabdārthāḥ puro dhāvanti | yat siddhapraṇidhānā yoginaḥ paśyanti, tatra vācā vicaranti kavayaḥ ity anantā mahākaviṣu sūktayaḥ (iti) |*
>
> On this topic, people have said: "Even when a great poet is asleep, Sarasvatī shows him words and meanings. But someone who is not a great poet, turns a blind eye to these, even when awake. For great poets are blind from birth to the apparent acts of others, but have divine vision with regard to acts that are not apparent. Neither three-eyed Śiva nor thousand-eyed Indra sees what poets see even when their eyes are closed. In the mirror of poets' minds is reflected the universe. Words and meanings—out of their sheer desire to be first—run before the eyes of these great souls, saying, 'How in the world will we be shown?' Well-said stanzas are inexhaustible in great poets because poets enact in their speech what yogis practicing deep meditation see."
>
> *Kāvyamīmāṃsā*, 197

Rājaśekhara, in addition to identifying Sarasvatī as the divine source of poetic speech, ascribes such speech to poets' "brilliance" (*pratibhā*): "Brilliance is that which makes multitudes of words, meanings, and ornaments appear, in the mind, as another sort of speech altogether—as speech of this [poetic] type. For someone who lacks brilliance, a host of [perceptible] objects seems imperceptible. But, for someone who has brilliance, a host of objects seems perceptible even if it is imperceptible" (*yā śabdagrāmam arthasārtham alaṅkāratantram uktimārgam anyad api tathāvidham adhihṛdayaṃ pratibhāsayati sā pratibhā | apratibhasya padārthasārthaḥ parokṣa iva, pratibhāvataḥ punar apaśyato 'pi pratyakṣa iva |*) (*Kāvyamīmāṃsā*, 43). Because brilliance enables poets to perceive what other people cannot, Rājaśekhara considers this quality alone to be poetry's prerequisite: "[A poet] always should have closeby a case for slate and chalk, a covered box, palm leaves or birchbark with pens and pots of ink, palm leaves with copper tacks, and well-cleaned work surfaces. 'For that is the foundation of the craft of poetry,' say teachers. 'On the contrary, only brilliance is its foundation,' says a scion of the Yāyāvara family [i.e. Rājaśekhara]" (*tasya sampuṭikā*

31 The word *mahākavayo* is misprinted as *mahakavayo* in the *Kāvyamīmāṃsā*'s main text, but in Sharma's commentary the corresponding word, *mahākavayaḥ*, appears correctly (*Kāvyamīmāṃsā*, 197, 197n).

saphalakakhaṭikā, samudgakaḥ, salekhanīkamaṣībhājanāni tāḍipatrāṇi bhūrjatvaco vā, salohakaṇṭakāni tāladalāni, susammṛṣṭāḥ bhittayaḥ, satatasannihitāḥ syuḥ | 'tad dhi kāvyavidyāyāḥ parikaraḥ' iti ācāryāḥ | 'pratibhaiva parikaraḥ' iti yāyāvarīyaḥ |) (*Kāvyamīmāṃsā*, 163).

Although Rājaśekhara does not explicitly link brilliance and Sarasvatī, he portrays them as affecting poets in similar ways: brilliance and Sarasvatī both extend poets' awareness to areas that usually would be beyond the reach of poets' senses, and, by bringing the components of poetry into poets' minds, provide poets with the special language required to express what they perceive. Therefore, perhaps by instilling brilliance in poets, Sarasvatī causes them to create and consequently is celebrated herself:

> *tadāha—"sarasvatī sā jayati prakāmaṃ devī śrutiḥ svastyayanaṃ kavīnām |*
> *anarghatām ānayati svabhaṅgyā yollikhya yat kiñcid ihārtharatnam ||"*

> In this regard, someone has said:
> "Glory in the highest to that goddess Sarasvatī, who is speech itself (the path to prosperity for poets),
> who, by depicting in her own way anything—in this world—that is a gem among objects, renders it priceless."
>
> *Kāvyamīmāṃsā*, 226

Sarasvatī is associated with brilliance here by Sharma as well. Glossing "'in her own way'" (*svabhaṅgyā*) as "'by means of brilliance'" (*pratibhayā*), he observes of Sarasvatī's action, "This is the power of brilliance, because of which, words and meanings—despite being common to all people—reach some pinnacle of pricelessness" (*pratibhāyā eṣa prabhāvo yatsarvajanasādhāraṇā api śabdārthau kāmapi anarghatākoṭīm āsādayataḥ |*[32]) (*Kāvyamīmāṃsā*, 226n).

Poets who possess brilliance, according to Rājaśekhara, deserve just as much praise as the verse that they produce:

> *atrāhuḥ—"nīcair nārthakathāsarge yasya na pratibhākṣayaḥ |*
> *sa kavigrāmaṇīr atra śeṣās tasya kuṭumbinaḥ ||"*

> On this matter, people have said:
> "He whose brilliance does not diminish in the course of creating narratives about subjects that are not base,

[32] I translate the adjective *yatsarvajanasādhāraṇā* as if it modifies the noun *śabdārthau*, because I believe that Sharma predicated this plural adjective of this dual noun. Without assuming this error, I see no way to construe this sentence.

> is the chief of poets in this world. All the other poets are his attendants."
>
> *Kāvyamīmāṃsā*, 126

The prestige of brilliant poets is based on the originality that sets them apart from others:

> *śabdārthoktiṣu yaḥ paśyed iha kiñcana nūtanam |*
> *ullikhet kiñcana prācyaṃ manyatāṃ sa mahākaviḥ ||*
>
> Whoever—in this world—sees something new in terms of words, meanings, and sentences
> as he depicts something old, let that great poet be esteemed.
>
> *Kāvyamīmāṃsā*, 195

This fresh vision that great poets have is rooted, in turn, in their brilliance, an implication that Sharma brings to light as he comments on this couplet's second line: "Whoever 'depicts' (i.e. shines on) 'something' (i.e. that which is indescribable) 'priorly' (i.e. first) in that way, 'let that great poet be esteemed' (i.e. let him be lauded)" (*tathā kiṃcanānirvacanīyaṃ prācyaṃ*[33] *prathamam ullikhet pratibhāyāt sa mahākaviḥ manyatām anumodyatām |*) (*Kāvyamīmāṃsā*, 195n). In glossing the verb *ullikhet* ("he should depict") with the verb *pratibhāyāt* ("he should shine on"), Sharma does not provide a synonym so much as point to the *pratibhā* by whose virtue poets innovate.

If Sarasvatī nurtures this brilliance by which poets attain acclaim, then her status as their "'path to prosperity'" (*svastyayanaṃ*) makes sense (*Kāvyamīmāṃsā*, 226). But why, then, does she herself—in Rājaśekhara's initial narrative—need a guide to find her way back to her baby, Kāvyapuruṣa? Why is the goddess of knowledge not in the know herself? The answers to these questions concern the covert reason behind the encounter of Sarasvatī and Vālmīki. This interaction, in addition to occasioning human beings' goddess-given gift of poetry, represents the daily routine of poetic composition that Rājaśekhara recommends.

This routine has four parts:

> *aniyatakālāḥ pravṛttayo viplavante tasmād divasaṃ ... yāmakrameṇa caturddhā vibhajet | sa prātar utthāya kṛtasandhyāvarivasyaḥ sārasvataṃ sūktam adhīyīta | tato vidyāvasathe yathāsukham āsīnaḥ kāvyasya vidyā*

33 Sharma understands *prācyaṃ* (literally, "prior" or "ancient") differently than I do. Whereas I read *prācyaṃ* as an adjective ("old") modifying the pronoun *kiñcana* ("something"), he takes *prācyaṃ* as an adverb ("priorly") modifying the verb *ullikhet* ("he should depict").

upavidyāś cānuśīlayed āpraharāt | na hy evaṃvidho 'nyaḥ[34] *pratibhāhetur yathā pratyagrasaṃskāraḥ | dvitīye kāvyakriyām | upamadhyāhnaṃ*[35] *snāyād aviruddhaṃ bhuñjīta ca | bhojanānte kāvyagoṣṭhīṃ pravarttayet | kadācic ca praśnottarāṇi bhindīta | kāvyasamasyādhāraṇā, mātṛkābhyāsaḥ, citrā yogā ity āyāmatrayam | caturtha ekākinaḥ parimitapariṣado vā pūrvāhṇabhāgavihitasya kāvyasya parīkṣā | rasāveśataḥ kāvyaṃ viracayato na ca vivektrī dṛṣṭis tasmād anuparīkṣet | adhikasya tyāgo, nyūnasya pūraṇam, anyathāsthitasya parivarttanaṃ, prasmṛtasyānusandhānaṃ cety ahīnam |*

Those undertakings whose times are not fixed fall apart. Therefore, one should divide his day ... into a series of four periods of three hours each.

[A poet] should rise with the sun, should worship with prayers, and should chant a hymn to Sarasvatī. Then he should sit comfortably in his study and, for the remainder of the period, should practice the poetic arts and crafts repeatedly. For the cause of brilliance is nothing else but constant self-cultivation.

During the second period, he repeatedly should practice composing poetry. Shortly before noon, he should bathe and should eat food that agrees with him.

When he has finished eating, he should meet with others to discuss poetry. And sometimes he should break into the conversation, with questions or answers. Comprehending how to complete incomplete stanzas, memorizing mystical diagrams made from certain letters of the alphabet, and various applications—the trio of three-hour periods should end with these.

During the fourth period, he—either alone or with a group limited to a few—should examine the poetry composed during the earlier part of the day. But a person composing poetry does not have discernment with regard to it, because he is under the influence of his feelings. Therefore, he should examine his poetry after everyone else does. Omitting what is extraneous, filling in what is lacking, rearranging what is out of place, and inserting what has been forgotten—these bring the routine of composition to a close.

Kāvyamīmāṃsā, 167–168

[34] In the *Kāvyamīmāṃsā*'s main text, *evaṃvidho 'nyaḥ* is misprinted as *evaṃvidhonyaḥ* (*Kāvyamīmāṃsā*, 167).

[35] The word *upamadhyāhnaṃ* is misprinted as *upamadhyānhaṃ* in the *Kāvyamīmāṃsā*'s main text, but appears correctly in Sharma's commentary (*Kāvyamīmāṃsā*, 167, 167n).

Several activities in which a poet engages over the course of his day correspond to certain of Sarasvatī's own acts in the story about the birth of her son (*Kāvyamīmāṃsā*, 24–26, 27, 29). These correspondences suggest that she symbolizes an eloquent poet striving to produce poetry.[36]

Such a poet's day breaks with diligent devotion to a divinity and with assiduous study of the disciplines pertaining to poetry. The poet praises Sarasvatī so that she will be pleased enough to enable him to compose poetry; and he, in order to develop the brilliance necessary to do so, practices poetic skills. Similarly, Sarasvatī venerates Brahmā so that he will beget her a baby who personifies poetry; and she, in addition to the prayers that she presumably addresses to Brahmā, offers him austerities that also demonstrate her commitment to her cause.

As a result of her efforts, Sarasvatī bears Kāvyapuruṣa. After she spends some time holding him, she leaves him on a rock face and takes a bath. A poet is correspondingly productive during the second stage of his day, during which he is dedicated to composing poetry. But, toward the end of this phase, he leaves off his work—which probably is inscribed with chalk on the sort of slate that Rājaśekhara counts among poets' supplies (*Kāvyamīmāṃsā*, 163)—and bathes.

Before the poet comes back to his composition, he seeks out other poets who can help him hone his poetic craft. While he himself may be able to assist them with some poetic issue, he, as only one person, most likely knows less than do they, as a group. Therefore, during the third part of his day, he focuses on following the other poets' lead, in an effort to obtain information that ultimately will enhance his own poetry.

Sarasvatī likewise requires assistance before she returns to Kāvyapuruṣa. As her guide, Vālmīki represents two types of poetic resources. First, he—by taking her to her infant, Poetry Personified—stands for the aforementioned "avenue of eloquence" (*sārasvataṃ vartma*) that leads poets to their own nascent narratives (*Kāvyamīmāṃsā*, 91). The two *itihāsa*s at this avenue's origin, Vālmīki's *Rāmāyaṇa* and Vyāsa's *Mahābhārata*, provide in their contents the raw materials from which Rājaśekhara and his contemporaries can construct compositions at the road's end (*Kāvyamīmāṃsā*, 15–16, 114). Second, Vālmīki—by bringing Sarasvatī to Uśanas' abode—symbolizes the assistance that a poet receives from peers during the third part of his day, before turning back to his own composition. By virtue of Vālmīki's involvement in her quest for Kāvyapuruṣa, Sarasvatī has access to two poets who have varying degrees of experience: Uśanas, who already has become a poet; and Vālmīki, who is about to become one. While Vālmīki gets the gift of poetic speech from Sarasvatī after reuniting her with her son, Uśanas

[36] The following seven paragraphs will appear in a somewhat different form in Pathak, forthcoming.

has acquired such speech from Kāvyapuruṣa himself, in return for taking care of this infant, and consequently is called a *kavi* (poet) (*Kāvyamīmāṃsā*, 29, 28). The sages' common craft also is emblematized by their shared blood. Uśanas' father, Bhṛgu, is identified as an ancestor of Vālmīki in the *Rāmāyaṇa*, *Mahābhārata*, and other texts.[37]

Uśanas' classification as a *kavi* and Uśanas' association with the *Rāmāyaṇa*'s Vālmīki recall Uśanas' own role in another *itihāsa*. In the *Mahābhārata*, where he repeatedly is referred to as Kāvya (Kavi's son),[38] Uśanas is most famous for his unusual affiliations with rebirth and revival. Early in the work, he accidentally swallows his student Kaca, who becomes a son of Uśanas by breaking out of his belly (*Mahābhārata* 1.71.33, 48–49). Later on, Uśanas is ingested whole by Śiva, who becomes Uśanas' father by ejaculating him (hence his other name, Śukra [Semen]) (*Mahābhārata* 12.278.19–20, 29–36). Robert P. Goldman rightly relates both rebirths to Uśanas' ability to bring the dead back to life, though Goldman elaborates on only the initial instance of this relationship.[39] Here, the link is explicit: only by conferring his "knowledge of revivification" (*vidyām ... jīvanīṃ*) on Kaca can Kāvya ensure his own survival after he is forced to give birth and thereby to allow Kaca to be reborn (*Mahābhārata* 1.71.46). In the second case, however, rebirth and revival are connected only indirectly: Uśanas, by propitiating Śiva with praise (*Mahābhārata* 12.278.28–29), persuades the god to release him, and thus has used his own wits to secure for himself a second lease on life. Effectively, Uśanas revives himself by causing himself to be reborn.

Uśanas' associations with rebirth and revival are relevant to his appearance in Rājaśekhara's story about Sarasvatī. In this regard, the fact that someone known as a poet has the power to revive the dead is understandable. Take, for example, such successors of Uśanas as the poets whom Rājaśekhara holds up as exemplars, Vālmīki and Vyāsa—authors who speak animatedly about any of the long-gone people populating accounts of the way things had been. Yet Uśanas makes himself most symbolically useful in Sarasvatī's story by representing rebirth. When she sees her son for the second time, at Uśanas' ashram, Kāvyapuruṣa is dramatically different than he was when with her previously. When they first meet, he acts like an adult, standing upright and greeting her in verse. He behaves like a baby solely at her behest, just before she leaves him for her bath. But, when Sarasvatī and Kāvyapuruṣa reunite, he remains infantile,

37 On this identification, see Goldman 1976:97–101.

38 In addition to being named Kāvya Uśanas and Uśanas Kāvya, he specifically is said to be the son of Kavi (*kaviputra*) (*Mahābhārata* 1.71.6, 10; 1.78.25; 1.79.2, 24; 1.80.21; 1.77.15; 1.71.20). Kavi is either Bhṛgu himself, who also is identified as Uśanas' father, or Bhṛgu's son (*Mahābhārata* 1.78.37, 1.60.40).

39 Goldman 1977:90–91.

ready to be suckled as he lies on her lap after she picks him up. Through his transformation, he is as if reborn.

There is an analogous change in the poetry to which a poet returns during the fourth period of his day. This change is anticipated by a shift in the poet's own perspective. Just after he creates his composition, he cannot assess it critically. Much as Sarasvatī sings out of joy the praises of her newborn boy, the poet feels too positively toward his creation to see its shortcomings. After he has spent some time away from his work, however, and other poets have looked his effort over, he sees it in a new light. Just as the interventions of Uśanas and Vālmīki bring Sarasvatī to a place where she provides the breast milk that her baby needs to thrive, the comments of other composers show a poet the ways in which he can improve his work, and through the ensuing process of revision his poetry takes another shape. Moreover, the mindset that the poet's critics, when they examine his composition, should have is the compassionate one for which Uśanas and Vālmīki both are known long before the story of Kāvyapuruṣa is told: Uśanas, "as a consequence of his compassion" (*nimitte karuṇātmake*) (*Mahābhārata* 12.278.7d), is kind to the demons opposing the gods; and Vālmīki feels compassion for the crying crane whose hunter he curses (*Rāmāyaṇa* 1.2.9–15, 26–28).

Although Rājaśekhara acknowledges in his *Kāvyamīmāṃsā* Vālmīki's poetic expertise, calling him a *kavi* and embodying through him the aid that poets obtain from their peers, Rājaśekhara separates Vālmīki's *Rāmāyaṇa*—as well as *kavi* Vyāsa's *Mahābharata*, the other *itihāsa* that he mentions by name—from the poetry of his own period. This poetry offers a new outlook on the topics treated by those accounts of the way things had been and by other human-made *śāstras*. For Rājaśekhara, this difference in approach between the *kāvya*s of his day and the *itihāsa*s of old is the distance along the avenue of eloquence between the beginning of this road, the *Rāmāyaṇa* and *Mahābhārata*, and the poems of his contemporaries and himself, which constitute this path's conclusion. Even though the poet's and his cohorts' compositions comprise some of the same speech and story elements as do the earlier accounts, these later efforts evince a brilliance that is all their own by combining these elements in other ways.

His vision of poetry thus diverges from that of Ānandavardhana, who imagines an infinite path of poetry interconnecting *kāvya*s old (including the *Rāmāyaṇa* and *Mahābhārata*) and new. While Ānandavardhana adduces Vālmīki's and Vyāsa's works as evidence of the poetic concepts that he wishes to convey, even implying—in anticipation of Rājaśekhara's explication—that the *Mahābhārata* is a *śāstra*, he does not distinguish these exemplary poems from their successors in his time. Rather than relegate the *Rāmāyaṇa* and *Mahābhārata* to the arid reaches of a faraway past, he observes in these poems, as in those of his period, the flowing of evocative emotional essences.

Whether the *Rāmāyaṇa* and *Mahābhārata* are considered *kāvyas* (à la Ānandavardhana) or *itihāsas* (in the manner of Rājaśekhara), neither category is entirely adequate, as attested by each exegete's occasional use of another rubric. Actually, these scholars follow the example that the two texts themselves set individually, as each work refers to itself primarily in one way, but adopts additional self-designations as necessary. Nevertheless, the strategy of especially emphasizing one term is suitable if that term aligns with an interpreter's analytical aims, as do the terms used by Ānandavardhana and Rājaśekhara. Yet, in cases where critics seek to capture with one word both the age-old insight of an *itihāsa* and the aesthetic appeal of a *kāvya*, a third term is required. The overarching appellation adopted by twentieth-century connoisseurs of the *Rāmāyaṇa* and *Mahābhārata*, who want to have on hand as staples the traditional stories of these *itihāsas* and to eat the fresh-flavored cakes of these *kāvyas* too, is "epic." This designation demands more attention, for a term of Classical Greek origin that is transferred to the strikingly different terrain of ancient India not only takes much along when departing, but also acquires a lot upon arriving.[40]

The Continuing Connection of the *Rāmāyaṇa* and *Mahābhārata* in the Twentieth Century

Twentieth-century critics, in categorizing the *Rāmāyaṇa* and *Mahābhārata* as epics,[41] all take after E. Washburn Hopkins (1857–1932), the philological pioneer whose work informed English-speakers of these poems. Hopkins not only refers to the poems as "epics" and to their authors as "epic poets,"[42] but also reveals that he orients himself to these texts by turning to their Greek analogues. True to his training as a classicist (he taught Latin at Columbia University and Greek at Bryn Mawr College before becoming a Sanskrit professor at Yale University), Hopkins contrasts the *Mahābhārata* and the *Rāmāyaṇa* thus: "beside the huge and motley pile that goes by Vyāsa's name stands clear and defined the little Rāmāyaṇa of Vālmīki, as (in this respect) besides Homer's vague Homerica stands the distinct Argonautika of Apollonius."[43] Although Hopkins overtly views Vyāsa as "[t]he Hindu Homer," as the "*poiētēs epôn*" who "out-Homers Homer,"[44] Hopkins implicitly cloaks Vālmīki with the Homeric mantle as well, by likening the composition of the *Mahābhārata* and *Rāmāyaṇa* to the making of

40 An earlier version of the current chapter's remainder has appeared in Pathak 2013:44–52.

41 Kane 1966:11; Nooten 1978:49; J. D. Smith 1980:48; Shulman 2001:21; Brockington 1998:1.

42 Hopkins 1901:58, 244; 1915:1, 11.

43 Hopkins 1901:58.

44 Hopkins 1901:379, 4, 58.

the *Iliad* and *Odyssey*: "As the two Greek epics were both based to a certain extent on the general rhapsodic phraseology of the day, so the two Hindu epics, though there was without doubt borrowing in special instances, were yet in this regard independent of each other, being both dependent on previous rhapsodic and narrative phraseology."[45]

After Hopkins, scholars evince varying levels of self-consciousness in classifying the Sanskrit poems as epics. While Sanskritists P. V. Kane, Barend A. van Nooten, and John D. Smith do not mention the connection between the term "epic" and Homer's works, historian of religions David Shulman and Sanskritist John Brockington do—and Brockington advances still farther by suggesting that this relationship is worthy of further study.

Both Shulman and Brockington see the Sanskrit texts in the light of their Greek antecedents. Shulman recognizes that the *Rāmāyaṇa* and *Mahābhārata*'s complementarity recalls that of "the prototypical epic poems of Homer," the *Iliad* and *Odyssey*.[46] Brockington is similarly explicit in associating the *Mahābhārata* and the *Iliad*. He observes "broad similarities between the battles of the *Mahābhārata* and the *Iliad*," remarking that "the whole of India took part" in the fighting featured in the *Mahābhārata*, "in the same way that in the *Iliad* all the Greek world took part in the siege of Troy."[47] Brockington also interrelates the *Rāmāyaṇa* and the Homeric works, albeit less conspicuously. In the course of explaining away inconsistencies in the *Rāmāyaṇa* narrative, he adduces the "even Homer nods" aphorism. And, as Brockington describes the tendency of the *Rāmāyaṇa* to refer to precious metals rather than the baser ones that already were employed by the time the poem was composed, he cites "adherence to the older pattern on precisely this point" as "a well known feature of Homer."[48]

Even more importantly, Brockington raises a question that anyone studying the Sanskrit poems today should attempt to answer: "It is ... worth asking from the start whether designation of the *Mahābhārata* and ... *Rāmāyaṇa* as 'epics' affects our understanding of them, generating expectations derived from ideas about the *Iliad* and *Odyssey*."[49] To respond to Brockington's query, I will draw from the resources of metaphor theories from the fields of philosophy and literary criticism.

45 Hopkins 1901:65.
46 Shulman 2001:23.
47 Brockington 1998:77, 26.
48 Brockington 1998:386, 411.
49 Brockington 1998:1.

Metaphor and the Sanskrit "epics"

I turn to these theories because identifying the implications of asserting that the *Rāmāyaṇa* and *Mahābhārata* are epics requires recognizing that this assertion is a metaphor. The statement's metaphorical aspect stems from the fact that the term "epic" is inextricable from the *Iliad* and *Odyssey*. Characterizing the Sanskrit poems as "epics," then, constrains their definition, in the manner (mutatis mutandis) mentioned by Slavicist David E. Bynum. For Bynum, "the name 'epic' is only a more or less metaphorical expression as applied to oral poetry in many parts of the modern world," because the term indicates a "long verse narrative sharing qualities of the *Iliad* and *Odyssey*" and excludes "the peculiar features of particular modern [poetic] traditions."[50]

Yet the metaphorical equation of poems with epics does more than merely reduce non-Greek narratives to the characteristics that these texts have in common with Homeric works. Three of this equation's implications are indicated by theories of metaphor.

The first implication enables the act of discerning that the equation indeed is a metaphor. Implicit in this kind of equation—in the analysis of philosopher Jacques Derrida[51]—is the "primitive meaning" of the equation, the equation's original import, which makes patent the equation's metaphorical nature. Thus, the primitive meaning of the equation of the Sanskrit poems with epics is that the *Rāmāyaṇa* and *Mahābhārata* are equivalent to the *Iliad* and *Odyssey*. But—as the equation becomes current and the Sanskrit compositions commonly come to be called "epics"—this primitive meaning is "forgotten," and "[t]he metaphor is no longer noticed." By this point, the primitive meaning has been supplanted by a less particular "proper meaning": hence the *Rāmāyaṇa* and *Mahābhārata* are epics insofar as this pair of Sanskrit works are long verse narratives.[52]

The process of retrieving an equation's primitive meaning and thereby of perceiving the equation as a metaphor has been portrayed metaphorically itself in the image of a resurrection. Literary critic I. A. Richards, for instance, speaks of "wak[ing] ... up" metaphors that seem "stone dead," and philosopher Paul Ricoeur similarly refers to the "reanimation" or "rejuvenation of dead metaphors."[53] But I think that this recognition process is characterized more aptly by a metaphor that captures the reversal of the memory failure discussed

50 Bynum 1976:45, 54, 45.

51 Derrida 1974:8–9.

52 I do not mean to imply here that all genre classifications necessarily are metaphors, merely those taxonomies in which the generic term has been coined with such a small number of species in mind that the term, to be used in another context, must be transferred across significant cognitive space.

53 Richards 1936:101; Ricoeur 1977:291, 292.

by Derrida: to discern a metaphor, then, is to remind an amnesiac metaphor that it is a metaphor.

Once the metaphorical aspect of the equation of Sanskrit poems with epics is remembered, the equation's second and third implications become apparent. If its first implication is its possession of a primitive meaning, then the equation's second implication is that the primitive meaning accentuates those of the Sanskrit poems' characteristics that accord with this meaning. Therefore, to equate the *Rāmāyaṇa* and *Mahābhārata* with epics is not only to suggest that the Sanskrit poems are equivalent to the *Iliad* and *Odyssey* (which is the primitive meaning of the aforementioned equation), but also to foreground those of the Sanskrit works' features that are analogous to attributes of the Greek works. The metaphorical equation—to borrow an image from philosopher Max Black[54]—thus functions as a filter composed of stripes of clear and opaque glass: if the Sanskrit poems are the night sky and their features are stars, then the stars most clearly visible through the filter (which stands for the equation of the Sanskrit poems with epics) align with the lines of clear glass in the filter (which represent the attributes of the Greek poems that evidence the equation's primitive meaning).

Yet those of the Sanskrit poems' characteristics that have no Greek counterparts are not obscured for long. Indeed, the third implication of the metaphorical equation of the *Rāmāyaṇa* and *Mahābhārata* with epics is that the semantic domain of the term "epic" expands to encompass the Sanskrit compositions' unique characteristics. This broader definition of "epic" ensues from a productive tension inherent in the predication that makes the metaphor possible. Two theorizations of this type of tension indicate how it operates with respect to the Sanskrit poems. According to Ricoeur, "the tension [is] between an 'is' and an 'is not,'" between the "literal interpretation restricted to the established values of words" in a statement (this interpretation being that the Sanskrit poems are epics in the original Greek sense, by virtue of resembling the *Iliad* and *Odyssey*) and the "metaphorical interpretation resulting from the 'twist' imposed on these words in order to 'make sense' in terms of the statement as a whole" (this interpretation being that the Sanskrit poems are not epics in the original Greek sense, but are epics in some other sense).[55] Philosopher Monroe C. Beardsley elaborates on the process whereby predicative tension produces the metaphorical interpretation. Just as the term "tension" itself denotes stretching as well as conflict, "the clash between sameness and difference" in a metaphor "twist[s]" the meaning of the predicate nominative that is attached metaphorically to a

54 Black 1962:39, 41.

55 Ricoeur 1977:248, 296.

subject.[56] Consequently, the original sense of the predicate nominative "epics" shifts from "poems similar to the *Iliad* and *Odyssey*" to a new connotation that conforms to the two Sanskrit works that constitute the subject, namely, "poems resembling the *Rāmāyaṇa* and *Mahābhārata*."

Reminding the amnesiac equation of the Sanskrit poems with epics that it is a metaphor, then, does not—contrary to Bynum's contention—simply highlight the Sanskrit poems' correspondences to their Greek analogues. The "entities" between which a metaphor "posit[s] an illuminating resemblance" are not—pace anthropologist Fitz John Porter Poole—"apparently disparate,"[57] but actually are so; and their differences, which also are elucidated by the metaphor, are as enlightening as their similarities. More precisely, the interplay of likeness and unlikeness in the epic metaphor for the Sanskrit poems provides a guide to exploring attributes of the *Rāmāyaṇa* and *Mahābhārata* that the *Iliad* and *Odyssey* do not exhibit, as well as the characteristics that the Greek and Sanskrit poems share.

The *Rāmāyaṇa* and *Mahābhārata* as epics like and unlike the *Iliad* and *Odyssey*

Qualities common to the Greek and Sanskrit epics

The *Rāmāyaṇa* and *Mahābhārata* are epics in the original Greek sense insofar as they display traits analogous to those of the *Iliad* and *Odyssey*. Thus the Sanskrit epics are immense, intricate works that arise from line repetition, ring composition, and episode multiplication; and that use the same metrical language and treat some of the same themes, by virtue of belonging to the same storytelling tradition.

As to the form of the Sanskrit poems, both are enormous. Although the *Mahābhārata* (with a total of almost 75,000 verses in its eighteen *parvans* [books]) is a "great epic" in comparison with "the little epic" of the *Rāmāyaṇa*,[58] the latter (which contains just under 20,000 verses in its seven *kāṇḍas* [parts]) is lengthy itself. Unsurprisingly, these sizeable works include certain lines more than once and elaborate on the events that compose the poems' contents. Moreover, each epic's story line comes full circle and, by the inclusion of additional incidents, is extended along the way.

The *Rāmāyaṇa* is ringed by two pairs of "pictures of ideal society"[59] and by two portrayals of the ritual during which the poem itself is recited. At the

56 Ricoeur 1977:196; Beardsley 1962:294.
57 Poole 1986:421.
58 Hopkins 1901:58.
59 Brockington 1998:400.

beginning of the *Rāmāyaṇa*, as Nārada informs Vālmīki about Rāma, the celestial sage describes the prosperity of Rāma's people and the monarch's entry into heaven, images that reappear at the *Rāmāyaṇa*'s end. Not long after Nārada departs, Vālmīki has his disciples Kuśa and Lava recite the *Rāmāyaṇa* to Rāma at his horse sacrifice (*aśvamedha*); and the poem revisits the ritual context of the princes' performance, soon before re-presenting the ultimate successes of Rāma's reign. The image of "righteous rule" also recurs in Kuśa and Lava's rendition: between the bookends that are the scenes of Rāma's horse sacrifice, Kuśa and Lava praise both Rāma's father, Daśaratha, and Rāma himself for doing right by the subjects in their sovereignty, Ayodhyā.[60]

While three narrative rings enclose the *Rāmāyaṇa*'s main events, the *Mahābhārata* is encircled by two rings that relate to the sacrifice at this poem's center: "The epic opens [and closes] with Janamejaya's snake sacrifice, which provides the setting for its narration; the action proper commences with the *rājasūya* [royal consecration], which is so fatefully interrupted by [the monarch] Yudhiṣṭhira's defeat at the dice-game;[61] the main narrative is then concluded by the Aśvamedha, the other, even greater sacrifice of kingship; and ... [between these two royal sacrifices that are recounted between the snake sacrifice's scenes is] the awesome sacrifice of battle."[62] The *Mahābhārata*'s narrative thus has been arranged to have a ripple effect that enlarges the poem plot's ritual dimensions. The sacrificial war at the core of the *Mahābhārata* story is compassed most closely by the *rājasūya* and *aśvamedha* observances and more remotely by the serpent ceremony that surrounds them.

Separating each set of concentric circles whose diameters compose the *Rāmāyaṇa*'s or *Mahābhārata*'s story line are tangential tales that diverge in many directions from this plot line. The multiplication of such narrative interludes in both poems leads one critic to conclude: "The available texts of the two Sanskrit epics are thus—and this is especially true of the *Mahābhārata*—gargantuan hodge-podges, literary pile-ups on a grand scale."[63] While I, too, believe that the *Rāmāyaṇa* and the *Mahābhārata* probably were pieced together from a number of sources, I do not intend to suggest that the authors of these works assembled their contents at random. Rather I would argue that the epic authors incorporated into the plots of their poems tangential tales that illuminated important aspects of the poems' central stories.

60 Brockington 1998:400–401. Here, Brockington refers to only one of the three rings surrounding the *Rāmāyaṇa* story—the circle comprising Daśaratha's and Rāma's kingships—and not to the loops including Kuśa and Lava's sacrificial recitation and Rāma's celestial ascension, respectively.

61 For discussion of this interruption and of similar occurrences, see Minkowski 2001.

62 Brockington 1998:45–46. The sacrificial aspects of the Mahābhārata war have been analyzed by Hiltebeitel (1990:287–296, 312–335).

63 J. D. Smith 1980:50.

The similar developments of the *Rāmāyaṇa* and the *Mahābhārata* result from a shared tradition at the levels of tongue and tale alike. The epics speak not the classical Sanskrit of later courtly literature, but an earlier idiom that is sparer in style and is not governed rigidly by the grammatical rules that crystallize only subsequently. Moreover, as Hopkins has observed,[64] both works employ many of the same poetic formulae.

The *Rāmāyaṇa* and the *Mahābhārata* overlap narratively as well as linguistically. While the *Rāmāyaṇa* notes a number of characters that the *Mahābhārata* describes in more detail, the *Mahābhārata* offers its own rendition of Rāma's story and also relates tales about other actors in the *Rāmāyaṇa*. These narrative interconnections probably reflect the epics' reliance on the same stock of older stories, in addition to the epics' influence on each other. Other evidence of this stock includes the verses that texts other than the two epics cite that appear to be from them but are not.[65]

Even though the "ground of literary allusion"[66] that the *Rāmāyaṇa* and *Mahābhārata* have in common is located in the particular context of ancient India, the epics cover four of the themes that the *Iliad* and *Odyssey* explore.

First, the *Rāmāyaṇa* and *Mahābhārata* treat the hero's need to separate himself from his usual social surroundings. The two works highlight the forest exiles of the warriors who are the epics' heroes, because being displaced from their regular royal roles affords these rulers opportunities to marshal the martial resources that the men need ultimately to defeat their foes.

Second, the Sanskrit epics address the destabilization of social order by strife, for the two poems feature families torn apart that cannot be restored in the wake of war. In the *Rāmāyaṇa*, Rāma, in deference to Daśaratha, relinquishes the right to rule Ayodhyā to his younger half-brother (and Daśaratha's son) Bharata and agrees to be exiled to the forest for fourteen years. While there with Rāma, Sītā is abducted by Rāvaṇa, whose refusal to return her brings about bloodshed across the country. By the time Rāma reclaims his kingdom, Daśaratha is long dead and Sītā is soon to be banished by Rāma through no fault of her own. In the *Mahābhārata*, Yudhiṣṭhira, his four brothers, and Draupadī (the wife of all five) are forced to go to the forest for twelve years and to spend another year incognito, after his cousin Duryodhana cheats him out of his kingdom—Indraprastha—during a dice match. The hostilities that erupt worldwide when Duryodhana refuses to return Indraprastha eradicate almost the entire family.

64 For his catalogue of parallel phrases in the *Rāmāyaṇa* and the *Mahābhārata*, see Hopkins 1901:403–445.

65 Hopkins 1901:64–65.

66 Hopkins 1901:79.

Third, each Sanskrit poem spotlights its hero's ability to reorder his life in the aftermath of societal ruptures. Thus, the *Rāmāyaṇa*'s Rāma becomes king and eventually embraces the sons whom Sītā bore during her banishment. The *Mahābhārata*'s Yudhiṣṭhira, too, is crowned and reigns righteously over the other survivors of warfare.

Fourth, the *Rāmāyaṇa* and *Mahābhārata* underscore the mortal constraints on their heroes by exploring the extents of their god-given gifts. Rāma (a human manifestation of Viṣṇu) and Yudhiṣṭhira (the human son conceived by mortal Kuntī once she coupled with immortal Dharma) attest that the epic "world of men [has] close kinship with the gods."[67] Simultaneously, however, the heroes' mortality circumscribes their exceptional success. Although Rāma gets rid of Rāvaṇa and thus outdoes the gods, sets a moral example for his Ayodhyan subjects over his long reign, and leads them to heaven at the end of his life, he cannot bring Sītā back to the human world once she has buried herself alive. In like manner, Yudhiṣṭhira cannot keep his brothers and Draupadī from predeceasing him and from falling temporarily into an illusory hell, even though he has demonstrated righteousness (which his divine father personifies) regularly enough to earn the honor of ascending into heaven in his human body. The ends of Rāma and Yudhiṣṭhira thus illustrate the challenge of achieving within the confines of the human condition.

At the same time that the *Rāmāyaṇa* and *Mahābhārata* resemble the *Iliad* and *Odyssey*, these Sanskrit works remain distinct from the Greek ones. The characteristics particular to the Sanskrit poems constitute their contribution to the category of epic.

Distinctive qualities of the Sanskrit epics

At least three traits set apart the Sanskrit epics from their Greek analogues. The first is formal and invites consideration of the second and third, which concern content.

The *Rāmāyaṇa* and *Mahābhārata*'s most prominent formal feature is their repeated embedding of narratives within narratives. One such story that the *Rāmāyaṇa* nests is the account of Rāvaṇa's rise to power in the epic's seventh part. The sage Agastya tells this tale within the tale told by Kuśa and Lava, which itself appears in the tale told by an unnamed narrator. The tendency to embed tales is even more marked in the *Mahābhārata*.[68] For instance, the action on the

67 Hopkins 1915:3.

68 Accordingly, the term that the *Mahābhārata* uses most often for itself—*ākhyāna* (or "tale")—calls attention to the *upākhyānas* (or "subtales") that the poem incorporates. See Hiltebeitel 2005:466–476.

battlefield in books 6 through 9 is recounted by Saṃjaya—the charioteer-bard of Duryodhana's father, Dhṛtarāṣṭra—in the story recounted by Vaiśaṃpāyana in the story recounted by Ugraśravas in the story recounted by an unidentified narrator.[69]

Two types of material that are taken up in the embedded tales of the Sanskrit epics reflect the poems' particular devotional and didactic thrusts. Theologically speaking, the *Rāmāyaṇa* and *Mahābhārata*'s pointed polytheism preserves a pantheon that includes Vedic deities such as Indra (the gods' king), Agni (the fire god), Yama (the god of the dead), and Varuṇa (the water god)—four divinities also known as Lokapālas (World Protectors)—while promoting Viṣṇu above them all. Evidence of this Vaiṣṇavite preference occurs in the aforementioned inset stories.

For instance, the *Rāmāyaṇa*'s Rāvaṇa narrative, which Rāma hears after he has done away with this demon, both protects and perfects Viṣṇu's reputation. This account, by describing the boon Brahmā bestowed on Rāvaṇa that made him invulnerable to all beings except humans and other mammals, explains why mighty Viṣṇu had to become a man to destroy the demon.[70] Additionally, the Rāvaṇa account extols Viṣṇu implicitly by expounding on the power of the enemy whom Rāma defeated readily. Indeed, lesser deities than Viṣṇu—namely, the Lokapālas Kubera (the god of wealth), Yama, Varuṇa, and Indra—had lost to Rāvaṇa in battle. Moreover, the Rāvaṇa narrative makes Rāma's victory seem to be a matter of course. Immediately after relating, early on in the story, that Viṣṇu slew a slew of Rāvaṇa's ancestors who were stronger than their demonic descendant, Agastya reveals to Rāma that he is Viṣṇu and has been born on earth to dispose of demons.

As for Saṃjaya's wartime tale, its most famous excerpt is the *Bhagavadgītā* (*Song of the Lord*)—the dialogue, in the *Mahābhārata*'s sixth book, between Yudhiṣṭhira's brother Arjuna and their cousin Kṛṣṇa, who is another human manifestation of Viṣṇu and has been giving military advice to Yudhiṣṭhira and his brothers. Arjuna and Kṛṣṇa's conversation begins when Arjuna balks at killing his kinsmen in battle. Kṛṣṇa convinces Arjuna to rejoin the fray, not simply by citing Arjuna's soldierly obligations, but also by recasting his military

[69] Sanskritist Christopher Z. Minkowski (1989:420) suggests that this unnamed narrator is Vyāsa, for Minkowski argues that Vyāsa's identification as "a transcendent figure in the epic" obviates the "infinite regression of frames, each one the story of the previous narration." But I imagine the anonymous narrator as someone who has heard the story from Ugraśravas and is relating it at some later time—because seeing the narrator as such accentuates the antiquity of the story, in keeping with its self-presentation as an *itihāsa*.

[70] To vanquish Rāvaṇa's army, Rāma enlisted the aid of monkeys. The popular notion that Rāma received ursine, as well as simian, assistance probably postdates Vālmīki's *Rāmāyaṇa* (Goldman 1989).

service as a form of Vaiṣṇava worship. "Emphasis on the deity [Viṣṇu] reaches its climax ... in the theophany in the [*Bhagavadgītā*'s] eleventh chapter, where Kṛṣṇa reveals to Arjuna his universal form (the *viśvarūpadarśana*), after he has identified himself in the previous chapter with the most essential aspects of every part of the cosmos. This revelation produces in Arjuna a spirit of humble adoration, summed up as the way of devotion (*bhakti*)."[71] Even though Arjuna, to resume a familiar relationship with Kṛṣṇa, appears to forget this reborn deity's dazzling self-display, it throws a different light on the events of the epic, casting into relief their religious features. Specifically, Viṣṇu's temporary reemergence implicitly rebroaches the question of why he has been reborn as a man to begin with. According to the *Mahābhārata*'s opening book, his human rebirth is a response to that of demons who intend to overrun the earth. When the distressed goddess of the earth beseeches Brahmā to lighten her load, he tells the gods to take birth themselves as men to oppose their demonic foes. Before doing so, the divinities ask Viṣṇu to supervise their effort, which he does after becoming Kṛṣṇa. By enabling Yudhiṣṭhira and his similarly godlike brothers to win the cataclysmic war, Kṛṣṇa relieves the earth of her burden and ensures that righteousness will prevail.

In addition to Viṣṇu narratives, the Sanskrit epics embed stories whose primary purpose is to promote proper human conduct. Among the occasions when these moral tales are told are the forest exiles of the epics' heroes, who, by being distanced from their realms during those periods, are freed to reflect on how to behave even better. Rāma, for example, is reminded by Sītā, at the beginning of their exile in *Rāmāyaṇa* 3, that he should use violence only to protect others and not to terrorize those who have not provoked him. To convey her point, she tells him about an ascetic who becomes so attached to a sword that Indra has given him that he grows to enjoy attacking others without cause. A similarly instructive story for Yudhiṣṭhira in *Mahābhārata* 3 emphasizes munificence and asceticism. The visiting Vyāsa narrates to the monarch how a man named Mudgala, who gets by merely by gleaning rice, goes without food so that he can host hospitably a hungry hermit who actually is Durvāsas in disguise. For satisfying this infamously irascible sage, Mudgala is granted the right to go to heaven in his human body. Knowing that he will fall from heaven as soon as he finishes relishing the karmic fruit of his beneficence, however, leads him to eschew heaven in favor of performing austerities by which he can gain the even greater reward of release from the round of rebirth.

[71] Brockington 1998:274–275. For more on this theophany, see Hiltebeitel 1990:114–121, 124–128, 139, 257–258, 310 and Laine 1989:115–116, 168, 226–230, 232–234, 240–242, 244–249, 272.

These and the other parables in the *Rāmāyaṇa* and the *Mahābhārata* also point to the texts' broader tendency to incorporate more explicit teachings about ritual and moral subjects: "The two great Epics of India, the Mahābhārata and the Rāmāyaṇa, contain (particularly the first) numerous passages bearing on many topics of Dharmaśāstra,"[72] the body of treatises on *dharma*. But, as Kane hints here, this pattern of interpolation is much less pronounced in the *Rāmāyaṇa*, which contains "nothing corresponding to the material of the *Śānti* and *Anuśāsana parvans* [books 12 and 13 of the *Mahābhārata*] with their pronouncements on ethical and social issues, discourses on [such philosophies as] Sāṃkhya and Yoga, and so on."[73] Even so, other elements of the *Rāmāyaṇa* made it nearly as influential a religious authority as the *Mahābhārata*: "The Rāmāyaṇa is a Kāvya, yet, on account of the noble ideals that it sets up in the chief characters, it was very popular and is relied upon as a source in digests on Dharma, though not so frequently and profusely as the Mahābhārata."[74] This lingering indication of a difference between the Sanskrit epics points to parts of their interrelationship to which I have yet to turn.

United by their interest in *dharma*, the *Rāmāyaṇa kāvya* and the *Mahābhārata itihāsa* nevertheless depict this ideal differently. Yet their disparate approaches to *dharma* do not ensue solely from the works' distinct functions as dissimilar types of traditional texts. In fact, the contrasting ways in which the *Rāmāyaṇa* and the *Mahābhārata* portray *dharma* resemble the varying takes of the *Iliad* and the *Odyssey* on their own ideal, *kléos*. The intercultural similarity of these intra-cultural differences suggests that they reflect certain features of the epic genre itself. To make out these generic features, I will look more closely in Chapter 3 and Chapter 4 at the Greek and Indian dichotomies to which the features give rise.

72 Kane 1966:11.

73 Brockington 1998:441.

74 Kane 1966:53. References to the *Rāmāyaṇa* and the *Mahābhārata* in these *dharma* texts are recapitulated in Kane 1966:49–50, 58.

3

Listening to Achilles and to Odysseus

Poetic Kings on the Ideal of *Kléos* in the Homeric Epics

THE CONTRASTING CONSTRUALS OF *KLÉOS* in the *Iliad* and the *Odyssey* are embodied by the poems' bickering protagonists, Achilles and Odysseus, in the first song that Demodocus sings in *Odyssey* 8.72–82. In this performance, the singer does not specify the heroes' quarrel's source, but rather leaves it open to his audience's speculation. The very vagueness of the disagreement's grounds foregrounds the heroes' difference itself, however the *Odyssey*'s hearers choose to explain it.

Nagy discerns in Demodocus' song a distinction, not just between Achilles and Odysseus, but also between the *Iliad* and the *Odyssey*.[1] Each poem, as a member of the *kléa andrôn* class, consists in a particular *kléos* that contrasts with the *kléos* constituting the other poem. Each *kléos* can be characterized by scrutinizing the hero whose glory it is. In this manner, Nagy distinguishes Achilles' (and the *Iliad*'s) *kléos* of *bíē* and Odysseus' (and the *Odyssey*'s) *kléos* of *mêtis*.[2]

I concur with Nagy that the *Iliad*'s *kléos* and the *Odyssey*'s *kléos* can be differentiated on the basis of the respective attributes of Achilles and Odysseus. However, I do not agree that these attributes are *bíē* and *mêtis*.[3] Rather, I regard the royal roles of the heroes as reflecting the kinds of *kléos* characteristic of their poems—both the poems that the heroes themselves perform and the poems that contain their entire stories.

Indeed, the heroes cut quite different kingly figures. Whereas Achilles forsakes his country, Phthia, so that he can head the Achaean effort to conquer Troy, Odysseus journeys back from Troy so that he can reclaim his throne on the isle of Ithaca. While Achilles goes abroad to garner glory for giving up his life in

1 Nagy 1999:59.

2 Nagy 1999:45–46, 47, 48–49.

3 Even Nagy (1999:317–318, 319–321) himself breaks down his dichotomy between Iliadic *bíē* and Odyssean *mêtis*, in observing that *bíē* operates in the *Odyssey* as well as in the *Iliad*.

the course of taking over another area, Odysseus, the rightful sovereign of his realm, returns home to find fame.

The two kings thus seek distinct kinds of *kléos*, and the epics about them vary accordingly. Moreover, the epics give away their respective endings, capturing the different sorts of glory that are in store for their heroes, by having them perform disparate poems themselves. The songs that Achilles and Odysseus sing when displaced from the lands that they should command signal the disparity not only between the fames for which the rulers aim, but also between the attitudes with which they—and the epics that immortalize them—approach their ends.

Understanding the performances of Achilles and Odysseus as portents of these rulers' poetic glories would seem to have a precedent within the *Odyssey* itself. The heroes' argument here can be seen as a competition between their inchoate renowns (i.e. as a clash of the qualities characteristic of Achilles and Odysseus that ultimately will cause their exploits to be the subjects of songs); and Agamemnon delights in this strife, because it is a sign from Zeus' son Apollo that Troy will fall to the Achaean forces[4]—an event that ensures that both Achilles and Odysseus will be celebrated in song forever. Therefore, the heroes' quarrel (which, in the absence of any identifiers, can be generalized to comprise the heroes' competing performances, poetic and otherwise) amounts to an expression of the essences of two opposing incipient poems and anticipates the coexistence of the contrasting complete epics that will keep alive Achilles' and Odysseus' memories, namely, the *Iliad* and the *Odyssey*.

For those onlookers here like Agamemnon who have yet to see Achilles and Odysseus achieve the successes for which these men are to become famous, their altercation is but part of a prophecy starting to come to fruition. However, for those who hear of the heroes' conflict long after it and their acts that follow have become part of the poetic tradition, this prefiguration of the *Iliad* and the *Odyssey*'s distinction is not prophetic but proleptic. In the ears of an audience already aware of how the narratives of the *Iliad* and the *Odyssey* have unfolded, the arguing of Achilles and Odysseus resounds as prolepsis, a "narrative maneuver that consists of narrating or evoking in advance an event that will take place later."[5]

In like manner, the rulers' poetic performances provide prolepses of the kinds of *kléos* that these kings will achieve ultimately. In fact, the narratives that the kings themselves share with others suggest the sorts of stories that eventually will be told about these monarchs. Thus, the rulers regale their listeners

4 On this oracular passage's allusive nature, see Jong 2001:8.73–82n.

5 Genette 1980:40.

with tales that differ. Achilles recites an account abbreviated so much in the *Iliad*, as simply to be classified among the *kléa andrôn*. Yet his performance, in the company of his companion Patroclus, of a story that already is complete and esteemed indicates that Achilles' securing his own self-sacrificing glory, at Troy, is a foregone conclusion that the *Iliad* assumes and does not need to portray. By contrast, Odysseus composes a triad of extended poems that dwell on his failures to conquer other realms, but that explain how he will obtain fame upon reclaiming his home on Ithaca at the end of the *Odyssey*.

The disparity between Achilles' rhapsodic recitation and Odysseus' bardic compositions is illuminated by narratological theory. Specifically, cultural critic Mieke Bal's division of prolepses into explicit "announcements" and implicit "hints"[6] offers terms by which to distinguish—on the one hand—Odysseus' overt predictions of his glorious homecoming in the prophecies that he interlaces with his poems, from—on the other hand—the unstated connection between Achilles' little-described rendering and the fame that he is fated to claim while invading Troy. The implicit prolepsis of the glory Achilles achieves as a royal conqueror—in the *Iliad*'s mere mention of his rendition, at Troy, of *kléa andrôn*—is consistent with the epic's confidence in his impending poetic immortalization upon his death on the Trojan battlefield. So too does the *Odyssey*'s uncertainty about Odysseus' ability to live out his days illustriously, away from the sea, agree with the explicit prolepses expressed in the prophecies surrounding his accounts about the fame waiting for him at home. The *Odyssey*, as if to reassure its audience of Odysseus' fated fame, features him repeatedly professing his imminent success on Ithaca—even as the *Iliad*, in its surety of Achilles' glorious destiny far from Phthia, dispenses with the details of his rhapsody.

Together, Achilles in the *Iliad* and Odysseus in the *Odyssey* compose a complete portrait of kingship in its capacity to represent *kléos* poetically.[7] The pair of poetic communities that brought these kings into being not only may have been well aware of each other's efforts, but also may have worked together to create alternative depictions of their central ideal—portrayals that could appeal to disparate audiences. I regard *kléos* as a religious ideal because the Homeric epics pose it as a partial answer to the existential query of what happens to human beings after they die—one of the cross-cultural religious questions that I have discussed in the Introduction. In the Conclusion, I will treat the different

6 Bal 1997:97.

7 The poetic power of Homeric kingship as a representation of heroic glory rests—at least in ancient times—on the historical reality of kingship in Archaic Greek society. The relationship between this reality and its poetic depiction has been studied most extensively by classicist Robert Drews (1983:99–105, 108–115, 129–131) and historian Pierre Carlier (1984:137–138, 210–214, 503–505, 509–511).

ways in which hearers of the *Iliad* and the *Odyssey* may perceive their heroes, but for now allow me to limn each of these Homeric kings in his capacity to embody the *kléos* that his society held dear.

Achilles as a Rhapsode Far from Phthia

Achilles articulates this glorious ideal of *kléos* even as he refrains from fighting at the fore of the Achaean forces attempting to take over Troy, as members of the embassy sent to soothe his wounded pride encounter him:

> *Murmidónōn d' epí te klisías kaì nē̂as hikésthēn,*
> *tòn d' heûron phréna terpómenon phórmingi ligeíēi,*
> *kalē̂i daidaléēi, epì d' argúreon zugòn ē̂en,*
> *tḕn áret' ex enárōn pólin Ēetíōnos oléssas·*
> *tē̂i hó ge thumòn éterpen, áeide d' ára kléa andrō̂n.*
> *Pátroklos dé hoi oîos enantíos hē̂sto siōpē̂i,*
> *dégmenos Aiakídēn, hopóte lḗxeien aeídōn.*
>
> They came upon the Myrmidons' shelters and ships
> and lighted on him delighting in the clear sounds of a
> beautifully wrought, silver-bridged lyre
> that he had got from the spoils of Eëtion's city after destroying it.
> With the lyre, his heart's delight, [Achilles] was singing of the
> glorious deeds of men;
> and only Patroclus was sitting opposite him in silence,
> waiting for the moment when this scion of Aeacus would cease
> singing.
>
> *Iliad* 9.185–191

What frees Achilles to present this impromptu recital is his double displacement. Having been called away from his kingdom in Phthia to combat at Troy, he has been driven away from the naval warfare there by his anger at Agamemnon, who has stolen from Achilles his slave woman Briseïs (*Iliad* 1.335–344).

Instead of a scepter or a spear, then, Achilles grabs a lyre. Yet his performance's significance is conveyed as much by the presence of his silent friend as by the summary of the song's contents. Patroclus' presence has one of two senses: he either intends to begin singing when Achilles ends, or serves solely as Achilles' audience.[8]

[8] M. W. Edwards 1987:16.

On the latter interpretation, Patroclus, like the approaching embassy members, attends to Achilles' song and is eager for it to end—not out of any interest in its contents, but out of a wish for Achilles to come back to battle. In light of the tremendous toll that the Trojan conflict will exact from both sides, the musical interlude implies that Achilles, a man whom only a few can hear singing, will be famous for effecting destruction so widespread that only a few will survive him.[9]

But taking so broad a view of the havoc that ensues from Achilles' reentry into the fray requires overlooking his specific monarchical aspirations and their poetic representation. An important part of this representation is Achilles' interaction with Patroclus, an implicitly reciprocal performance whose significance emerges on the observation that both men are to play poets here and that, in doing so, "they are *re*producing, not producing[,] epic poetry."[10] At this point, the *Iliad* does not simply signal that any poet contributing to epics of its type—by virtue of being indebted to an earlier poetic tradition—is "recomposing [such works] in performance,"[11] but additionally anticipates a later distinction between poets who are the primary authors of such epics and performers who re-present these works long after the works have been in existence.

The bards belonging to the first category are the *aoidoí*—specialists in song (*aoidḗ*) that are identified as such in the *Iliad* and the *Odyssey* (see, for instance, *Iliad* 24.720 and *Odyssey* 1.325), and that probably were prevalent by the time of the poems' composition in the late eighth century BCE. In fact, I believe that each of the Homeric epics was composed by a community of *aoidoí*. In support of such a "model of the multiform epic bard," humanist John Miles Foley notes: "The very multiformity of 'Homer the epic poet' as represented in the ancient sources—from the various lives of Homer through accounts from Herodotus, Plutarch and Proclus—argues for a legendary rather than a real, documentary figure. Instead of seeking to determine which of the disparate histories is true, or trying to reduce their obvious inconsistencies to one archetypal story from which others must have evolved, we would do better to understand Homer as an anthropomorphisation of the epic tradition, a name for the art and practice of epic poetry."[12]

Contrasting with the Homeric *aoidoí*, creators of the Homeric epics, are the *rhapsōidoí*, reciters of complete epics such as those of Homer (i.e. those that have been composed by the Homeric *aoidoí*), who are brought to light by Pindaric and Herodotean passages I have cited in Chapter 1. The earliest explicit mention of *rhapsōidoí* occurs in connection with Cleisthenes' cessation of Homeric recitation

9 Buchan 2004:107–109.

10 Seidensticker 1978:13n32.

11 Wilson 2002:101.

12 Foley 2004:186.

in section 5.67.1 of the *Histories*, a text that dates from the latter half of the fifth century BCE. Yet the presence of such Homeric performers appears to predate their designation as *rhapsōidoí*. The *Nemean* 2.2 reference to the Homeridae as "singers of epic poems pieced together" (*rhaptôn epéōn … aoidoí*) suggests that, by the late sixth century BCE, *aoidoí* were beginning to evince capacities to recite epics already completed, as well as abilities to add substantially to inchoate works of this type. And, if the *Iliad*'s depiction of the singing Achilles is indicative of the poetic practices of its time, *aoidoí* of a rhapsodic variety actually may have been present even then.

In any event, even though the lyre (*phórminx*) of an *aoidós*—rather than the staff (*rhábdos*) of a *rhapsōidós*—is what Achilles holds,[13] he is better described as a rhapsode than as a bard. And so, too, is Patroclus classified in the following passage:

> The esthetics of rhapsodic sequencing, where each performer takes up the song precisely where the last one left off, are in fact built into the contents of Homeric poetry: much as rhapsodes sing in sequence, each one taking his turn after another ('Plato,' *Hipparchus* 228b and Diogenes Laertius 1.57), so also the *Iliad* represents the heroes Patroklos and Achilles as potentially rhapsodic performers of epic.[14]

Even though rhapsodic reciters may be recomposing in performance—and thereby may be contributing to the previously composed poems that have been passed down to them—this activity of theirs is distinct from that of the prior bardic poets responsible for much of the content that the reciters have received. Even if the Homeridae are in the same line of poetic transmission as the *aoidoí* known collectively as Homer, the difference between the two groups' efforts is well worth observing and is anticipated in the *Iliad* itself. Indeed, Achilles' Iliadic rhapsody belies Havelock's dissolution of this distinction:

> The conditions in oral society under which the Homeric poems came into existence make it impossible for the critic to distinguish between creative composition and mechanical repetition, as though these represented two categories mutually exclusive, the first of which was superseded by the second. … At all stages of the Homeric process, now lost in the mists of anonymity, we should speak only in hyphenated terms of the composer-reciter, the singer-rhapsode.[15]

13 For further discussion of the distinct implications of these different poetic implements, see Burkert 2001:101–102.

14 Nagy 1996a:71.

15 Havelock 1978:11.

Given that "the hero [Achilles] ... sings himself into the [*Iliad*] epic,"[16] it is important—*pace* Havelock—to note the type of singer that Achilles is styled, so as to understand what his singing signifies.

Achilles' Rhapsodic Recitation: A Prolepsis of His *Kléos* of Conquest

When Achilles renders *kléa andrō̂n*, he clearly evokes the epic that centers on his own glory.[17] Moreover, the fact that he acts as a rhapsode rather than as a bard hints at the early fixity of his fame. In this scene, the *Iliad* does not merely indicate that his glorious deeds are worthy of being incorporated into the songs of *aoidoí*, but also emphasizes that the illustriousness of his future acts is established so well already that they will persist in poetic form long enough to be recited by performers like *rhapsōidoí*. Even as an Achillean epic is anticipated, it appears to have assumed its complete form.

Such a sudden development suits a hero who is semi-divine himself. As the son of Thetis, Achilles is well aware of his imminent demise in a war away from home, and of his heroic death's attendant reward of eternal glory:

> *mḗtēr gár té mé phēsi theà Thétis argurópeza*
> *dikhthadías kē̂ras pherémen thanátoio télosde.*
> *ei mén k' aûthi ménōn Trṓōn pólin amphimákhōmai,*
> *ṓleto mén moi nóstos, atàr kléos áphthiton éstai·*
> *ei dé ken oíkad' híkōmi phílēn es patrída gaîan,*
> *ṓletó moi kléos esthlón, epì dēròn dé moi aiṑn*
> *éssetai, oudé ké m' ō̂ka télos thanátoio kikheíē.*
>
> For my mother, Thetis, the goddess with silver feet, tells me that
> two different destinies are taking me to the moment of my death:
> if I stay here and wage war around the Trojans' city,
> then my homecoming will have been lost but I will have undying
> glory;
> but, if I go home to my beloved fatherland,
> my noble glory will have been lost, though I will have a long life
> without the moment of my death quickly coming upon me.
>
> *Iliad* 9.410–416

[16] Andersen 1992:20.

[17] Segal 1994:124; Cairns 2001:30–31.

Even though Achilles frames this pair of fates as apparent alternatives, I do not think that the hero's early death in battle is something that he ultimately is able to select freely over an immediate departure from Troy.[18] In presenting this second outcome, Achilles considers what his life would continue to be, were he not constrained already to effect the first. Yet his consideration of this continued life is not simply "[c]ounterfactual,"[19] for this hypothetical existence provides the poetic images for his inevitable, impending death.

The fame that he is fated to attain on the battlefield is associated with his premature and predestined passing, an event of which he appears to have been apprised since childhood. He tells Thetis that she has borne him to be "short-lived" (*minunthádión*) (*Iliad* 1.352), which means not that he is mortal, but that he has little time left to live.[20] He seems to have learned of this limit on his life from Thetis herself, assuming that her tendency to remind him of his looming death—as she does thrice (*Iliad* 1.414–418, 18.95–96, 24.131–132) even after he has acknowledged it—has been longstanding. And he acts accordingly: "Dedicated from the outset—one might say by nature—to a beautiful death, he goes through life as if he were already suffused with the aura of the posthumous glory that was always his goal."[21] Although his temporary withdrawal from the Trojan War may call into question "the very possibility of any equivalence in the structure of exchange of life for *kleos* ... in the insistence on the enormity of the stake,"[22] his eventual reentry into the fray—with a vengeance as predestined—confirms the *Iliad*'s tight embrace of this ideal.

Achilles himself idealizes the war that will confer *kléos* upon him, and eschews this conflict temporarily only when he feels that it is not being conducted correctly. His indictment of Agamemnon as this commander makes plain his designs on Briseïs highlights the reward structure undergirding the current martial moral code. Agamemnon, by dint of his superior military position, is entitled to a better prize than is Achilles, even though Achilles has engaged in a far greater share of the fighting (*Iliad* 1.165–168). While Achilles can countenance this inequity, he cannot tolerate Agamemnon's renegation of the warrior norm that prizes cannot be removed once awarded (*Iliad* 1.125–126, 229–230, 299). On the basis of Agamemnon's imminent offense of seizing the desirable Briseïs after she already has been won, Achilles determines that his commander is not merely avaricious (i.e. "the most rapacious" [*philokteanṓtate*] or

18 In other words, "Achilles' choice is a false choice" (*[l]e choix d'Achille est un faux choix*) (Frontisi-Ducroux 1986:58).

19 Burgess 2009:52.

20 Slatkin 1991:34–35.

21 Vernant 1991:51.

22 Lynn-George 1988:153.

"preoccupied with profit" [*kerdaleóphron*]), but altogether "shameless" (*anaidés*) (*Iliad* 1.122, 149, 158). Agamemnon's ill-gotten gain of this spoil is Achilles' loss of his very honor. Knowing that he is being dishonored unjustly, Achilles no longer wishes to fight on the Trojan battlefield to accrue booty for Agamemnon and therefore threatens to retreat to Phthia (*Iliad* 1.244, 355–356, 412, 169–171).

After Achilles raises the initial specter of his departure in the *Iliad*'s opening book, he goes on in book 9 to suggest to Agamemnon's embassy members a possible countermeasure that is beyond their control. Achilles stipulates that he will reenter the war against the Trojans only when their crown prince, Hector, fights his way to the ships of the Myrmidons, Achilles' people, and sets these vessels on fire (*Iliad* 9.649–655). The Phthian ruler seems to keep open for the embassy the possibility of his homecoming to reinforce his persistent rebuke of his Mycenaean commander, who has dismissed him "as if [he] were an unhonored wanderer" (*hōs eí tin' atímēton metanástēn*) (*Iliad* 9.648) by taking the liberty to appropriate Achilles' concubine without her or his consent (*Iliad* 9.367–369).

Achilles rearticulates his righteous indignation at Agamemnon's treatment of him "as if [he] were an unhonored wanderer" (*hōs eí tin' atímēton metanástēn*) (*Iliad* 16.59) as he asks Patroclus to wear the divine armor in Achilles' possession to lead the Myrmidons to battle against the Trojans (*Iliad* 16.64–70). Although Achilles urges Patroclus to protect the Achaeans' homecoming from their enemy, Achilles anticipates being able to sail back to Phthia only after he and Patroclus together have defeated the Trojans. On this assumption, Achilles instructs Patroclus only to beat the Trojans back from and to keep them from burning the Phthian ships and not to engage the hostile forces at Ilium without him. Were Patroclus himself to best the Trojans there, then Achilles would lose the chance to sack their city and to win back Briseïs as an award from the Achaeans, who in their gratitude would gift him anew as well (*Iliad* 16.80–90). If Patroclus were to cost Achilles this opportunity, then the Phthian king would be even "more unhonored" (*atimóteron*) (*Iliad* 16.90).

Achilles, however, is poised to claim *kléos* for himself by avenging Patroclus' death at the hands of Hector. Achilles acknowledges his impending act as his fate:

> *nûn d' eîm', óphra phílēs kephalē̂s oletē̂ra kikheíō,*
> *Héktora· kē̂ra d' egṑ tóte déxomai, hoppóte ken dḕ*
> *Zeùs ethélēi telésai ēd' athánatoi theoì álloi.*
> *oudè gàr oudè bíē Hēraklē̂os phúge kē̂ra,*
> *hós per phíltatos éske Diì Kroníōni ánakti·*
> *allá he moîra dámasse kaì argaléos khólos Hḗrēs.*
> *hṑs kaì egṓn, ei dḗ moi homoíē moîra tétuktai,*

keísom' epeí ke thánō· nûn dè kléos esthlòn aroímēn,
kaí tina Trōïádōn kaì Dardanídōn bathukólpōn
amphotérēisin khersì pareiáōn hapaláōn
dákru' omorxaménēn hadinòn stonakhē̂sai epheíēn,
gnoîen d' hōs dḕ dēròn egṑ polémoio pépaumai·

And now I will go to overtake Hector, the killer of a man dear to me,
for I will accept my death at the moment whenever
Zeus and the other immortal gods choose to accomplish it.
For not even powerful Heracles escaped his death,
despite being the dearest to Lord Zeus, son of Cronus.
Rather, fate felled him, as did the vexing rage of Hera.
So, too, I—if indeed a similar fate has been fixed for me—
will lie still when I die. But now allow me to win noble glory,
and to send one of the full-chested Trojan or Dardanian women
to moan vehemently while wiping off tears
from her soft cheeks with both hands.
And allow them to know for how very long I have ceased and
desisted from the war.

Iliad 18.114–125

Achilles knows full well that reentering the war will lead to his decease, because Thetis has already revealed that he will succeed Hector in death (*Iliad* 18.96). Hence, Achilles connects to his own acceptance of his fated demise his requital against Hector (*Iliad* 18.114–116). The Phthian recognizes the inexorability of his dire destiny, likening it to the end of Heracles (*Iliad* 18.117–121). Here Achilles implies that, if such a fate can befall a semi-divine being who—by virtue of having been fathered by the immortal ruler (Zeus) rather than a mortal one (such as Peleus)—is even higher in status than Achilles, then he, too, as a mere great-grandson of Zeus, will die soon, despite having a divine mother. Before Achilles accrues *kléos* as a consequence of his own death in combat, he will make a widow out of Hector's wife, Andromache, who indeed will be in tears and in the company of other Trojan women when she mourns him (*Iliad* 18.121–125, 22.515, 24.746).

At the same time that Achilles alludes to Andromache's laments, he evokes the women whom he and Patroclus plundered from the cities that they were sacking (*Iliad* 18.341–342). These "full-chested Trojan and Dardanian women" (*Trōiaì kaì Dardanídes bathúkolpoi*), observes Achilles while mourning Patroclus, "will wail for nights and days while shedding tears" (*klaúsontai núktas te kaì ḗmata dákru khéousai*) for him (*Iliad* 18.339–340). In making this observation, Achilles is aware that he and Patroclus alike have been destined to die at Troy (*Iliad* 18.329–330). While Achilles' Ilian end will ensue in *kléos* for him, Patroclus will attain only an accessory renown as Achilles' companion, rather than the fame of a storied warrior. When the Phthian king explains that his promise to Patroclus' father, Menoetius, "to bring back his glorious son to Opoeis" (*hoi eis Opóenta periklutòn huiòn apáxein*), their city, has rung hollow, Achilles himself remarks that "Zeus does not accomplish all the aims of humans" (*ou Zeùs ándressi noḗmata pánta teleutâi*) (*Iliad* 18.326, 328). Instead of acquiring *kléos* at the sacking of Ilium, as well as his share of the attendant spoils, Patroclus dies beforehand and will be bewailed immediately and only by women whom he and Achilles carried off in the past, rather than eventually and additionally by concubines who could have belonged to these men in the future to enjoy for the remainders of their lives. Aptly, Patroclus, prior to his demise, appears with Achilles as he sings *kléa* such as his own to come (*Iliad* 9.189–191). Yet Patroclus, despite his proximity to Achilles, does not sing *kléa* himself, as if to underscore that his own glory will be postponed eternally. While he plays the part of the next rhapsode in the symbolic performance of Achilles' *kléos*, Patroclus' own song is forestalled forever.

By contrast, Achilles' own untimely demise in Troy, with its guarantee of undying glory, is a gift from Zeus. Hence, when Achilles is seen in the act of reciting men's fames, in the manner in which he himself will be sung, he is said to be the "scion of Aeacus" (*Aiakídēn*) (*Iliad* 9.191). This epithet emphasizes Achilles' proximity to Zeus,[23] who is the father of Achilles' paternal grandfather, Aeacus, and makes possible Achilles' poetic immortalization. Although Achilles attributes his dire destiny to the gods in general ("... for I will accept my death at the moment whenever / Zeus and the other immortal gods choose to accomplish it" [*... kêra d' egṑ tóte déxomai, hoppóte ken dḕ / Zeùs ethélēi telésai ēd' athánatoi theoì álloi*] [*Iliad* 18.115–116, 22.365–366]), the hero singles out Zeus here because this deity, by deciding what to dispense from his containers of banes and benefits (*Iliad* 24.527–528), determines the quality of a mortal's lot in life and death. The best destiny from Zeus for which a human can hope is mixed (*Iliad* 24.529–530), as is illustrated by the case of Achilles' father, Peleus, who has received divine favors such as prosperity, riches, kingship over the Myrmidons, and a goddess for a wife, but has sired only one short-lived son who will not be able to care for Peleus in his old age (*Iliad* 24.534–540, 19.322–325). In citing Peleus' situation, Achilles, the current king of the Myrmidons (*Iliad* 1.180; 16.211; 24.448–449, 452), alludes to his own situation, for he also receives divine assistance—as evinced both by his inheritance of the immortal horses and godly armor that divinities have

23 Schein 1984:122n8.

given to his father (*Iliad* 16.145–154; 19.399–400; 16.380–381, 866–867; 17.441–444, 194–197; 18.82–84) and by the replacement of this armor by the immortal smith, Hephaestus, thanks to the intercession of Thetis (*Iliad* 18.457–461). In continuing parallel to Peleus, Achilles has already been separated from and will not be able to enjoy an old age in the care of his son, Neoptolemus (*Iliad* 19.326–327).

But the benefit of being subject as a human to some of Zeus' "banes" (*kakȏn*) (*Iliad* 24.528) is that Achilles can attain *kléos*. According to Helen, the semi-divine daughter of Zeus (*Iliad* 3.199, 237–238), Zeus has set a "baneful fate" (*kakòn móron*) upon Hector's brother Paris and her so that they may become a subject of song for people, even in the future (*Iliad* 6.357–358). Similar renown will redound to Zeus' mortal great-grandson, despite being doubtful while Achilles is in danger of drowning ignominiously in the waters of Scamander when this river rises to war with the Phthian. Certainly, Achilles' subsequent prayer to his great-grandfather for succor is answered finally by Zeus' son Hephaestus and his drying fire, at the behest of his mother—Hera—Zeus' wife and sister (*Iliad* 21.272–283, 328–355). With the support of such immortals, Achilles is able to live up to his illustrious patriline, which he vaunts well in advance of his encounter with Scamander, just before slaying Asteropaeus—the grandson of Axius, another river (*Iliad* 21.184–202, 140–142).

The imagery employed to describe the fire that Hephaestus deploys for Achilles against Scamander sheds light on the hero's own glory:

> *prȏta mèn en pedíōi pûr daíeto, kaîe dè nekroùs*
> *polloús, hoí rha kat' autòn hális ésan, hoùs ktán' Akhilleús·*
> *pân d' exēránthē pedíon, skhéto d' aglaòn húdōr.*
> *hōs d' hót' opōrinòs Boréēs neoardé' alōȇn*
> *aîps' anxēránēi· khaírei dé min hós tis etheírēi·*
> *hȍs exēránthē pedíon pân, kàd d' ára nekroùs*
> *kȇen· ho d' es potamòn trépse phlóga pamphanóōsan.*
> *kaíonto pteléai te kaì itéai ēdè murîkai,*
> *kaíeto dè lōtós te idè thrúon ēdè kúpeiron,*
> *tà perì kalà rhéethra hális potamoîo pephúkei·*
> *teíront' enkhélués te kaì ikhthúes hoì katà dínas,*
> *hoì katà kalà rhéethra kubístōn éntha kaì éntha*
> *pnoiȇi teirómenoi polumḗtios Hēphaístoio.*

> First, the fire was set on the plain and burned the many dead bodies
> that thronged around it after having been killed by Achilles;
> and the entire plain was dried up and the sparkling water was halted.
> And, just as when at harvest time the north wind dries a newly
> watered orchard

quickly and delights the man who tills it,
thus was the entire plain dried up as [Hephaestus] burned through
the dead bodies.
He then turned the shining flame toward the river.
Elms and willows and tamarisks burned.
Clover burned, and rushes and galingale,
all of which had grown profusely around the river's pretty streams.
Eels and fish were afflicted, jumping out along the eddies,
along the pretty streams here and there,
while afflicted by the blast of Hephaestus, who was crafty in many
ways.

Iliad 21.343–355

Hephaestus contributes here to Achilles' *kléos* by enabling the hero to best "the protective river of Troy"[24]—and thus to battle the city's inhabitants while free of this formidable natural obstacle (*Iliad* 21.359–360). Yet the agricultural simile for Hephaestus' act illuminates another facet of Achilles' fame. At first glance, comparing the furnace effect of Hephaestus' conflagration to a fast, wind-driven evaporation favorable to crops (*Iliad* 21.343–349) may appear bizarre, particularly in light of the Scamander River's necessity to "the fertility of the Trojan plain, and hence [to] the life of Troy as a whole."[25] But the coupling of the destructive and the productive in this comparison recalls Achilles' own juxtaposition above of the death that threatens him at Troy and the life that he has left behind in Phthia (*Iliad* 9.410–416). Moreover, the barrier between these two states breaks down when considered in connection with *kléos*: fighting to the death at Troy will destroy Achilles, but will produce his glory, while living in Phthia has allowed him to produce wealth and ultimately acclaim for his heir, but has promised to destroy Achilles' own prospects for fame.

Not merely antithetical,[26] but also analogous, existences, both Achilles' life in Phthia and his death at Troy betoken both production and destruction. And the fact that Achilles experiences these states sequentially, living in Phthia initially and dying at Troy finally, implies that the first state can inform the second. Hence the productive start that Achilles has made amid the Myrmidons provides the terms in which is expressed his quest for a self-destructive yet illustrious end among the Trojans.

He carries Phthia with him when he wields the shield specifically crafted by Hephaestus for Achilles' return to arms. The alter ego of Phthian king Achilles

24 Whitman 1958:139.
25 Taplin 1992:228.
26 King 1987:107–108.

whom this immortal smith forges from his heavenly alloy (*Iliad* 18.474–475) is the ruler featured in one of the shield's inner scenes:

En d' etíthei témenos basilḗïon· éntha d' érithoi
ḗmōn oxeías drepánas en khersìn ékhontes.
drágmata d' álla met' ógmon epḗtrima pîpton éraze,
álla d' amallodetê̄res en elledanoîsi déonto.
treîs d' ár' amallodetê̄res ephéstasan· autàr ópisthe
paîdes dragmeúontes, en ankalídessi phérontes,
asperkhès párekhon· basileùs d' en toîsi siōpê̄i
skê̄ptron ékhōn hestḗkei ep' ógmou gēthósunos kê̄r.
kḗrukes d' apáneuthen hupò druï̀ daîta pénonto,
boûn d' hiereúsantes mégan ámphepon· hai dè gunaîkes
deîpnon eríthoisin leúk' álphita pollà pálunon.

And inside [Hephaestus] placed a king's property, and there laborers
were reaping with the sharp sickles that they had in their hands.
While some swaths were falling to the earth, one after another, in a row,
others sheaf-binders were binding together with bands.
Three sheaf-binders took their positions; then, behind them,
boys gathering the fallen swaths by the armful
gave them to the sheaf-binders, without stopping; and among them, in silence,
stood the king, holding his scepter and rejoicing to the core at the reaping row.
Apart from them, heralds were preparing a feast beneath an oak tree
and were attending to the great bull that they had sacrificed. The maidservants
strewed plenty of white barley for the laborers' main meal.

Iliad 18.550–560

I regard the "property" (*témenos*) (*Iliad* 18.550) over which this ruler presides not as "the kind of privilege which any great *basileus* [or king] might hope to return to after the war, the kind which Achilles might have had if he had chosen long life instead of a glorious death,"[27] but as the very patrimony that this hero has been constrained to enjoy only briefly. On this view, Phthia looms not as a potential destination, but as a piece of a completed—if fleeting—past. And this land is named aptly, assuming that its appellation "is motivated by the theme of vegetal

[27] Taplin 1980:8.

death as conveyed by the root **phthi-**."[28] Although the king of Phthia, Achilles, grew like a shoot after he had been born to Thetis, who tended him like a tree in the sunniest spot of an orchard (*Iliad* 18.56–57, 437–438), his life will be cut short in the Trojan War. And Phthia, without its king, will languish as Peleus withers away in his old age, waiting for Neoptolemus to return to his roots—from Scyrus, the island where he is being reared (*Iliad* 19.326–327)—and to take over.

Thus, fertile Phthia (*Iliad* 1.155), memorialized on Achilles' shield, already has started to disappear after suffering his departure. The soldered kingdom, even in its metal plenitude, is an emblem of the insufficiency that he seeks to sow elsewhere. Just as he himself no longer can enjoy the abundance of his distant homeland, he aims to make the plenty of Troy nothing but imaginary to its inhabitants as well. Hence the losses that he inflicts upon them are conveyed by images of copiousness that no longer will be seen in the Trojan country.

The simile that evinces this tendency most expressly finds Achilles simultaneously on the battlefield and on the threshing floor:

hōs d' hóte tis zeúxēi bóas ársenas eurumetṓpous
tribémenai krî leukòn eüktiménēi en alōêi,
rhímpha te lépt' egénonto boôn hupò póss' erimúkōn,
hṑs hup' Akhillêos megathúmou mṓnukhes híppoi
steîbon homoû nékuás te kaì aspídas· haímati d' áxōn
nérthen hápas pepálakto kaì ántuges haì perì díphron,
hàs ár' aph' hippeíōn hopléōn rhathámінges éballon
haí t' ap' epissṓtrōn· ho dè híeto kûdos arésthai
Pēleḯdēs, lúthrōi dè palásseto kheîras aáptous.

And, just as when a man yokes broad-fronted bulls
to trample white barley on a well-built threshing floor,
and the husked grain soon appears under the feet of the loud-
  bellowing bulls,
like so, below great-hearted Achilles, his uncloven-hooved horses
were trampling dead bodies and shields at once. The whole axle
had been spattered beneath with blood, and the railing around the
  chariot,
which drops of blood—from the horses' hooves and from the wheel
  rims—struck.
But Peleus' son was speeding on, to attain honor;
and, with gore, he spattered his unhandleable hands.

Iliad 20.495–503

[28] Nagy 1999:185.

The threshing action of Achilles' immortal horses calls to mind the reaping scene depicted on his divine shield (*Iliad* 18.550–557). Both events involve grain—at least figuratively, if not literally: in fact, threshing is what must happen to the barley in order for humans like the reapers who have harvested it to consume it (*Iliad* 18.559–560). Furthermore, the productiveness of these imagined acts forms a mold for the real destruction around them. As Achilles speeds over the lifeless bodies beneath his horse-drawn vehicle, he is akin to the man guiding yoked oxen across the husks from cut stalks that are to be crushed. The thresher in this simile, like the reapers on Achilles' shield, embodies this king's ability to increase his country's yield. As the shield reveals, laborers of this agricultural variety provide the might that he presumably has overseen in Phthia, and thus may be seen as an extension of his own strength. However, on the battlefield in Troy, where Achilles brandishes his shield as he leads not laborers but warriors, this king will visit his own destiny of a lost country on another ruler whose city he wants to spoil. Moreover, just as the metal Phthia of Achilles' shield becomes a symbol of all that will be lost in Troy, so too the aforementioned blast sent from Hephaestus in Achilles' behalf (*Iliad* 21.346–349) evokes a northern breeze pleasing to the kind of farmer who once was found in Phthia, in Achilles' employ, but whose services no longer will be needed in a soon-to-be desolate Troy. Trojans will fall not only like the trees that Hephaestus burns down (*Iliad* 21.349–350), but also like Achilles himself, whose own growth—as Thetis bemoans (*Iliad* 18.54–60, 436–441)—will be cut short. But, before then, Achilles will keep mowing down Trojans. Even though the corpses crushed under his chariot in the threshing simile above are dead already, the blood that these bodies leave on his hands hints that, before reaching his end, he will continue to kill in force—as he, like "divinely kindled fire" (*thespidaès pûr*), already has been doing by the time that Hephaestus discharges his "divinely kindled fire" (*thespidaès pûr*) near Scamander (*Iliad* 20.490, 21.342).

The extent of this devastation in Troy is betokened by the lyre that Achilles has brought there from Thebe,[29] where he has rehearsed the destruction of a productive land (*Iliad* 9.185–188). In addition to having killed Thebe's ruler Eëtion, Achilles has slain all seven of Eëtion's sons and thus an entire generation of his heirs (*Iliad* 6.416, 421–423). Furthermore, the Phthian has done so among these Thebans' oxen and sheep (*Iliad* 6.424)—that is, on a pasture that presumably will be less green now that it no longer can be overseen by its king.

Priam's city faces a similar fate. On the day when Achilles once anticipated reaching Phthia after leaving Troy, Achilles instead stays there and extinguishes the Trojans' leading light, Hector,[30] having slain by then many of

29 Zarker 1965:114.

30 Mueller 1984:47.

Hector's forty-nine brothers and half-brothers as well (*Iliad* 9.356–363; 24.248–262, 477–479). In the absence of Priam's most illustrious son and Troy's most ardent defender (*Iliad* 6.403, 22.507, 24.499), the future of Ilium and its inhabitants dims, as the newly widowed Andromache—the "dire-fated" (*ainómoron*) daughter of "ill-fated" (*dúsmoros*) Eëtion—and the now bereft Priam alike are all too painfully aware (*Iliad* 22.479–481; 24.723–742, 777–781):

> As the reader approaches the end of the poem, the visions of the future fate of the city increase in clarity and pathos. Priam foresees the fall of Troy, the slaughter or enslaving of its inhabitants, and his own death (xxii, 59-71); he prays that he may die before his eyes behold the sacking of the city (xxiv, 244-246). In like manner Andromache after Hector's death bewails her fate and that of [their son] Astyanax (xxii, 485-507). She later laments the bondage and toil that will await her and the other captives, and with unerring prophetic vision she even foresees the death of Astyanax, whom some Achaean may seize and hurl from the wall (xxiv, 725-738).
>
> Thus the reader has a vivid picture of the events which are to happen after the close of the *Iliad*. The poem ends on a quiet note, the funeral of Hector, but the later events—the death of Achilles and the fall of the fated city—have impressed themselves upon the consciousness of the reader almost as vividly as if the poet had extended his epic to include them.[31]

Even though Achilles will be killed by divine Apollo and human Paris (*Iliad* 22.359–360) and will not live to see Troy sacked by fellow Achaean Odysseus, an event anticipated in the *Iliad* and celebrated in the *Odyssey*,[32] the Phthian's fate is inseparable from that of Ilium, whose downfall he is and whose name gives rise to the rubric for the epic praising his exploits.

So, I assert not that "[e]pic can only be hinted at and anticipated in the *Iliad*,"[33] but that epic need only be hinted at and anticipated in the *Iliad*. Given the inexorability of Achilles' fate as an invader, and this destiny's inextricability from the destruction of Troy, Achilles' *kléos* of conquest is assured even before he assails the city's walls, and thus is the implicit subject of a song that has been finished long before it is performed by its protagonist. Far less certain is the glory of Odysseus in the *Odyssey*, a goal that the Ithacan king treats repeatedly in stories that question whether he can attain it, even while they incorporate explicit announcements of its inevitability.

31 Duckworth 1933:31–32.

32 Haft 1990:38, 41, 42, 45–55.

33 Redfield 1994:36.

Odysseus as a Bard on Scheria and Ithaca

Like Achilles, Odysseus acts like a poet. However, unlike Achilles, who performs in the manner of a rhapsode, Odysseus assumes the character of a bard.

The first occasion for Odysseus' bardic behavior is the feast hosted by Phaeacian ruler Alcinous. At this event, Odysseus seems to substitute for Phaeacian singer Demodocus.[34] Just after giving this *aoidós* a piece of meat to eat and asking him to sing more about the Achaeans who fought at Troy (*Odyssey* 8.477–478, 492–495), Odysseus (who himself just has dined) tells his own tale of the Achaeans' trip from Troy (*Odyssey* 9.1–12.453) and captures the attention of Demodocus' audience. About halfway through Odysseus' story, Alcinous affirms that "... upon [Odysseus] is shapeliness of words ... / and [that he] ha[s] skillfully told [his] story, as when a singer does so" (*soì ... épi mèn morphḕ epéōn, ... / mûthon d' hōs hót' aoidòs epistaménōs katélexas*) (*Odyssey* 11.367, 368).[35] Accordingly, at this point in and at the end of Odysseus' story, his listeners "... [a]re all speechless in silence / and spellbound ..." (*... pántes akḕn egénonto siōpêi, / kēlēthmôi d' éskhonto ...*) (*Odyssey* 11.333–334, 13.1–2).

Odysseus strikes similar bardic poses after he has made his way home to Ithaca, where, in action and in station, he has much in common with the *aoidós* Phemius. For both men, taletelling is a matter of survival. In the guise of an elderly beggar, Odysseus approaches Antinous—Penelope's most brutal suitor—and asserts that "[he] will make [Antinous] glorious throughout the boundless earth" (*egṑ ... ké se kleíō kat' apeírona gaîan*) (*Odyssey* 17.418), if Antinous gives him better food than the other suitors have given him. Odysseus, in making this promise, evokes Phemius, who sings of the "deeds of men and gods ... that singers make glorious" (*érg' andrôn te theôn te, tá te kleíousin aoidoí*) (*Odyssey* 1.338). In addition to taking on the singer's role as raconteur and sharing with Antinous a false story about going to Egypt with plundering pirates, being sent to Cyprus, and then coming to Ithaca (*Odyssey* 17.414–476), Odysseus demonstrates the duress under which Phemius operates. When Odysseus reproves Antinous for insulting him and for telling him to stay away from Antinous' table, this irascible suitor throws a footstool at and hits him (*Odyssey* 17.445–463). This blatant abuse that Odysseus—as a performer—suffers at the hands of his unwilling patron probably resembles the implicit violence threatened by the new patrons of Phemius, "who s[i]ng[s] before the suitors because they forc[e] him to" (*hós rh' ḗeide parà mnēstêrsin anánkēi*) (*Odyssey* 1.154). Seemingly Phemius is subject to such compulsion, because he, like Odysseus, sings for his supper.

34 Thalmann 1984:170–171; Wyatt 1989:241–242; Beye 1993:172–173.
35 Segal 1994:86.

Even though unfortunate circumstances necessitate Phemius' and Odysseus' command performances, the men are consummate entertainers. While recalling the experience of hearing one of incognito Odysseus' Cretan tales, his Ithacan host Eumaeus observes:

> *hōs d' hót' aoidòn anḕr potidérketai, hós te theỗn èx*
> *aeídēi dedaồs épe' himeróenta brotoîsi,*
> *toû d' ámoton memáasin akouémen, hoppót' aeídēi·*
> *hồs emè keînos éthelge parḗmenos en megároisi.*
>
> Just as when a man beholds a singer, who
> sings to mortals delightful things in songs that he has learned from the gods,
> and they are insatiably eager to hear him whenever he sings,
> like so, [the Cretan] charmed me as he sat in my home.
>
> *Odyssey* 17.518–521

Similarly enchanting are "the many other charms for mortals" (*pollà ... álla brotỗn thelktḗria*) that Phemius has in his repertoire (*Odyssey* 1.337).

The talents that he and Odysseus evince distinguish them from other dependents. Even though Odysseus himself, as the unnamed Cretan, notes that he is a *ptōkhós* (beggar) (*Odyssey* 17.18), the swineherd Eumaeus begs to differ as he explains why he (the Syran king's son who had been kidnapped by Phoenician traders who went on to sell him as a slave to Odysseus' father [*Odyssey* 15.403, 412–413, 415–416, 474–475, 482–483]) has brought this man to Odysseus' palace:

> *tís gàr dḕ xeînon kaleî állothen autòs epelthồn*
> *állon g', ei mḕ tỗn hoì dēmioergoì éasi,*
> *mántin ḕ iētễra kakỗn ḕ téktona doúrōn,*
> *ḕ kaì théspin aoidón, hó ken térpēisin aeídōn;*
> *hoûtoi gàr klētoí ge brotỗn ep' apeírona gaîan·*
> *ptōkhòn d' ouk án tis kaléoi trúxonta hè autón.*
>
> For what man coming from another place himself invites another stranger,
> unless [this stranger] is one of those men who work for the people—
> a prophet or a healer of illnesses or a woodworker
> or, in fact, an inspired singer, who delights by singing?
> For these are the very men who are invited all over the boundless earth,

> but no one would invite a beggar, who would eat him out of house
> and home.
>
> *Odyssey* 17.382–387

Eumaeus—in justifying his invitation of the Cretan itinerant—devotes a longer description to the epic singer than to the other popular practitioners, and places the singer in the prominent final position on the practitioner list. Given that Eumaeus goes on to compare the Cretan pauper to an *aoidós* (*Odyssey* 17.518–521), the swineherd probably regards him as an *aoidós* (at least in his present effect, if not in his current employment).

Acting like a bard, both on the Phaeacian land, Scheria, and on Ithaca, affords Odysseus the creative capacity to craft his past as he sees fit. This ability becomes necessary symbolically in the wake of the Trojan War, when the hero strives for a different kind of glory as he turns from distant conquests to the disorder in his house. Instead of rhapsodizing assuredly like Achilles, who—while performing—already is poised to claim *kléos* for fighting to the death to take over Troy, Odysseus sings uncertainly of the hindrances to his homecoming. As he creates custom-made narratives about the particular hardships that he has had to overcome to take back his throne, he attaches to his compositions predictions of his triumph, which are required to shore up its sureness. Thus, at the same time that he resembles an *aoidós*, he is akin to a *mántis* (prophet). By taking on the roles of these two types of traveling tradesmen—that is, by fashioning his future as well as his past—Odysseus ensures that the people on whom he has relied previously will work with him to reestablish his rule.

Odysseus' Bardic Compositions: Prolepses of His *Kléos* of Restoration

The first supporter whom Odysseus sounds out about his restoration is Alcinous. Although Odysseus has met this Phaeacian monarch only on the previous evening, before performing like a poet at Alcinous' court, by the time of this performance Alcinous already has hosted Odysseus for the night, has lavished valuable presents upon him, and has promised him conveyance to his homeland (*Odyssey* 7.207–225, 335–347; 8.389–397, 424–432; 7.191–196, 317–328; 8.26–36, 555–557). Now, then, at the mercy and under the protection of a powerful and benevolent sovereign, Odysseus lets down his guard and shares with the court an unvarnished narrative of his recent trials. While his performance follows that of Demodocus, Odysseus' story contrasts sharply with the *aoidós*' account, in character as well as in content. Whereas Demodocus recounts what amounts to the rationale for the *kléos* that he already has ascribed to Odysseus—namely, his engineering of the sack of Troy by leading the Achaean charge from the Trojan Horse—Odysseus describes what is initially a dilatory voyage on which he is unable to achieve any *kléos*, a journey comprising conflicts with more powerful peoples (Cicones and Lotus-Eaters) and beings (Cyclopes and Laestrygones), from whom he flees (*Odyssey* 8.73–74, 499–521; 9.1–10.202).

Yet the tide turns for Odysseus when he decides to set sail for the underworld: appropriately, his Hades journey occurs at the center of his thirteen adventures, being both preceded and succeeded by six others.[36] Odysseus—on the recommendation of immortal sorceress Circe (*Odyssey* 10.487–495, 503–540)—seeks in Hades the advice of deceased Theban *mántis* Teiresias, who states:

> *nóston dízēai meliēdéa, phaídim' Odusseû·*
> *tòn dé toi argaléon thḗsei theós· ou gàr oḯō*
> *lḗsein ennosígaion, hó toi kóton éntheto thumôi,*
> *khōómenos hóti hoi huiòn phílon exaláōsas.*
> *all' éti mén ke kaì hō̂s kaká per páskhontes híkoisthe,*
> *aí k' ethélēis sòn thumòn erukakéein kaì hetaírōn,*
> *hoppóte ke prō̂ton pelásēis euergéa nē̂a*
> *Thrinakíēi nḗsōi, prophugṑn ioeidéa pónton,*
> *boskoménas d' heúrēte bóas kaì íphia mē̂la*
> *Ēelíou, hòs pánt' ephorâi kaì pánt' epakoúei.*
> *tàs ei mén k' asinéas eáais nóstou te médēai,*
> *kaí ken ét' eis Ithákēn kaká per páskhontes híkoisthe·*
> *ei dé ke sínēai, tóte toi tekmaírom' ólethron*
> *nēḯ te kaì hetárois· autòs d' eí pér ken alúxēis,*
> *opsè kakō̂s neîai, olésas ápo pántas hetaírous,*
> *nēòs ep' allotríēs· dḗeis d' en pḗmata oíkōi,*
> *ándras huperphiálous, hoí toi bíoton katédousi*
> *mnṓmenoi antithéēn álokhon kaì hédna didóntes.*
> *all' ē̂ toi keínōn ge bías apotíseai elthṓn·*
> *autàr epḕn mnēstē̂ras enì megároisi teoîsi*
> *kteínēis ēè dólōi ḕ amphadòn oxéï khalkō̂i,*
> *érkhesthai dḕ épeita, labṑn euē̂res eretmón,*
> *eis hó ke toùs aphíkēai hoì ou ísasi thálassan*
> *anéres, oudé th' hálessi memigménon eîdar édousin·*
> *oud' ára toì ísasi néas phoinikoparḗious,*
> *oud' euḗre' eretmá, tá te pterà nēusì pélontai.*
> *sē̂ma dé toi eréō mál' ariphradés, oudé se lḗsei·*

[36] Finley 1978:76.

hoppóte ken dḗ toi sumblḗmenos állos hodítēs
phḗēi athērēloigòn ékhein anà phaidímōi ṓmōi,
kaì tóte dḕ gaíēi pḗxas euêres eretmón,
rhéxas hierà kalà Poseidáōni ánakti,
arneiòn taûrón te suôn t' epibḗtora kápron,
oíkad' aposteíkhein érdein th' hieràs hekatómbas
athanátoisi theoîsi, toì ouranòn eurùn ékhousi,
pâsi mál' hexeíēs· thánatos dé toi ex halòs autôi
ablēkhròs mála toîos eleúsetai, hós ké se pephnēi
gḗrai húpo liparôi arēménon· amphì dè laoì
ólbioi éssontai· tà dé toi nēmertéa eírō.

You seek your honeyed homecoming, illustrious Odysseus,
but a god will make it difficult for you, for I cannot imagine that
you will escape the notice of the Earth-Shaker, who has harbored anger at you in his heart
and continues to be rankled because you blinded his own son [Polyphemus].
But you still may reach home, even as you suffer afflictions,
if you are willing to curb your desire and that of your comrades
when you first bring your well-made ship
to Thrinacia Island—after you have eluded the blue-violet sea—
and you come upon the grazing cattle and fat sheep
of Helius, who sees everything and hears everything.
If you leave these unharmed and keep in mind your homecoming,
even as you suffer afflictions, you still may come home to Ithaca;
but, if you harm them, then I predict your destruction
and that of your ship and comrades. And—even if you yourself escape—
you will come home with afflictions after a long time, having lost all of your comrades,
on a ship that is not your own; and at home you will come upon woes,
reckless men who devour your livelihood,
while wooing your godlike wife and tendering bride-prices.
Yet, to tell you the truth, you will avenge the wrongdoing of those very men after you come home;
but—after you have killed the suitors in your hall,
either by guile or in plain view with honed bronze—
then and only then grab a well-constructed oar and proceed

until you reach people who do not know the ocean
and do not eat food mixed with salt,
and thus do not know red-prowed ships
nor well-constructed oars, which are the wings of ships.
And I will tell you of a sign that is very easy to discern and that will
  not elude you:
at the very moment when another traveler, upon encountering you,
says that you are carrying a winnowing fan on your shining shoulder,
right then plant your well-constructed oar in the earth,
sacrifice fine offerings to Lord Poseidon—
a ram and a bull and a boar, the mate of sows—
and return home and offer holy hecatombs
to the immortal gods who inhabit widespread heaven,
to each one in the proper order. And death of a very gentle sort will
  come upon
you yourself away from the sea, doing you in
when you are worn out by a pleasant old age; and, all around you,
  your people
will be prosperous. I am telling you the truth.

Odyssey 11.100–137

The events that Teiresias sees and foresees place Odysseus' fate and fame in stark contrast with those of Achilles. Whereas Achilles is favored by Hephaestus, who blasts his fire to help the Phthian repel the Scamander River in Troy (*Iliad* 21.349–355), Odysseus has angered ocean god Poseidon, who has hindered the Ithacan's homecoming—roiling the sea enough to disperse the remnants of Odysseus' raft as he approaches the coast of Scheria—and who perturbs Odysseus enough on his way there that, upon arriving, he takes refuge in a much smoother river (*Odyssey* 11.102–103; 5.291–296, 313–332, 366–370; 7.270–277; 5.388–457; 7.278–282). Before reaching Scheria, Odysseus suffers the loss of his crewmen when he cannot prevent them from feeding on sun god Helius' livestock on Thrinacia (*Odyssey* 12.353–419). Achilles himself, however, wreaks havoc on the royal owners of the oxen and sheep that he finds when he sails to Thebe; and thus is free to loot this land as he pleases (*Iliad* 6.416, 421–427). And, at Troy, whose people war with Achilles on sea as well as on land, he garners glory for heroics that keep him from coming home to Phthia ever again (*Iliad* 18.94–125). But Odysseus will be renowned not only for returning to Ithaca but also for wresting it away from the avaricious young men who have overrun it and for restoring it to its prewar prosperity once he has introduced worship of

Poseidon and the other Olympians to a faraway landlocked people unfamiliar with the sea (*Odyssey* 11.113–114, 115–120, 136–137, 121–134).

Even the scenes surrounding the necromancy cast Odysseus' life and death into relief from those of Achilles. In the fertile Phthia on Achilles' shield, maidservants "stre[w] ... white barley" (*leúk' álphita ... pálunon*) (*Iliad* 18.560) while preparing to nourish the laborers who have been working the king's land (*Iliad* 18.559–560). But, in the underworld, Odysseus "strew[s] white barley" (*álphita leukà pálunon*) (*Odyssey* 11.28) that will not be eaten by Teiresias and the other blood-drinking dead as they arrive to provide information that will help the Ithacan win back his kingdom (*Odyssey* 11.28–50). Immediately after Odysseus disperses the fruitless seed, he promises the dead that in his uncertain future on Ithaca he will sacrifice to them a "sterile cow" (*steîran boûn*) (*Odyssey* 11.30), which contrasts with the "great [and likely fertile] bull" (*boûn ... mégan*) (*Iliad* 18.559) that the heralds on Achilles' shield offer in their prosperous king's realm (*Odyssey* 11.29–31; *Iliad* 18.558–559), which is permanently fixed in the present as a testament to Phthia's past.

Ithaca and Phthia's divide is illuminated further by Odysseus' recently deceased mother, Anticleia. She informs him of the decrepitude that has crept up upon his father, Laertes, who—in his sorrow for his long-gone son—eschews the city for the country, comfortable bedding for fireside ashes, and royal raiment for rags (*Odyssey* 11.187–196). Yet Laertes will be rejuvenated after Odysseus comes back to Ithaca from the dead, rids his palace of Penelope's overweening pursuers, and reclaims his name and ancestral land (*Odyssey* 24.365–382). So, even as Anticleia describes the decay that has beset her husband—and, by extension, Ithaca[37]—in Odysseus' absence, her speech anticipates the regeneration that her son will reintroduce upon his return to the island. Associated as she is here both with the absence of Odysseus' glory from his languishing kingdom as he battles at Troy and with the resurgence of this fame when Odysseus returns to Ithaca and sets everything right, Anticleia aptly goes by a bivalent name, and thus is known as a lady who is opposed, as well as akin, to *kléos*. But, while Odysseus' *kléos* is connected to the condition of his kingdom and precursor, Achilles' is not. In fact, after the Phthian's glorious death, his father and predecessor, Peleus, is likely to decline so rapidly that he will resemble not only the bereaved Trojan leader Priam (*Iliad* 24.485–506), but also the enfeebled Ithacan king in Anticleia's account. Thus, what lies in Laertes' past by the end of the *Odyssey* looms in Peleus' future by the end of the *Iliad*.[38] Indeed, even before Achilles dies, Thetis describes Peleus as having been worn out by his woeful old age (*Iliad* 18.434–435).

37 Austin 1975:102–103.

38 This paternal parallel has been elaborated by classicist Anthony T. Edwards (1985:52–59).

The *kléos* of conquest that Achilles embodies in the *Iliad* is put to rest in the *Odyssey* even more overtly when Odysseus encounters him in the underworld. When the heroes meet in Hades, the deceased Achilles does not suffer Odysseus' efforts to glorify Achilles' wartime sacrifice, but demurs:

> *mḕ dḗ moi thánatón ge paraúda, phaídim' Odusseû.*
> *bouloímēn k' epárouros eṑn thēteuémen állōi,*
> *andrì par' aklḗrōi, hôi mḕ bíotos polùs eíē,*
> *ḕ pâsin nekúessi kataphthiménoisin anássein.*
>
> Do not speak gently to me of my death, illustrious Odysseus.
> I would rather be on fertile soil, hiring myself out as a laborer to
> another—
> to a man having little land and not much to live on—
> than be king over all the dead, who have perished.
>
> *Odyssey* 11.488–491

These words of Achilles often have been interpreted as evidence of a change of heart on his part, a second-guessing of his so-called choice to leave Phthia to seek fame at Troy.[39] While I agree that Achilles' stance represents a questioning of the Iliadic *kléos* of conquest, I think that such fame's uncertainty stems from a change not in his motivation, but in his very location.

While he would rather be alive than be dead, he wants to relive the end of his life (when he strove for glory in war), not his life's penultimate part (when he ruled over his people in Phthia). When the specter of Achilles speaks longingly of laboring on fertile land that is not his own (*Odyssey* 11.489), he refers metaphorically to his term as a grim reaper on the battlefield in faraway Troy, which—like Achilles' homeland, Phthia, as memorialized on his shield—is "fertile" (*eribṓlaki*) (*Iliad* 24.86, 1.155). The man whom the shadowy Achilles imagines hiring him (*Odyssey* 11.490) is Agamemnon, who lacks land and sustenance in the ironic sense that he wants to increase his already immense holdings abroad, and to take not only Troy itself, but also its spoils (*Iliad* 2.225–240, 9.135–138). Achilles' postmortem portrayal of Agamemnon as "a man having little land" (*andrì ... aklḗrōi*) (*Odyssey* 11.490) recalls, yet counters, this ruler's Iliadic characterizations of himself as "... not ... / ... be[ing] prizeless" (*... mḕ ... / ... agérastos éō ...*) and as "... neither plunderless ... / nor propertyless ..." (*oú ... alḗïos ... / oudé ... aktḗmōn ...*) (*Iliad* 1.118, 119; 9.125, 126). Agamemnon's second self-description is echoed by Odysseus (*Iliad* 9.267, 268), whose repetition of its alpha-privative compounds while negating their language of lack accents Agamemnon's avarice. But both

39 For further discussion of this position, see Schmiel 1987:35.

Agamemnon's and Odysseus' uses of these terms occur in lists of the gifts that Agamemnon has authorized his embassy to give to Achilles as recompense for Agamemnon's offense against him (*Iliad* 9.119–157, 259–299). Thus, Agamemnon itemizes his holdings at the moment when he is willing to confer some of them to Achilles. Were Agamemnon to cede what he promised to Achilles, then the Mycenaean ruler would be closer to being in need, given his great greed. At the same time that the dead Achilles satirizes his former commander's acquisitiveness, the Phthian warrior may also be expressing here his regret that he did not serve under a ruler less voracious than Agamemnon. Still, Achilles' shade deems being under Agamemnon's command at Troy better "than be[ing] king over all the dead, who have perished" (*ḕ pâsin nekúessi kataphthiménoisin anássein*) (*Odyssey* 11.491). Continuing to reign over Phthia—the domain that is named for death itself, and that is home to people whose own hopes for glory in war are dead unless these Phthians go elsewhere—would be worse for Achilles than working for Agamemnon would be, because only in the latter state could Achilles act again to garner undying fame in battle, the only kind of *kléos* that the *Odyssey*, as well as the *Iliad*, allows him.

Although his aspirations have not changed after his death, his permanent position in the underworld has relegated him, as well as his Iliadic glory, to the periphery of the *Odyssey*. This shift also evinces itself in the fate of Neoptolemus, of which the dead Achilles must learn from the living Odysseus (*Odyssey* 11.492–507). He has escorted Achilles' son from Scyrus to Troy, where Neoptolemus has proved to be a formidable warrior (*Odyssey* 11.508–509, 513–521). Yet, in surviving the city's sacking and in sailing toward his homeland on a ship laden with goods (*Odyssey* 11.533–537), Neoptolemus has more in common with the Ithacan than with Achilles. To highlight the link between Odysseus and Neoptolemus, Anthony T. Edwards describes "how closely the Wooden Horse is identified with Odysseus and his heroism," and observes that, "in his summary of Neoptolemus' exploits at Troy, Odysseus stresses the young hero's obedience to him in the Wooden Horse, and the importance of that strategem as the final action of the war."[40] Yet, even before Odysseus wends his way home from Troy and becomes famous for restoring Ithaca to its prewar glory, Neoptolemus becomes famous himself for returning Phthia to its Achillean prosperity: "Kingship and marriage crown the maturation of Neoptolemos. He has succeeded Akhilleus as king of the Myrmidons ([*Odyssey*] 4.9) and, when Telemakhos arrives at Sparta, [Helen and Menelaus' daughter] Hermione is about to depart to become [Neoptolemus'] bride ([*Odyssey*] 4.3ff)."[41] More precisely, Hermione will be on her way "to the

40 A. T. Edwards 1985:31, 32. For further evidence of Odysseus and Neoptolemus' connection, see A. T. Edwards 1985:59–67, 68.

41 Felson 1997:71.

glorious city of the Myrmidons, over whom [her intended] rule[s]" (*Murmidónōn protì ástu periklutón, hoîsin ánassen*) (*Odyssey* 4.9). Neoptolemus' renown, despite differing in nature from Achilles' own (given that Achilles gains glory for dying in a distant war fought to return Helen to her Spartan home, whereas Trojan War veteran Neoptolemus attains fame for restoring his homeland, Phthia, where he will live with his wife, Helen's daughter, after she arrives from Sparta), nevertheless remains a source of paternal pride and pleasure for Aeacus' scion (*Odyssey* 11.538–540).

For Odysseus, however, the Odyssean *kléos* of restoration is far more uncertain. The contrast in character between Odysseus' and Achilles' fames is conveyed by their distinct connections to denizens of Thebes and Thebe, the homonymous cities of the regions of Boeotia and Mysia, respectively. Whereas the *Iliad*'s *kléos* of conquest and the ease of its accomplishment by Achilles are emblematized by the lyre that he has taken in the course of killing Theban king Eëtion and his heirs, the *Odyssey*'s *kléos* of restoration and the difficulty of its achievement by Odysseus are represented by the contents of the prophecy presented by Theban *mántis* Teiresias. While the dangers of which the prophet warns his auditor hover like specters over the remainder of the Ithacan ruler's ill-fated journey, the lyre's sweet strains imply that the Phthian king can refrain from concerning himself with the manner in which his own fames will live on after he is gone. Achilles' rhapsody signifies the certainty of his glory as a conqueror and requires no accompaniment other than that provided by the Theban lyre, his prior prize. But Odysseus' bardery, fraught with the uncertainty of whether he will survive his woes and will achieve glory as his homeland's restorer, requires reinforcement of a prophetic variety. Odysseus hears about his future restoration from a Theban prophet whom he has reached by journeying away from Troy, a city that he helped to conquer in the past. Conversely, Achilles sings on a lyre that he got in the past by conquering Thebe, and his song anticipates his future victory at Troy.

Before performing narratives, both Achilles and Odysseus have had access to divine foreknowledge of their futures. The two heroes, however, have had different types of access. Achilles hears directly of his death—from his mother, the goddess Thetis. Odysseus, in contrast, hears indirectly of his death—from Apollo, the god who has enabled Teiresias to prophesy. Given that the heroes have been granted prescience divinely from disparate distances, these men address the future differently in their performances: Achilles—implicitly and affirmatively, confident in the firsthand account that Thetis has offered to him; while Odysseus—explicitly and interrogatively, not having spoken himself with Apollo but having had to rely on Teiresias to relay this immortal's message. Although Teiresias, as a prophet, is regarded as an authority by his society,

Odysseus differs from semi-divine Achilles, because the Ithacan interacts less directly than does the Phthian with the divinity who reveals his future. Achilles also has a less formal relationship with his mother, Thetis (with whom he himself can converse), than does Odysseus with Apollo (whom the Ithacan must consult through an intermediary, such as Teiresias).

Odysseus—by incorporating the prophecy of Theban Teiresias, who foresees the Ithacan's success—bolsters on Scheria the story that he himself tells. His temporary assumption of Teiresias' prophetic persona is effective rhetorically as assurance of Ithaca's restoration. After hearing the portion of Odysseus' woeful tale following the prophecy's rearticulation, Alcinous—on the recommendation made by his queen, Arete, immediately after she hears from Odysseus about Teiresias and the women in Hades—is moved to encourage every Phaeacian man in Odysseus' audience to contribute a bronze tripod and cauldron to the Ithacan and thus to his cause (*Odyssey* 11.138–332, 378–640; 12.1–453; 11.336–352; 13.3–22). With the Phaeacians' generous support, he can set forth on the final leg of his postwar journey home, and can replenish the stores that have been plundered by the suitors there.

Although quoting Teiresias and thereby gaining the complete confidence and assistance of Alcinous on Scheria have allowed Odysseus to increase his odds of regenerating Ithaca, he still needs to learn whether he can continue to count on the loyal herdsman and the loving queen whom he forsook for war at Troy an entire score of years before. Upon returning to Ithaca, then, Odysseus seeks to assess the interest that Eumaeus and Penelope have in Odysseus' reappearance, as well as to explain what he has been through while absent. To present his past and future in ways that enable him to attain his two aims, he once again plays both poet and prophet. In relating what has happened to him on his way home from Troy, and in stating what will happen upon his return to Ithaca, he reconnects surreptitiously with the people whose help he needs to achieve the victory at home on which his glory depends. Thus, Odysseus' "narratives, true to the mixture of truth and falsehood they involve, succeed as evocations of Odysseus as someone absent, as someone remembered in the past or hoped for in the future, but not as indications of his presence."[42]

The disguised Odysseus' stories—of what has been and what will be—concern a pair of personae, the unnamed Cretan and the Cretan Aethon. Yet, even though these beggars' apparently lying tales seem (at first listen) to warrant the long-standing belief that they (like epic poems) are distant from the truth,[43] they actually lie quite close to it.

42 Murnaghan 1987:167.

43 The tradition of suspicion of Odysseus for this reason has been delineated by classicist W. B. Stanford (1963:95).

For instance, the tale that the unnamed Cretan tells Eumaeus, in his hut, strikingly echoes in its woes the story that Odysseus has shared with Alcinous, at his court. Importantly, the source of all these sorrows is Zeus, who—in the *Odyssey* as in the *Iliad*—is believed to dole out good and bad things to human beings.[44] At *Odyssey* 1.347–349, for example, Telemachus declares that Zeus is responsible for giving what he wishes to each person, not the bards who sing of these gifts. Indeed, as the bardic Cretan recalls his experiences—i.e. losing his inheritance by lots to the legitimate sons of his wealthy father, leading Achaean soldiers in the Trojan War, seeking the protection of the king of Egypt after an abortive expedition there, being enslaved by a Phoenician trader, being captured by Thesprotian sailors, and escaping at Ithaca—he attributes his travels and travails to Zeus (who plotted the Trojan campaign, sabotaged the Egyptian expedition, and destroyed the Phoenician ship) (*Odyssey* 14.191–359). Similarly, to the Phaeacians, Odysseus waxes poetic on his homecoming's hindrance by gales sent by this storm god (*Odyssey* 9.67–69, 259–262; 12.312–315).

Yet the adversity that Odysseus suffers at Zeus' hands can be seen as a means of creating the circumstances under which the Ithacan attains *kléos*. Stated another way, "[b]y exposing Odysseus to Poseidon's pain, Zeus 'odysseuses' Odysseus; that is, makes it possible for him to earn his incomparable identity."[45] Zeus—by making certain that Odysseus and his crew are sent by storms to the lands of the Lotus-Eaters, Cyclopes, and Helius (*Odyssey* 9.82–104, 259–278; 12.312–355)—ensures that only Odysseus will survive to arrive at Scheria, in a pitiable enough condition to arouse Alcinous' compassion and generosity. With the Phaeacian monarch's support, Odysseus can make a fresh start on Ithaca while working for the fame linked to the renewal of his kingdom.

To achieve this aim, the Ithacan ruler must confirm that he has allies at home. Hence the instrumentality of all of his tall tales here: "The Cretan Lies provide more than simple entertainment, for they are intimately connected with Odysseus' recent return to Ithaca and his desire to regain his hearth, wife, and throne. If he is to succeed, Odysseus must have time to gather information and allies, to test the loyalty of others."[46] The narrative that he shares with Eumaeus, then, needs to reveal whether the swineherd remains loyal to him, and not to give away prematurely the particulars of his restoration plan. Therefore, the story incorporates an indirect encounter with Odysseus: the unnamed Cretan reports having heard about him from his Thesprotian host, Pheidon (*Odyssey* 14.321–333)—an episode included to elicit the sympathy the Ithacan sovereign hopes that his servant still has for him. Happily for Odysseus, Eumaeus responds with

44 M. W. Edwards 1987:128–129.

45 Dimock 1989:260.

46 Haft 1984:299.

affection for him and with skepticism toward the Cretan. While Eumaeus does not believe that his master can be on his way home—and is convinced instead that Odysseus has died ingloriously in the stormy sea—the swineherd speaks of having had his hopes of Odysseus' return raised and dashed in the past by a guileful traveler, and of not wanting to repeat that experience (*Odyssey* 14.363–387).

Yet, Eumaeus is taken in by the remainder of the Cretan's tale (*Odyssey* 14.360–362). And the swineherd is right to be taken in, because the ostensibly fictive story that the Cretan, in the manner of a poet, has presented also can be read as a cryptic prediction of what Odysseus actually will do—a prediction that the Cretan has delivered as if he were a prophet. Eumaeus himself hints that the Cretan may be playing this double role, for the occupations with which the swineherd starts and ends his speculation on the Cretan's specialty are the *mántis* and the *aoidós* (*Odyssey* 17.384, 385). In acting like both practitioners at once, the Cretan relates a narrative that is masked. On its face, the account sounds like a doleful poem whose Cretan protagonist randomly loses his livelihood, wages a distant war, seeks a sovereign's support upon failing to loot his land, and suffers at sea. Yet, unraveling the Cretan's yarn as such a poem reveals it to be the complete opposite of a prophecy of the strategies that Odysseus will employ to regain and to restore his kingdom and thus his glory. In fact, the Ithacan ruler ultimately protects his patrimony, by standing—with his father and son—against the kinsmen of the suitors slain in his own palace with the assistance of Eumaeus, among others; replenishes the plundered royal estate with spoils from Scheria and from Ithaca; and propitiates Poseidon, in order to die peacefully among the prosperous Ithacan people (*Odyssey* 24.496–515; 16.227–232; 23.355–358, 277–284).

Odysseus' juxtaposition of poetry and prophecy continues as he faces Penelope alone for the first time since he left her for Troy. In meeting with her, as with Alcinous and with Eumaeus, Odysseus tests her fidelity while providing her with reassurances that he will return gloriously. But his poetic and prophetic activities intensify in front of her, because of the closeness of his relationship to her and because of the necessity of its success to his efforts to restore his royal family as well as his patrimony.

When he, in the guise of Aethon, interacts with his queen in book 19, he acts first as an *aoidós*, then as a *mántis*, then simultaneously as an *oneiropólos* (dream interpreter) and an *oiōnopólos* (bird-omen interpreter), and finally as both a *mántis* and an *aoidós*.

Aethon starts by behaving like a bard. When Penelope asks Aethon who he is, he praises her, evades her question, and—when she persists—tells her a false story about being from Crete and seeing Odysseus there after the Troy-bound Achaeans had been thrown off course (*Odyssey* 19.102–202, 214–248). But Aethon, before beginning his narrative, is sincere as he lauds Penelope and her husband:

ô gúnai, ouk án tís se brotôn ep' apeírona gaîan
neikéoi· ê gár seu kléos ouranòn eurùn hikánei,
hṓs té teu è basilêos amúmonos, hós te theoudè̂s
andrásin en polloîsi kaì iphthímoisin anássōn
eudikías anékhēisi, phérēisi dè gaîa mélaina
puroùs kaì krithás, bríthēisi dè déndrea karpôi,
tíktēi d' émpeda mêla, thálassa dè parékhēi ikhthûs
ex euēgesíēs, aretôsi dè laoì hup' autoû.

My lady, no mortal on the boundless earth
could have quarrel with you, for certainly your glory reaches wide-
spread heaven—
as does that of a blameless king, a god-fearing man who,
as the lord among many noble men,
upholds good laws; and the black earth bears
wheat and barley, and the trees are loaded with fruit,
and the sheep bear young continuously, and the sea provides fish
because of his good leadership; and his people thrive under him.

Odyssey 19.107–114

That Odysseus is the "blameless king" (*basilêos amúmonos*) whose "trees are loaded with fruit" (*bríthēisi ... déndrea karpôi*) and whose "sheep bear young continuously" (*tíktēi ... émpeda mêla*) makes sense because of the abundance of his orchards and flocks of sheep and because Aethon goes on to extol Odysseus' regalia (*Odyssey* 19.109, 112, 113; 24.336–344; 14.100; 19.224–235). But Aethon does not name the absent king whom he glorifies, and thus cannot ensure that the ruler's name will live on. Nonetheless, Aethon's praise of Penelope suggests that his poetry resembles that of Demodocus in its efficacy. Aethon's declaration that no one "could have quarrel with" (*neikéoi*) the queen, whose "glory reaches widespread heaven" (*kléos ouranòn eurùn hikánei*), recalls Demodocus' song about the "quarrel" (*neîkos*) of Odysseus and Achilles, a song whose "glory ... reached widespread heaven" (*kléos ouranòn eurùn híkane*) (*Odyssey* 19.108; 8.75, 74). Moreover, as Penelope reacts to Aethon's yarn, she parallels Odysseus in his response to Demodocus' ballad about the Trojan War. Although the Phaeacian *aoidós* sings of the Achaean victory at Troy, the Ithacan king grieves rather than rejoices:

Taût' ár' aoidòs áeide periklutós· autàr Odusseùs
tḗketo, dákru d' édeuen hupò blephároisi pareiás.
hōs dè gunè̄ klaíēisi phílon pósin amphipesoûsa,

hós te heē̂s prósthen pólios laō̂n te pésēisin,
ásteï kaì tekéessin amúnōn nēleès ē̂mar·
hē mèn tòn thnḗiskonta kaì aspaíronta idoûsa
amph' autō̂i khuménē líga kōkúei· hoi dé t' ópisthe
kóptontes doúressi metáphrenon ēdè kaì ṓmous
eíreron eisanágousi, pónon t' ekhémen kaì oïzún·
tē̂s d' eleeinotátōi ákheï phthinúthousi pareiaí·
hṑs Oduseùs eleeinòn hup' ophrúsi dákruon eîben.
énth' állous mèn pántas elánthane dákrua leíbōn,
Alkínoos dé min oîos epephrásat' ēd' enóēsen,
hḗmenos ánkh' autoû, barù dè stenákhontos ákousen.

Of these very things, the glorious bard sang. But Odysseus
melted, and, beneath his eyelids, tears steeped his cheeks.
And—just as a woman embraces and wails over her beloved husband,
who has fallen before his city and people
while warding away the pitiless day from his city and children,
and she, upon seeing him laboring to take his last breaths,
throws her arms around him and shrieks shrilly, but the men behind
her
strike her with their spear shafts on the back and shoulders
and carry her away into slavery to suffer labor and sorrow,
and her cheeks waste away with the most piteous grief—
like so, Odysseus shed pitiful tears beneath his brows.
In shedding his tears, he eluded the attention of everyone else there
except Alcinous, the only one who looked at and took notice of him
while sitting near him, because of having heard him groaning
grievously.

Odyssey 8.521–534

Penelope sorrows similarly as she hears Aethon's story:[47]

Íske pseúdea pollà légōn etúmoisin homoîa·
tē̂s d' ár' akouoúsēs rhée dákrua, tḗketo dè khrṓs.
hōs dè khiṑn katatēket' en akropóloisin óressin,
hḗn t' Eûros katétēxen, epḕn Zéphuros katakheúēi·
tēkoménēs d' ára tē̂s potamoì plḗthousi rhéontes·
hṑs tē̂s tḗketo kalà parḗïa dákru kheoúsēs,

[47] The melting metaphors used in *Odyssey* 8.522 and 19.204 for these weeping episodes have been likened to one another by classicist Irene J. F. de Jong (2001:19.204–209n).

klaioúsēs heòn ándra parēmenon. autàr Odusseùs
thumôi mèn goóōsan heèn eléaire gunaîka,
ophthalmoì d' hōs ei kéra héstasan ēè sídēros
atrémas en blephároisi· dólōi d' hó ge dákrua keûthen.

He made the many lies that he told seem like truths,
and, as she listened, her tears flowed and her body melted.
Just as snow melts on mountain peaks,
snow that the East Wind melts when the West Wind showers it down,
and—as it melts—the flowing rivers flood,
like so, her beautiful cheeks melted as she showered tears
and lamented her husband even as he sat beside her. But, although Odysseus
pitied his weeping wife in his heart,
his eyes stared ahead as if made of horn or iron,
unmoving under his eyelids; and, with deceit, even he concealed his tears.

Odyssey 19.203–212

As Penelope mirrors Odysseus' sorrow, she herself resembles the apparently Trojan widow to whom he has been compared already. The horror of the Trojan War is brought home to Penelope when she hears the name of her absent and perhaps dead husband on the lips of Aethon, the apparent brother of Odysseus' brother-in-arms. Here, as the Cretan Aethon, Odysseus departs from his earlier self-disclosure (as the unnamed Cretan) that he was fathered by Castor (Hylax's son), and instead claims to be Minos' grandson, Deucalion's son, and the younger brother of Idomeneus, whom Aethon identifies as Odysseus' close friend and fellow fighter (*Odyssey* 14.199–206, 19.178–191). Penelope's reaction to hearing from Aethon of the hardships her husband faced in Crete as he tried to embark for Troy in harsh weather (*Odyssey* 19.185–189, 199–201)—namely, her ability to share Odysseus' own despair at Demodocus' Trojan War reminder—confirms for Odysseus that she will be receptive to his return and helpful to him as he strives to make Ithaca thrive once again. Odysseus will achieve glory by leaving behind the lives that he and other Achaeans have destroyed at Troy and by recreating on Ithaca a kingdom that produces as well as it has in the past. Odysseus' departure from the Iliadic ideal is revealed by his identification with the war widow. Indeed, hearing about winning Achaeans leads him to lament like the wives of the warriors whom Achilles will have killed to obtain *kléos* (*Iliad* 18.121–125). These women include Hector's wife, Andromache, whose natal and marital homelands of Thebe and Troy, respectively, have been and will be pillaged—in effect—by

Achilles, when he collects handsome ransoms for two of the kingdoms' most prominent inhabitants: Eëtion's widowed queen, who is Andromache's mother and dies—apparently in childbirth—shortly afterward; and King Priam's most heroic son to have died, Hector (*Iliad* 22.515; 6.425–428; 24.493–502, 572–579). Unlike Achilles' widow-making strikes, Odysseus' widow-like outcry indicates that he now is ready to tend to the hurts that his own wartime absence has inflicted on his queen and kingdom.

Although Odysseus is not yet ready to reveal himself to Penelope, he does offer her solace in the form of prophecy. In fact, in his forecasts of his own emergence and her suitors' demise, he bears a striking resemblance to the *mántis* Theoclymenus. As Aethon, Odysseus promises:

> *... émpēs dé toi hórkia dṓsō.*
> *ístō nûn Zeùs prôta, theôn húpatos kaì áristos,*
> *histíē t' Oduséos amúmonos, hèn aphikánō·*
> *ê mén toi táde pánta teleíetai hōs agoreúō.*
> *toûd' autoû lukábantos eleúsetai enthád' Odusseús,*
> *toû mèn phthínontos mēnós, toû d' histaménoio.*
>
> ... Nevertheless, I will give you my word.
> Let Zeus, highest and best of the gods, now be my witness first;
> and the hearth of blameless Odysseus, to which I come.
> I swear that all these things will come to pass as I tell you.
> Within this very month Odysseus will come here,
> as one month ends and the next begins.
>
> *Odyssey* 19.302–307

In its opening text, Aethon's prediction—which is "almost the same" as one that he utters to Eumaeus in regard to Odysseus' return (*Odyssey* 14.158–162)[48]—evokes a prophecy that Theoclymenus makes on the basis of a bird omen (*Odyssey* 17.160–161):

> *... emeîo dè súntheo mûthon·*
> *atrekéōs gár toi manteúsomai oud' epikeúsō.*
> *ístō nûn Zeùs prôta theôn xeníē te trápeza*
> *histíē t' Oduséos amúmonos, hèn aphikánō,*
> *hōs ê toi Oduseùs ḗdē en patrídi gaíēi,*
> *hḗmenos è hérpōn, táde peuthómenos kakà érga,*
> *éstin, atàr mnēstêrsi kakòn pántessi phuteúei·*

[48] Podlecki 1967:20.

... But listen to my words,
for I will prophesy to you precisely and will not hold back anything.
Let Zeus, first of the gods, now be my witness—and the table of
hospitality
and the hearth of blameless Odysseus, to which I come—
to the fact that Odysseus already is in his fatherland,
staying still or moving while learning of these evil acts,
and he is planting evil for all the suitors.

Odyssey 17.153–159

The connection between both prognostications is strengthened when they elicit the identical reaction from Penelope:[49]

Tòn d' aûte proséeipe períphrōn Pēnelópeia·
aì gàr toûto, xeîne, épos tetelesménon eíē·
tôi ke tákha gnoíēs philótētá te pollá te dôra
ex emeû, hōs án tís se sunantómenos makarízoi.

Wise Penelope replied to him,
"If only your word would be accomplished, my guest,
then soon you would know my favor and so many gifts
from me that anyone who met you would say that you were blessed."

Odyssey 17.162–165, 19.308–311

That Penelope is equally welcoming to her guests is unsurprising, given the similarity of their circumstances. Like Theoclymenus, who has fared away from his fatherland, Hyperesia (*Odyssey* 15.224, 272, 252–256), Odysseus journeys far from his home during much of the *Odyssey*; and, even when he is home, his beggar disguise distances him from his customary way of life. Moreover, both men bring Penelope happy news. While Aethon actually is not a *mántis* and merely can attest to alter ego Odysseus' intention to emerge on Ithaca, Theoclymenus is inspired to prophesy the tremendous penalty Odysseus will exact from the suitors there once he is fully aware of their wicked acts. The extent of this penalty becomes clear in the vision that this prophet shares with the suitors the day after Penelope interviews Aethon:

toîsi dè kaì metéeipe Theoklúmenos theoeidḗs·
â deiloí, tí kakòn tóde páskhete; nuktì mèn huméōn
eilúatai kephalaí te prósōpá te nérthe te goûna,

[49] Harsh 1950:12; Amory 1963:102.

oimōgḕ dè dédēe, dedákruntai dè pareiaí,
haímati d' errádatai toîkhoi kalaí te mesódmai·
eidṓlōn dè pléon prothuron, pleíē dè kaì aulḗ,
hieménōn Érebósde hupò zóphon· ēélios dè
ouranoû exapólōle, kakḕ d' epidédromen akhlús.
Hṑs éphath', hoi d' ára pántes ep' autôi hēdù gélassan.
toîsin d' Eurúmakhos, Polúbou páïs, árkh' agoreúein·
aphraínei xeînos néon állothen eilēlouthṓs.

Then godlike Theoclymenus spoke among them:
"Poor wretches, what is this misfortune that you are suffering?
Your heads and faces and knees below are wrapped up in darkness,
and wailing has burst out, and your cheeks are coated with tears,
and the walls and the pretty pillars are bestrewed with blood!
The entryway is full of phantoms, and the courtyard is filled as well,
[with phantoms] going under the gloom of the netherworld. The sun
has disappeared from the sky, and a foul mist has spread all over!"
Thus he spoke, but all the [suitors] guffawed at him.
And Eurymachus, Polybus' son, began to speak among them:
"The stranger who just arrived from somewhere else is out of his
mind!"

Odyssey 20.350–360

The fact that Theoclymenus witnesses the future is confirmed by the correspondence between components of his vision (the bloody walls and pillars, the crowd of phantoms in the entryway and courtyard, and the foul mist) and actual events (the blood of the suitors spewing in Odysseus' palace hall, the pile of their corpses beside his courtyard doors, and the stench of the burning sulfur that he uses as a fumigant) (*Odyssey* 20.354–355, 357; 22.407; 23.49–51). And Aethon, while not having prophet Theoclymenus' access to the particulars of the suitors' future retribution, knows at least how Odysseus intends to dispose of these evildoers.

But, before Odysseus takes their lives, Aethon—by providing, in the manners of both an *oneiropólos* and an *oiōnopólos*, his own prediction of Odysseus' execution of Penelope's suitors—makes certain that she will countenance their killing. She asks Aethon to interpret her dream: the necks of twenty geese around her house are broken by a powerful eagle, who declares that the geese were Penelope's suitors, that he is Odysseus, and that he will kill the suitors. Aethon not only interprets this dream, as an *oneiropólos*, but also acts as an *oiōnopólos* (*Odyssey* 19.535–558), basing his prediction on information given by Odysseus the dream eagle, who reads himself. The *oiōnopólos* Halitherses similarly foretells the suitors' death at Odysseus' hands, by reading an eagle omen; and recalls prophesying, on Odysseus' departure for Troy, that the Ithacan would return alone and incognito twenty years later (*Odyssey* 2.146–176). Penelope, in her dream, weeps at the death of her twenty geese-suitors, because she is mourning the twenty youthful years that she was forced to live in Odysseus' absence and that she will not be able to relive with him upon his return—lost time that she will bemoan again, when she reunites with him (*Odyssey* 23.210–212). Birds likewise symbolize years for the *Iliad*'s Calchas (*Iliad* 2.303–332), a prophet who regards as the nine years that the Achaeans will suffer before sacking Troy the nine sparrows devoured by a snake that Zeus finally turns into stone.[50] Although Penelope laments in her avian dream the time with Odysseus that she has lost forever, she responds positively to Aethon's dream reading, wanting it to be correct and telling him of the archery contest she is planning that will spur Odysseus to reappear (*Odyssey* 19.569–581).

Aethon, at the end of his interaction with Penelope in book 19, makes a prediction for her as would a prophet; but, in doing so, elicits a reaction from her as would a poet. Upon hearing of her decision to hold the archery contest, Aethon tells her that she should do so and that Odysseus will return to her before her suitors string his bow and shoot an arrow through the iron of the twelve axes she will have had propped up (*Odyssey* 19.582–587). Aethon—in suggesting to her that Odysseus, with his bow, will best the suitors—supplements Theoclymenus' prophecies that Odysseus is at hand and he will send these younger men to their ends. Yet, Penelope's answer to Aethon ("If you, my guest, were willing to sit beside me in my hall / to delight me, sleep would not spread over my eyelids" [*eí k' ethélois moi, xeîne, parḗmenos en megároisi / térpein, oú ké moi húpnos epì blephároisi khutheíē*] [*Odyssey* 19.589–590]) seems like a reflex to a poetic, rather than a prophetic, stimulus. Penelope's rapt attention to Aethon's speech is reminiscent of the unsleeping Phaeacians' absorption in Odysseus' nocturnal storytelling, and Aethon appears able to delight his listener just as the bards Phemius and Demodocus delight theirs (*Odyssey* 11.333–334, 13.1–2, 1.345–347, 8.43–45).

The simultaneity of Aethon's yoretelling and foretelling anticipates the explicit link between poetry and prophecy that Hesiod would forge. In the proem to his *Theogony*, he details the process whereby poets like Phemius and Demodocus acquire "the inspired art of singing" (*théspin aoidḗn*) (*Theogony* 31–32; *Odyssey* 1.328, 8.498).[51] In fact, Hesiod claims to have experienced inspiration

50 Athanassakis 1987:261–262.

51 For further discussion of this process vis-à-vis these Homeric bards, see M. W. Edwards 1987:18–19.

firsthand: "... [the Muses] breathed their divinely sweet voice into me / so that I could make glorious the things that would be and the things that had been before" (... *enépneusan ... moi audḕn / théspin, hína kleíoimi tá t' essómena pró t' eónta*). Here Hesiod brings poetry even closer to prophecy than does Homer, for the Hesiodic *aoidós* not only is inspired by the Muses (who are Zeus' daughters and the followers of their choral leader, Apollo, who inspires prophecy), but also has access both to past and to future events, as does the Iliadic *mántis* and *oiōnopólos* Calchas ("who kn[o]w[s] the things that [a]re, the things that w[i]l[l] be, and the things that [were] before" [*hòs ḗidē tá t' eónta tá t' essómena pró t' eónta*] [*Iliad* 1.70]). Nagy regards the prophetic nature of the Hesiodic poet as a survival of "an earlier stage in which poet and prophet were as yet undifferentiated." Nagy writes:

> The words *mantis* and *kērux* [herald] ... had once been appropriate designations for an undifferentiated poet-prophet; after differentiation set in, the word *aoidos* filled the need for designating a general category, as distinct from *mantis* and *kērux*, which became specialized subcategories. ...
>
> ... Such a pattern of semantic evolution corresponds to what is known in linguistic theory as Kurylowicz's Fourth Law of Analogy: when two forms come into competition for one function, the newer form may take over that function while the older form may become relegated to a subcategory of its earlier function.[52]

Like Nagy's focus, Hesiod, Aethon may evoke poet-prophets of old. Yet, his hold-over eloquence concerning past events and future events has another source.

While "[h]e ma[k]e[s] the many lies that he t[e]l[ls] seem like truths" (*Íske pseúdea pollà légōn etúmoisin homoîa*) (*Odyssey* 19.203)—and thereby foreruns Hesiod's Muses, who "know how to tell many lies that seem like truths" (*ídmen pseúdea pollà légein etúmoisin homoîa*) (*Theogony* 27)—Aethon's speaking talent stems from his true status as a king. According to Hesiod:

> *hóntina timḗsousi*[53] *Diòs koûrai megáloio*
> *geinómenón te ídōsi diotrephéōn basilḗōn,*
> *tôi mèn epì glṓssēi glukerḕn kheíousin eérsēn,*
> *toû d' épe' ek stómatos rheî meílikha· ...*

52 Nagy 1990b:56, 56–57.

53 In *Theogony* 81, I, with West (1966, commentary on *Theogony*:81n), read *timḗsousi* (they honor) as the third-person plural form of the aorist short-vowel subjunctive.

Whomever—among kings nurtured by Zeus—great Zeus' daughters
honor
and look upon at the moment of his birth,
upon his tongue they pour sweet dew,
and honeyed words flow from his mouth ...

Theogony 81–84

As a monarch blessed thus, Odysseus—as the unnamed Cretan and the Cretan Aethon—can call up his own keenly observed accounts of having endured an arduous journey after the Trojan War, as well as articulate eloquently his intention to replenish his realm. As he prepares to take vengeance upon Penelope's pursuers, he personifies his strategic connection of narration and prediction:

... polúmētis Odusseús,
autík' epeì méga tóxon ebástase kaì íde pántēi,
hōs hót' anḕr phórmingos epistámenos kaì aoidē̂s
rhēïdíōs etánusse néōi perì kóllopi khordḗn,
hápsas amphotérōthen eüstrephès énteron oiós,
hṑs ár' áter spoudē̂s tánusen méga tóxon Odusseús.
dexiterē̂i d' ára kheirì labṑn peirḗsato neurē̂s·
hē d' hupò kalòn áeise, khelidóni eikélē audḗn.
mnēstē̂rsin d' ár' ákhos géneto méga, pâsi d' ára khrṑs
etrápeto. Zeùs dè megál' éktupe sḗmata phaínōn.

... [A]s soon as Odysseus, the man of many devices,
grasped the great bow and looked it over on every side—
just as when a man expert in the lyre and in the art of singing
easily stretches a string around a new peg,
after fastening the skillfully twisted strand of sheep gut at both
ends—
like so, Odysseus effortlessly strung the great bow.
Then he took it into his right hand and tried out the bowstring,
and it sang well under [his hand], like a swallow in voice.
A great grief now came over the suitors, and the flesh of every one of
them
changed color. And Zeus thundered loudly, showing his portents.

Odyssey 21.404–413

Here, Odysseus simultaneously evokes the lyre-playing poets Phemius and Demodocus and signals the imminent fulfillment of the recurrent prediction that Odysseus will return home and kill the suitors, whose execution he initiates with his great bow—an instrument with which he dispenses his justice (*Odyssey* 1.153–155; 8.261–262, 266; 22.8, 15–16). Moreover, the god who grants him glory for the victories of stringing his bow and hitting his target is Apollo (*Odyssey* 21.338, 22.5–7)—the only deity who, in addition to being a dread archer, accompanies poetry and inspires prophecy. He himself—in the *Homeric Hymn to Apollo* (ca. 690–640 BCE)—highlights his threefold status, making the following declaration shortly after he is born:

> *eíē moi kítharís te phílē kaì kampúla tóxa,*
> *khrḗsō d' anthrṓpoisi Diòs nēmertéa boulḗn.*
>
> May the lyre and the curved bow be dear to me,
> and I will prophesy to human beings Zeus' infallible will.
>
> *Homeric Hymn to Apollo* 131–132

Odysseus' invocation—prior to his own completion of a feat of archery—of the similarly poetic and prophetic Apollo becomes even clearer in light of the association of this deity's archery with pestilence followed by purification. Just as Apollo—with his arrows—inflicts acute illness upon errant communities and gives his surviving devotees the knowledge that they need to cleanse themselves of their offenses and thus to heal,[54] Odysseus—from his quiver and weapon stores—visits sudden death upon the wicked suitors in his midst and purifies his palatial premises immediately afterward with the aid of his servants (*Odyssey* 22.8–501). Fittingly, when Odysseus avenges the suitors' outrages, he does so "on a day consecrated to the archer god."[55] With Apollo's blessings, the arrows of sure-shooting Odysseus find their marks: suitor-intruders, whom he drives away from the doors trapping them in his own home. Once again, then, Odysseus contrasts with Achilles, who dies at the hands of Apollo and Paris, who kill the Phthian with arrows as he tries to invade the gates of Troy.[56]

When Odysseus is about to discard his beggar rags (*Odyssey* 22.1)—and, with them, the arduousness of his life at Troy, where he pretended to be a beggar before, in order to enter the city undetected and to kill a number of its residents (*Odyssey* 4.242–258)[57]—then he is ready to be the subject of actual poetry and prophecy rather than of Cretans' imitative speeches. As Theoclymenus has

54 Burkert 1985:145–148.

55 Jong 2001:20.276–278n. The timing of Odysseus' requital has also been remarked on by classicist William G. Thalmann (1984:176).

56 For further discussion of these events alluded to in the *Iliad* and treated at length elsewhere, see Burgess 2009:29, 38–39, 43, 44–45, 46–47.

57 The connection between Odysseus' beggarly turns has been observed by classicists Ignace Wieniewski (1924:123–124) and Hartmut Erbse (1972:97), as well as by Beye (1993:148).

prophesied (*Odyssey* 17.157–159), Odysseus shifts from a state of inaction (and impotence)—personified by an Aethon staring with eyes like horn or iron as he sits with a Penelope crying at his Cretan tale of meeting Odysseus (*Odyssey* 19.209–212)—to the powerful activity of stringing his bow containing horn (*Odyssey* 21.393–395) to shoot his arrow through the series of iron axes that she has had set up. The Ithacan ruler's impending realization of the suitors' predicted slaughter is portended at the end of the bowstringing passage, by Zeus' thunder, which echoes the thunder that he sounded earlier as a response to Odysseus' request for an external sign showing him that the gods supported his plan to exterminate the suitors (*Odyssey* 21.413; 20.97–121). In addition to bringing to pass the prophecy of his return and reinstatement, he, in taking hold of his bow, reclaims his kingly identity and thus attaches his own name to the blameless monarch whose *kléos* Aethon has characterized (*Odyssey* 19.109–114). Stated another way, "Odysseus' reassertion of his heroic persona and his restoration to wife, house, and kingship consist precisely in this movement from singer to actor. He (re-)creates *kleos* in song when he recites the *apologoi* [accounts] to Alcinous' court skillfully like a professional bard, but he finally wins *kleos* in deeds when he makes the warrior's bow sing like the poet's lyre."[58] When he (as Cretans) impersonates (in effect) a poet, he passes through an intermediary phase between song and action, repeatedly using his "singing" strategically to test Eumaeus' and Penelope's fidelity to him.

On the heels of these entertaining yet expedient efforts, Odysseus ultimately will find fame for replenishing his realm, which has been depleted by the suitors' depredations (*Odyssey* 23.356–358, 4.318–321, 14.89–95, 17.534–538, 18.274–280, 23.303–305). Appropriately, "[a]utumnal and winter pictures which had accompanied Odysseus' journey from Scheria to Ithaka—the windblown chaff, night frosts, fallen leaves, bitter storms—give way, on the day of vengeance, to the sounds and sights of nightingales, swallows, farmers breaking the soil or cutting grass, and pasturing cattle."[59] Moreover, the vernal, agricultural nature of Odysseus' glory is captured by a substance of his weapon (the bow that he was given, as a boy, by Iphitus, prince of Oechalia, when the two were working individually in Messene to recover rustled livestock—three hundred Ithacan sheep and twelve Oechalian mares nursing mule colts [*Odyssey* 21.11–23, 31–33]): horn that symbolically both is linked to and links Odysseus to the land where he will reap *kléos* as soon as his herds, flocks, fields, and orchards flourish again. Even the doors to the room where his bow has been stored while he has been away from Ithaca and at war (*Odyssey* 21.38–41) evoke the once-and-future peaceable

58 Segal 1994:109.

59 Austin 1975:247. For an enumeration of these signs of spring, see Austin 1975:246–253.

kingdom for which he will be known. These portals—when opened by his wife (and son's mother) Penelope, who has aroused Odysseus' potency in the past, and will do so again when she reunites with him on their live olive-tree bed made up by maids Eurynome (Widely Ranging or Ruling) and Eurycleia (Widely Glorious)—sound like a bellowing (and presumably virile) bull grazing on (ostensibly fertile) pastureland (*Odyssey* 23.289–296, 21.48–50). Odysseus ensures that he will live on in song by making sure that its makers are secure. Odysseus spares from the suitors' slaughter Phemius and Medon (the herald who gives the poet his lyre) and hence sustains these entertainers in the manner of Alcinous, who feeds and supports Demodocus and his lyre-provider, the herald Pontonous (*Odyssey* 22.375–377, 1.153–154, 8.65–71). Patronizing the Ithacan performers is part of Odysseus' larger restoration project: "Both in song and action, [his] task is to restore domestic, civic, and cosmic order. He reestablishes song and feasting as a sign of that order in his palace when the bard, spared from death by the grim warrior-king ([*Odyssey*] 22.330–[3]57), can once more play the accompaniment to joyful dancing and merriment as king and queen are about to be united ([*Odyssey*] 23.143–[1]45; 22.332b = 23.133b)."[60]

Thus, the glory of Odysseus that is preserved by Phemius and his successors differs from that of Achilles. Whereas the destructive *kléos* of conquest that the Phthian king seeks abroad requires him to give up a productive life in his own kingdom, the productive *kléos* of domestic restoration to which the Ithacan ruler aspires demands that he turn away from the destruction that he has wreaked on a distant land. Although Odysseus' eradication of the suitors probably is as gory as anything that he has seen or done on the Trojan battlefield, the *Odyssey* "insists upon the positive aspects of the hero's return and of the restoration of the past and thus of 'the proper order' which results from it."[61] In this light that illuminates, yet mitigates, the measures he takes to make sure that Ithaca regenerates, the suitors' deaths constitute the necessary, if bloody, cost of justice, security, and prosperity on the island.[62]

The two types of renown that redound to Achilles and Odysseus each contrast with an outcome of the life of Agamemnon, who commanded both men during the Trojan War—a double distinction drawn during the *Odyssey*'s second excursus into the underworld. Here, the shade of Achilles comments that "great glory for [Agamemnon's] son" (*sôi paidì méga kléos*) (*Odyssey* 24.33) remained hypothetical, rather than becoming real, because his father did not die on the Trojan battlefield (*Odyssey* 24.30–31, 34). As the shade of Agamemnon acquiesces to the spectral Achilles' account, a few of the circumstances that the

60 Segal 1994:109.

61 Olson 1995:183.

62 For an explanation of how the suitors have reaped what they have sown, see Segal 1994:221.

shadowy Agamemnon characterizes as having created Achilles' *kléos* are akin to conditions that Agamemnon himself was unable to fulfill. While this Mycenaean commander of the Achaeans met his doom near home, the Phthian ruler died in Troy (*Odyssey* 24.96–97, 36–37). Moreover, a consecrated host of Achaean spearmen heaped up for Achilles "a great and unblemished burial mound" (*mégan kaì amúmona túmbon*) (*Odyssey* 24.80) that would be seen from afar at that time and in the future, but no such memorial—not even a mere "burial mound" (*túmbon*) (*Odyssey* 24.32)—was erected to Agamemnon by the Achaeans (*Odyssey* 24.80–81, 83–84, 32, 34). Whereas Agamemnon did not manage to achieve any glory for his heir, Orestes, "... [Achilles] did not lose [his] name even after dying, but always ... / will have noble glory among all people ..." (*... sù mèn oudè thanṑn ónom' ṓlesas, allá toi aieì / pántas ep' anthrṓpous kléos éssetai esthlón ...*) (*Odyssey* 24.93–94) to leave as a legacy for Neoptolemus. In fact, Achilles, as the semi-divine son of a goddess, was celebrated in exceptional ways upon his death: he was lamented by Thetis and the other Nereids, who adorned him with immortal garments; the nine Muses sang his dirge; the golden funerary urn that contained his bones, intermingled with those of Patroclus, had been forged by Hephaestus and presented by Thetis as a gift from Dionysus, god of wine and revelry; and, at Thetis' request, gods had provided the fine prizes that she set aside for the winners of Achilles' funeral games (*Odyssey* 24.47–49, 58–61, 73–77, 85–92).

When the shadowy Achilles argues that Orestes inherited no glory from Agamemnon, the Phthian king's specter restricts the qualifications for Iliadic *kléos*. Earlier in the *Odyssey*, the *kléos* ascribed to Trojan War veteran Agamemnon had two sources. Odysseus averred before the Cyclops Polyphemus that the commander of the Achaeans had "the greatest glory beneath the sky" (*mégiston hupouránion kléos*), given "... [how] great a city he [had] sacked and / [how] many people he [had] killed ..." (*tóssēn ... diéperse pólin kaì apṓlese laoùs / polloús ...*) (*Odyssey* 9.264, 265–266). Furthermore, Agamemnon's brother Menelaus, who was away from their native land, Mycenae, when he learned of Agamemnon's death, "heaped up a burial mound for [him] so that he would have inextinguishable glory" (*kheû' Agamémnoni túmbon, hín' ásbeston kléos eíē*) (*Odyssey* 4.584). But the location of this funeral in Egypt (*Odyssey* 4.581–584) precluded Agamemnon's people from participating in the ritual. Its private rather than public nature, as well as its temporal and geographical distance not only from the Achaeans' taking of Troy but also from Agamemnon's freshly rendered remains in Mycenae, evidences the spectral Achilles' implication that Agamemnon did not claim *kléos*. Instead of having a hero's farewell in Ilium among the Achaean forces, as Achilles did within days after dying (*Odyssey* 24.43–46, 68–70), Agamemnon was mourned formally some seven years after he had been murdered upon his return to Mycenae from Troy, assuming that his "harmless homecoming" (*nóstos apḗmōn*) (*Odyssey* 4.519) had allowed him to disembark fairly soon after setting sail—certainly no more than a year later if the watchman who had alerted Agamemnon's killer to his target's arrival had been in position since the end of the Trojan War (*Odyssey* 4.519–528). Agamemnon's relatively quick trip contrasts with the arduous journey that had extended Menelaus' travel from Troy into an eighth year before he heard of Agamemnon's slaying and soon afterward redocked at Egypt, Menelaus' final stop on his way back to Mycenae (*Odyssey* 4.81–92, 460–586).

The fate that Zeus assigned to Agamemnon (*Odyssey* 24.96–97) is opposed to that of Odysseus. After this Ithacan king dispatches Penelope's suitors to the underworld, their shades attest to the ultimate success of her schemes and her husband's intent to keep anyone else away from her bed and his throne (*Odyssey* 24.98–190). Upon hearing the phantasmic suitors' report, the shadowy Agamemnon proclaims that Penelope, in her fidelity to Odysseus, has virtue whose "glory will never be destroyed" (*kléos oú pot' oleîtai*) and, in her prudence, will be the subject of "... a delightful song" (*... aoidḕn / ... kharíessan ...*) (*Odyssey* 24.196, 197, 198). But there will be only "a hateful song" (*stugerḕ ... aoidḕ*) (*Odyssey* 24.200) about Agamemnon's wife, Clytemnestra, who in Agamemnon's wartime absence from Mycenae took a lover, Aegisthus, and clandestinely convinced him to kill her husband (his cousin) when he returned to his homeland (*Odyssey* 1.35–36, 4.514–535, 11.409–430, 24.199–200), and who consequently "... will bestow a burdensome reputation / upon all women ..." (*... khalepḕn ... phêmin opássei / thēlutérēisi gunaixí ...*) (*Odyssey* 24.201–202). Clytemnestra's own infamy, embodied by the doomed bard whom Agamemnon had entrusted to protect her while he was in Troy, and whom Aegistus relegated to a desert island and thus rendered as the prey of birds (*Odyssey* 3.267–271), assures further that her husband will not have his own *kléos*, while Penelope's fame, forged in her defense of the home that she and Odysseus have made together, enhances that of her husband.

The disparate destinies of Agamemnon and Odysseus inform the efforts of their sons. When Orestes attains *kléos* for slaying Aegisthus and avenging Agamemnon (*Odyssey* 1.29–30, 298–300; 3.203–204), Agamemnon's son supersedes "his glorious father" (*hoi patéra klutòn*) (*Odyssey* 1.300; 3.198, 308), whose *kléos* for sacking Troy will be canceled by Achilles ten years after the sack (*Odyssey* 5.105–108), by the conclusion of the *Odyssey*. Even earlier, Menelaus—"in the eighth year" (*ogdoátōi étei*) after leaving Troy (*Odyssey* 4.82)—pays his last respects to Agamemnon in Egypt shortly before Agamemnon—"in the eighth" (*ogdoátōi*) year after his death (*Odyssey* 3.306)—is avenged by Orestes in Mycenae. Moreover, as seen in *Odyssey* 3.309–312, Menelaus (before moving on to his Spartan stronghold) actually arrives in Mycenae from Egypt—with cargo, as if in congratulatory celebration—on the very day when Orestes is hosting a funeral feast for "his hateful mother [Clytemnestra] and uncourageous Aegisthus" (*mētrós te stugerê̄s kaì análkidos Aigísthoio*) (*Odyssey* 3.310). In rightfully reclaiming the Mycenaean monarchy, Orestes is cited by Athena as a model for Telemachus (*Odyssey* 1.298–302), who too has a father of whose "great glory [this son] always ha[s] heard" (*méga kléos aièn ákouon*) (*Odyssey* 16.241)—a warrior who, like Agamemnon, took part in the taking of Troy. However, because Telemachus himself has no memory of Odysseus (*Odyssey* 4.112, 11.445–450), the son uses the phrase *kléos eurù* to mean "a far-reaching rumor" of his father when asking his garrulous senior Nestor of Pylus after Odysseus' whereabouts; whereas, on Ithaca, Penelope, uttering the same phrase at the same line position (just before the trochaic caesura), refers to her beloved long-gone husband's "widespread glory" (*Odyssey* 3.83; 1.344; 4.726, 816).

Even as Telemachus terms the rumor about his father *kléos* as well, as if to accent how far in the past his father's fame seems to him, Telemachus departs from Orestes' example. Rather than render his father's glory an even more distant memory while achieving *kléos* that is all his own, the Ithacan prince works to return his father to his rightful position on Ithaca's throne. From here, Odysseus can restore his kingdom and claim the *kléos* attendant upon its righteous rule. To attain this end, Odysseus rids his land of the pretenders to it. Upon slaying Penelope's suitors, he transforms "the far-reaching rumor" (*kléos eurù*) of their execution—whose spread through his capital he attempts to check by commanding Phemius to sing in accompaniment to what will seem to be a wedding feast in the palace to any onhearers outside (*Odyssey* 23.133–139)—to a reality that seals Odysseus' "widespread glory" (*Odyssey* 23.137), his phrase echoing and encompassing those of his son and wife as it occupies the same metrical place as did theirs. Thus, although Odysseus will be known for a different type of glory than is Achilles, both of the best of the Achaeans excel their erstwhile commander—a warrior who does not die in battle, as well as a monarch who cannot rule after returning from war.

The difference between the Achillean and Odyssean types of fame informs not only the poetic performances of the heroes, but also the epics that center on them. The *Iliad* and the *Odyssey* offer different solutions to the human problem of striving for poetic immortality against divinely sanctioned hostility: in stark contrast to the *Iliad*'s pat and patent answer of Achilles' ready, faraway glory (foreshadowed briefly in his own wartime rhapsody) is the *Odyssey*'s cryptic and tortuous response of Odysseus' hard-won fame at home (foretold and encoded repeatedly in his postwar, bardic odes). The Greek epics' Indian counterparts, the *Rāmāyaṇa* and the *Mahābhārata*, also pose through royal poetry distinct reactions to an issue facing the human beings inhabiting a universe ordered by gods. In the Indian instance, however, the poetic rulers perform for the epic heroes, who consequently listen to accounts that incorporate these protagonists' varyingly successful efforts to maintain *dharma*—and thus to do right in an increasingly immoral world.

4

Hearkening to Kuśa and Lava and to Nala

Poetic Monarchs on the Ideal of *Dharma* in the Hindu Epics

THE HINDU EPICS DIFFER further from their Homeric counterparts by featuring rulers who are not merely similar to poets, but actually are poets. Yet these figures are not the heroes of the Hindu epics, despite resembling these leading men in their displacement from their sovereignties. In fact, this resemblance between the royal poets and the epic heroes who hear them reflects the parallel approaches to *dharma* taken by the royal poems and the epics that embed these poems. More precisely, the hero of each epic attends to the performance of a ruler who—in his poetry, as well as in his very person—captures the experience that the hero will have as he strives to realize righteousness in his own realm.

I define *dharma*, both descriptively and prescriptively, as righteousness as it exists and will exist in the cosmos, and righteousness as it is maintained and should be maintained through practices associated with class (*varṇa*), stage of life (*āśrama*), gender, and society as a whole. As this definition indicates, I see *dharma* as an umbrella term, "a collective noun referring to the loose aggregation of all the particular *dharmas*."[1] In order to overspread these various moral imperatives, my definition of *dharma* is broad by necessity. I blur distinctions among the duties subsumed by this rubric[2] in favor of focusing on the relationship of *dharma* as a whole to the *Rāmāyaṇa* and the *Mahābhārata* and to the royal poems that these texts encapsulate.

These royal poems—in their correspondences to the contents of the epics containing them, contents comprising events likely to be well known to epic audiences even before they hear epic recitals conclude—are, like their Archaic Greek analogues, proleptic. Yet the Sanskrit poetic prolepses are explicit where

[1] Fitzgerald 2004a:679.

[2] For genealogies of the notions of *dharma* in the *Rāmāyaṇa* and the *Mahābhārata*, see, respectively, Brockington 2004:658–669 and Fitzgerald 2004b, introduction to bk. 12:103–127.

the Greek ones are implicit, and vice versa. While Achilles' rhapsodic performance merely hints at the ease with which he will achieve *kléos* in his conquest of Troy, Odysseus' bardic compositions announce in their incorporated prophecies how hard won will be the *kléos* to accrue to him upon restoring Ithaca. But the exuberant rhapsody of Kuśa and Lava in the *Rāmāyaṇa* announces how Rāma will attain *dharma* triumphantly, whereas the tortured bardery of Nala in the *Mahābhārata* merely hints at how Yudhiṣṭhira will fulfill *dharma* with difficulty.

Before I explore the implications of these intercultural epic differences, let me compare the poetic Indian sovereigns who are nevertheless reminiscent of the eloquent kings of Phthia and Ithaca.[3]

Kuśa and Lava as a Rhapsode Away from Ayodhyā

When Kuśa and Lava tell Rāma a triumphal tale about his own life—a tale that takes up nearly the entire *Rāmāyaṇa*—the twin princes do so in their capacity as a *kuśīlava*, or roaming rhapsode (*Rāmāyaṇa* 1.5.1–7.100.25, 1.4.4, 7.85.14). Yet the *Rāmāyaṇa*'s identification of the *kuśīlava* with Rāma's own sons is startling, given the way in which the approximately contemporaneous *Arthaśāstra*—a statecraft manual dating from the first or second century CE—depicts this poetic practitioner.

In the *Arthaśāstra*, "*kuśīlava*" is a classification that sometimes covers such other performers as singers and actors (*Arthaśāstra*[4] 1.2.13, 1.18.12, 1.21.16). But this treatise also specifies that *kuśīlavas* can be "itinerant mendicants and narrators" (*cāraṇā bhikṣukāś ca vyākhyātāḥ*) (*Arthaśāstra* 4.1.62). And, in other contexts, it suggests that *kuśīlavas* stray, rather than simply wander, for these roving rhapsodists somehow seem to set bad moral examples for their audiences. For instance, the injunction in *Arthaśāstra* 2.1.34 that actors, dancers, singers, musicians, jesters, and *kuśīlavas* should not interrupt other people's work implies that these entertainers encourage shirking. In fact, according to the *Śrīmūla*, pandit T. Ganapati Sastri's modern Sanskrit commentary on the *Arthaśāstra*, it requires *kuśīlavas* to remain in one place during the rainy season (*Arthaśāstra* 4.1.58), so that these rhapsodists do not disrupt the agricultural processes that have to happen then.[5] Therefore, an ideal kingdom would have neither outdoor nor indoor entertainment venues and would have nowhere in its villages to house *kuśīlavas* and other entertainers. Without their distractions, farmers would devote all their attention to their fields, and the kingdom's wealth, manpower, goods, and foods would increase (*Arthaśāstra* 2.1.33, 35).

3 Earlier versions of the following four sections have appeared in Pathak 2006:128–141, 142–145.

4 All translations of passages from this work are my own.

5 Kangle 1969–1972, critical and explanatory notes to pt. 2:4.1.58n.

Apparently, *kuśīlavas* do not just constrain the produce of a country, but also exert a bad influence on its king. The *Arthaśāstra*—instead of conceding that diversion for the king has the positive effect of providing employment for *kuśīlavas* and such others as craftsmen, artists, jesters, and traders—argues that the king, after seeking such diversion, starts to crave other things. As a result, he harasses his subjects—both by seizing for himself what they produce and the commodities that they give as gifts, and by allowing his favorites, too, to take these things (*Arthaśāstra* 8.4.21–23).

Given that *kuśīlavas*, in preventing people from carrying out their occupational obligations (and thus from fulfilling *dharma*), can do no right in the *Arthaśāstra*, why does this kind of performer appear in the *Rāmāyaṇa*—as its hero's heirs, no less? In my view, there are two reasons why the *Rāmāyaṇa* represents itself as being related by a *kuśīlava*.

First, this poetic performer's moral dubiousness lends itself to the epic's emphasis on Rāma's righteousness. The *Rāmāyaṇa*'s assertion of its hero's integrity is more difficult to dispute, if even the *kuśīlava* recounting Rāma's story cannot help but be special. Indeed, this narrative is recited by Rāma's own twin sons, who have been named—of course—Kuśa and Lava. As the *Rāmāyaṇa* divides the *kuśīlava*'s function between these characters, the epic creates the impression that these poetic performers are prototypical—that they are the ones for whom the *kuśīlavas* of ancient Indian society have been named, rather than the reverse. As a result, Kuśa and Lava's story's stock rises. The social status of the twins also indicates that they are no ordinary *kuśīlava*. Their position as *kṣatriyas* (reigning warriors), members of society's second-highest class, is much higher than that which *kuśīlavas* customarily occupy—the station of *śūdras*, or servants belonging to the bottom class of society (*Arthaśāstra* 1.3.8).

A second reason why Rāma's sons play the role of rhapsode is that the princes' capacity as a *kuśīlava* conveniently keeps them waiting in the wings as their father stays on center stage. The benefits to a kingdom of limiting *kuśīlava* activity justify some remove between a king who rules as well as Rāma does and the reciters of his tale, who—in spite of their royal ancestry—have been reared apart from their father, in the forest.

But why is this poetic role reserved for princes of such promise? On the strength of their paternity alone, Kuśa and Lava would seem to be capable of doing more than what the *Rāmāyaṇa* assigns them—to wit, telling their father's story and taking their respective seats on the thrones of Kosala and Uttarakosala (the southern and northern regions of Rāma's ancestral land) at a time of Rāma's choosing (*Rāmāyaṇa* 7.97.7, 17–19). Kuśa and Lava's relative obscurity results from the *Rāmāyaṇa*'s double balancing act. In the first place, the epic strikes a balance between elevating the *kuśīlava* and keeping him at a safe distance from the kingdom's administration. In the second place, the epic likens the princes to their father just enough to underscore his achievements without shifting focus to the twins' own.

Caught in both of these balances, Kuśa and Lava cannot move enough to be memorable in their own right. But they are in the perfect position to foreground their father's righteousness, on which these princes center their story. Kuśa and Lava relate that Rāma is relentlessly "righteous by nature" (*dharmātmā*) (*Rāmāyaṇa* 2.15.11, 2.18.25), as at least two of his acts exemplify. First, on the eve of his consecration as Ayodhyā's prince regent, Rāma agrees to relinquish this title to Bharata and to be exiled to the forest for fourteen years (*Rāmāyaṇa* 2.16.28). Second, Rāma, after ascending Ayodhyā's throne, banishes Sītā to Vālmīki's sylvan hermitage. By this banishment, Rāma counters the criticism that he—in taking Sītā back after she has been kidnapped, and thus touched, by Rāvaṇa—has set a bad example for his subjects. Although Rāma may appear to overstep the bounds of acceptable behavior, he—by virtue of being a human manifestation of Viṣṇu, the deity deemed the "best among the groups of gods" (*devagaṇaśreṣṭham*) (*Rāmāyaṇa* 6.105.5)—is beyond reproach. And, as Pollock has shown, Rāma's divinity is not simply tacked on to the text of the *Rāmāyaṇa*, but is interwoven throughout.[6]

Although Rāma's acts overshadow their telling by Kuśa and Lava—an event depicted only toward the epic's beginning and end (*Rāmāyaṇa* 1.4.27, 7.85.1)—the princes' striking likeness to Rāma and the princes' forest upbringing accentuate his righteousness. Kuśa and Lava, like their father, "know right from wrong" (*dharmajñau*) (*Rāmāyaṇa* 1.4.4, 2.18.19). This moral similarity is stressed by the identical twins' physical resemblance to Rāma, of whom they are the image (*Rāmāyaṇa* 1.4.10, 7.85.7). In addition, the twins were born to and brought up by Sītā in the ashram of Vālmīki, who taught these youths how to recite the *Rāmāyaṇa*, which he had composed (*Rāmāyaṇa* 7.58.1; 1.4.6, 1; 7.85.19). Consequently, the princes' very existence as forest-dwellers recalls Rāma's own forest exile as well as his banishment of his sons' mother, two events that evince his devotion to *dharma* above all else. Moreover, his morality—by motivating him to reject her and thus to displace their twins from Ayodhyā to Vālmīki's abode—permits the princes' performance of the *Rāmāyaṇa* for their father, for Kuśa and Lava probably would not have become the sage's students had they resided in the king's palace. Thus, *dharma* accomplishes its own articulation in epic.

Kuśa and Lava, then, reinforce Rāma's righteousness in four ways. First, the duo, by highlighting his divinity while telling his story, renders irreproachable his refusal to make moral compromises. Second, the princes' poem performance itself is predicated on their father's unflinching integrity, which lets the twins

6 Pollock 1984:516.

learn the epic from its mythological author. Kuśa and Lava also maintain Rāma's *dharma* by recounting the *Rāmāyaṇa* on a particular occasion, and by relating his future as well as his past.

Kuśa and Lava's recital is occasioned by Rāma's first horse sacrifice. By completing this rite known as "the king of sacrifices" (*kraturāṭ*) in verse 11.261 of the *Mānavadharmaśāstra* (a law book whose composition, roughly between 100 BCE and 100 CE, probably overlapped chronologically with those of the Sanskrit epics and the *Arthaśāstra*), Rāma ushers his realm into a prosperous period (*Rāmāyaṇa* 7.89.1–10). Kuśa and Lava, by performing the *Rāmāyaṇa* in this sacrifice's interstices (*Rāmāyaṇa* 7.85.4–5), create a continuum between the righteous conduct that Rāma already has exhibited and the similarly moral activity in which he is in the process of engaging. The twins extend this continuum even further by foretelling the righteous acts of Rāma's future. Given that these events begin right after the horse sacrifice ends (*Rāmāyaṇa* 7.App. I.13.36–51), the rhapsodists actually foresee their father's success as a sovereign and a celestial guide. So, by the end of the epic, he has heard that he will be righteous in the future, as he has been in the past, and that he will reap the attendant rewards. Therefore his fulfillment of *dharma* is a foregone conclusion: even before his death, his story has entered the poetic tradition.

As recited by Kuśa and Lava, Vālmīki's *Rāmāyaṇa* relates and anticipates Rāma's sustained moral attainment. Yet the princes' performance is not without precedent. In fact, the twins elaborate—in epic poetry—on the prophecy of which only their instructor, Vālmīki, was the initial human recipient. The mortal ascetic's ability to make this divine announcement into an epic that, by virtue of being passed down by him to its protagonist's progeny, already is certain to persist also foreruns and represents the enduring extent of Rāma's *dharma*.

Kuśa and Lava's Rhapsodic Recitation: A Prolepsis of Rāma's Unhindered *Dharma*

In the first chapter of the *Rāmāyaṇa*, Nārada reveals to Vālmīki the events of the epic. Toward the end of this disclosure, the celestial ascetic lists Rāma's present and future achievements as Ayodhyā's king:

> *prahṛṣṭamudito lokas tuṣṭaḥ puṣṭaḥ sudhārmikaḥ |*
> *nirāmayo arogaś ca durbhikṣabhayavarjitaḥ ||*
> *na putramaraṇaṃ kecid drakṣyanti puruṣāḥ kvacit |*
> *nāryaś cāvidhavā nityaṃ bhaviṣyanti pativratāḥ ||*
> *na vātajaṃ bhayaṃ kiṃcin nāpsu mañjanti jantavaḥ |*
> *na cāgnijaṃ bhayaṃ kiṃcid yathā kṛtayuge tathā ||*

aśvamedhaśatair iṣṭvā tathā bahusuvarṇakaiḥ |
gavāṃ koṭyayutaṃ dattvā vidvadbhyo vidhipūrvakam ||
rājavaṃśāñ śataguṇān sthāpayiṣyati rāghavaḥ |
cāturvarṇyaṃ ca loke 'smin sve sve dharme niyokṣyati ||
daśavarṣasahasrāṇi daśavarṣaśatāni ca |
rāmo rājyam upāsitvā brahmalokaṃ gamiṣyati ||

His subjects are happy and delighted, satisfied, well nourished, and really righteous.
They have no diseases nor disabilities, and have no famine to fear.
Men never are faced with the deaths of their sons,
and women, who never are widowed, remain true to their husbands.
As in the Winning Age, neither wind nor fire poses any danger,
nor are drowned creatures found floating on floodwaters.
Once he also has sponsored hundreds of horse sacrifices at which gold keeps heaping up,
and has given crores upon crores of cows to the knowledgeable (as custom requires),
Raghu's scion will start hundreds of royal lineages
and will turn each of the four classes toward its respective duties in this world.
After he has reigned for eleven thousand years,[7]
Rāma will go to Brahmā's world.

Rāmāyaṇa 1.1.71–76

Rāma ascends his throne after he has defeated Rāvaṇa and has returned to Ayodhyā (*Rāmāyaṇa* 6.116.54–58). Rāma's royal accomplishments are enumerated again—this time by Kuśa and Lava, at the end of the epic's sixth part:

rājyaṃ daśa sahasrāṇi prāpya varṣāṇi rāghavaḥ |
śatāśvamedhān ājahre sadaśvān bhūridakṣiṇān ||
ājānulambibāhuś ca mahāskandhaḥ pratāpavān |
lakṣmaṇānucaro rāmaḥ pṛthivīm anvapālayat ||
na paryadevan vidhavā na ca vyālakṛtaṃ bhayam |
na vyādhijaṃ bhayaṃ vāpi rāme rājyaṃ praśāsati ||
nirdasyur abhaval loko nānarthaḥ kaṃcid aspṛśat |

[7] Later in the *Rāmāyaṇa*, Rāma's reign is said to last for ten thousand years (see, in this regard, *Rāmāyaṇa* 7.89.5). Yet no manuscript used to construct the first volume of the epic's critical edition offers a variant of verse 1.1.76 to this effect. Hence the eleven-thousand-year figure in my reading here.

na ca sma vṛddhā bālānāṃ pretakāryāṇi kurvate ||
sarvaṃ muditam evāsīt sarvo dharmaparo 'bhavat |
rāmam evānupaśyanto nābhyahiṃsan parasparam ||
āsan varṣasahasrāṇi tathā putrasahasriṇaḥ |
nirāmayā viśokāś ca rāme rājyaṃ praśāsati ||
nityapuṣpā nityaphalās taravaḥ skandhavistṛtāḥ |
kālavarṣī ca parjanyaḥ sukhasparśaś ca mārutaḥ ||
svakarmasu pravartante tuṣṭāḥ svair eva karmabhiḥ |
āsan prajā dharmaparā rāme śāsati nānṛtāḥ ||
sarve lakṣaṇasampannāḥ sarve dharmaparāyaṇāḥ |
daśa varṣasahasrāṇi rāmo rājyam akārayat ||

Over the ten thousand years of his reign, Raghu's scion
sponsored hundreds of horse sacrifices featuring the best horses and abundances of gifts.
With the aid of [his half-brother] Lakṣmaṇa, powerful Rāma—whose arms extended all the way to his knees and whose shoulders were strong—
protected the earth.
No widows wailed, and neither predators
nor diseases posed a danger, while Rāma ruled his realm.
There were no robbers in the world, adversity did not impinge on anyone,
and old men never performed the funeral rites of youths.
There was all manner of happiness, and everyone was focused on doing right.
They, training their sights right on Rāma, did not hurt one another.
They each lived for a thousand years and had a thousand children,
but had neither diseases nor distress, while Rāma ruled his realm.
The trees always were flowering and fruitful as they extended their branches,
the rain god sent down showers at the right times, and the touch of the wind god was pleasant.
The people, who were satisfied with the very occupations in which they respectively engaged,
were focused on doing right and told the truth while Rāma ruled.
They all showed signs of success and were devoted to right-doing.
And, for ten thousand years, Rāma ruled.

Rāmāyaṇa 6.116.82–90

This passage, which is from Vālmīki's version of the *Rāmāyaṇa*, seems to revise Nārada's prophecy by suggesting that the period of Rāma's reign does not equal, but actually excels, the *kṛtayuga* (the Winning Age). The fact that his subjects live to be a thousand years old suggests that these people fare better than people who are alive during the *kṛtayuga*, who live to the age of four hundred (*Mānavadharmaśāstra* 1.83).

Indeed, the Vālmīki epic that Kuśa and Lava recite emphasizes Rāma's *dharma* further by specifying that the ten-millennium period of his reign that is associated with the acme of his people's prosperity actually will begin after his uncompromisingly right action drives his wife to her death. Even after his request that she prove her fidelity to him pushes her, as a measure of her steadfastness, to enter—and thus to be interred by—the earth (*Rāmāyaṇa* 7.88),[8] Rāma's land does not languish. Instead, his twin children sing that, on the heels of his initial *aśvamedha*, Rāma (rather than remarry) installs a golden Sītā to serve as his wife at all of his myriad succeeding sacrifices (*Rāmāyaṇa* 7.App. I.13.52–56; 7.89.1, 4–6); and the Ayodhyā of his highly ritualized reign's decamillennial duration elicits from its poetic immortalizers this by-now familiar description:

> *kāle varṣati parjanyaḥ subhikṣaṃ vimalā diśaḥ |*
> *hṛṣṭapuṣṭajanākīrṇaṃ puraṃ janapadas tathā ||*
> *nākāle mriyate kaścin na vyādhiḥ prāṇināṃ tadā |*
> *nādharmaś cābhavat kaścid rāme rājyaṃ praśāsati ||*

8 While Sītā here clearly leaves life on the surface of the earth forever, disappearing into the earth's depths on a descending throne (*Rāmāyaṇa* 7.88.11–16), the question of whether or not she thus has died is a vexed one in the *Rāmāyaṇa* textual tradition. Her fate is addressed by Brahmā in a brief passage (7.App. I.13.11*) that the southern recension (including four Devanāgarī manuscripts [D6.7.10.11]) interpolates into the important extract that all the manuscripts on which the critical edition's seventh volume is based include just after *Rāmāyaṇa* 7.88: "For pure, virtuous Sītā, who earlier was devoted only to you, / has gone happily to the netherworld of the serpents—by dint of her devotion to you. / She undoubtedly will reunite with you in heaven" (*sītā hi vimalā sādhvī tava pūrvaparāyaṇā | nāgalokaṃ sukhaṃ prāyāt tvadāśrayatapobalāt | svarge te saṃgamo bhūyo bhaviṣyati na saṃśayaḥ |*).

I think that the eight southern manuscripts (T1 G3 M2-5.8.10) that substitute *nākalokaṃ* (the world of heaven) for *nāgalokaṃ* (the netherworld of the serpents) in line 2 of this passage are right for two reasons. First, heaven makes more sense than the snakes' realm does as the object of the austerities that Sītā devotes to Rāma, a human manifestation of celestial dweller Viṣṇu. Second, when Rāma sets out for heaven himself, he already is accompanied by Śrī, the goddess who had been reborn as Sītā (*Rāmāyaṇa* 7.99.6). Śrī's appearance here implies that Sītā long before gave up her human body and returned to her celestial source. This post-death process is treated more explicitly at the end of the *Rāmāyaṇa*, where Rāma and his half-brothers enter Viṣṇu's body, and at the end of the *Mahābhārata*, where Yudhiṣṭhira and his wife and brothers enter the bodies of their originary divinities in heaven (*Rāmāyaṇa* 7.100.10; *Mahābhārata* 18.4.3, 5–7; 18.5.19).

The rain god sent down showers at the right times, food abounded,
and there was purity all around.
Happy, well-nourished people crowded the city and the country.
No one died before his time, no being was diseased,
nor was there any unrighteousness, while Rāma ruled his realm.

Rāmāyaṇa 7.89.9–10

In fact, the *dharma* of his realm can be considered the fruit of Sītā's earthing. In the *Rāmāyaṇa*, she is associated with Śrī, the divinity who personifies prosperity[9]—an association that aids in explaining the aforementioned persistence of Sītā's iconic presence at Rāma's munificent royal rituals. Given that the goddess Śrī is cast in the *Mahābhārata* (*Mahābhārata* 12.8.3–5, 12.94.12) as "a kind of consort of a good king,"[10] the *Rāmāyaṇa* sequence of Sītā's Rāma-incited sepulture and Ayodhyā's ensuing enrichment likely symbolizes the infusion of resources into a land that is ruled righteously. Moreover, Śrī favors Rāma even at the end of his reign, when she takes his side on his way to heaven.

In Kuśa and Lava's telling, Rāma eventually garners an even greater reward for his subjects than prosperity, after his "rigid"[11] righteousness claims yet another casualty. This time, Time/Death itself assumes the form of an ascetic who requires Rāma to execute anyone who overhears their secret conversation (*Rāmāyaṇa* 7.93.1, 13). When circumstances force Lakṣmaṇa to listen to part of this exchange, Rāma relinquishes Lakṣmaṇa's life (*Rāmāyaṇa* 7.95.9, 7.96.13). Rāma then acts on the recommendation that Time/Death has relayed to him from Brahmā, who has bidden Rāma to return to heaven and to rejoin him (*Rāmāyaṇa* 7.94.13). Rāma leads his people away from Ayodhyā into Sāntānikas, celestial spheres that resemble and adjoin Brahmā's world, which is Rāma's final destination (*Rāmāyaṇa* 7.100.14–17).

Kuśa and Lava, in developing Nārada's theme of Rāma's *dharma*, set forth in the *Rāmāyaṇa* an extended encomium that is a far cry from the anguished autobiographical accounts that Nala, as the *sūta* Bāhuka, articulates in the *Mahābhārata* after losing his throne. These elliptical utterances, in which Bāhuka blames himself for failing to do right by his wife and society, encapsulate the *Mahābhārata*'s qualms about actualizing *dharma* in an age of increasing immorality.

9 Sutherland 1989:73; Brockington 1998:445.

10 Fitzgerald 2004b, introduction to bk. 11:4.

11 As philosopher Bimal Krishna Matilal (1989:18) has observed, "The nature of *dharma* idealized by Rāma ... seems to have been very rigid."

Nala as a Bard in Ayodhyā and Vidarbha

Bāhuka's poetic performances are occasioned by Duryodhana's overthrow of Yudhiṣṭhira through a crooked dice match (*Mahābhārata* 2.67.19–21). At an especially desperate moment during his ensuing forest exile, Yudhiṣṭhira asks the sage Bṛhadaśva whether he knows of any monarch more unfortunate than the one in front of him (*Mahābhārata* 3.49.34). In response, Bṛhadaśva tells Yudhiṣṭhira the story of Nala, another king who—when cosmic *dharma* declines—loses his land, by dicing.[12] In this account the demon Kali[13] possesses Nala, who consequently gambles away his kingdom, Niṣadha, to his younger brother Puṣkara (*Mahābhārata* 3.56.1–3, 9–10, 18; 3.58.1; 3.61.45–47; 3.49.39–41), and can regain it only with the aid of another supernatural being. As Nala roams through the forest, he saves the life of the snake king Karkoṭaka, who rewards him by biting him and thereby transforming him into a stunted figure by the name of Bāhuka (*Mahābhārata* 3.63.11–14). No longer afflicted by Kali, who has been quelled by Karkoṭaka's venom, the now-disguised Nala can serve Ayodhyā's king, Ṛtuparṇa, who teaches him how to dice well and thus how to win back Niṣadha (*Mahābhārata* 3.64, 69–70).

To access the Ayodhyan sovereign, Nala—at Karkoṭaka's urging—works as Ṛtuparṇa's *sūta* (*Mahābhārata* 3.63.19, 3.68.6). In this role, Nala acts as both charioteer and bard, and hence resembles the *Mahābhārata*'s most famous *sūta*, Saṃjaya, who narrates the epic's battle books and drives Dhṛtarāṣṭra.

The double deftness of these *sūtas* seems to be an amalgam of two different textual traditions. In four late Vedic texts, the *Taittirīya* and *Maitrāyaṇī Saṃhitās* (which date roughly from 1000 to 800 BCE) and the *Taittirīya* and *Śatapatha Brāhmaṇas* (composed, respectively, during the ninth and eighth centuries BCE), the *sūta* is seen as a charioteer who is a part of his king's inner circle (*Taittirīya Saṃhitā* 1.8.9.1–2; *Maitrāyaṇī Saṃhitā* 4.3.8; *Taittirīya Brāhmaṇa* 1.7.3.1–6; *Śatapatha Brāhmaṇa* 5.3.1.1–12). Like others in this select group (whose members are known as the *ratnins* [jewel-bearers]), the *sūta* hosts a component of the king's *rājasūya* and accepts some of his sacrificial offerings. But, in the *Arthaśāstra*, the *sūta* serves as a bard instead of as a charioteer and is menial rather than ministerial. In the manual's list of king's servants salaried at 1,000 *paṇas* per year,[14] an

12 Bṛhadaśva, however, is not labeled as a poet. Rather he is one of several sage raconteurs from whom Yudhiṣṭhira hears during his forest exile. These storytellers have been studied by Sanskritist Annette Mangels (1994:91–93) and Hiltebeitel (2001).

13 On Kali's inclusion in the class of demons known as *asuras* (antigods), see Hiltebeitel 2001:223–224.

14 The *Arthaśāstra*'s critical editor, R. P. Kangle (1969–1972, critical and explanatory notes to pt. 2:5.3.3n), identifies the unit of currency implicit in *sūtra* (sentence) 5.3.3 (where salary amounts are mentioned for the first time), in his note to his translation of this text. Here Kangle hints that the *paṇas* are silver, rather than copper, coins. On the alloy used, see *Arthaśāstra* 2.12.24.

enumeration that includes the king's charioteer (*sārathi*) (*Arthaśāstra* 5.3.21), the *sūta* is grouped with the *paurāṇika* (legend reciter) and the *māgadha* (panegyrist). These three poetic practitioners preoccupied with the past are opposed to the *kārtāntika* (fortuneteller), *naimittika* (diviner), and *mauhūrtika* (astrologer)—three specialists who foretell the future (*Arthaśāstra* 5.3.13). Earning just 1,000 *paṇas* each year, the *sūta* is far poorer than a member of the ministers' council (who makes 12,000 *paṇas* a year), let alone the king's chief minister (whose annual salary is 48,000 *paṇas*) (*Arthaśāstra* 5.3.7, 3).

By further contrast, the bard—because of his lowly birth—is barred from the ruler's war room. The *sūta*, as the son of a *kṣatriya* (a male member of the kingly class) and a *brāhmaṇī* (a female member of the priestly class), is the product of a *pratiloma* (against-the-grain) marriage resulting from his ruler's inattentiveness to his own religious obligations (*Arthaśāstra* 3.7.28, 30). These obligations are specified primarily in chapters 7, 8, and 9 of the *Mānavadharmaśāstra*.[15] In addition to requirements of regality, the legal treatise spells out the social implications of the *sūta*'s humble origin. Because he is seen as one of society's *apasadas* (outcasts), and is thus excluded from all four classes of ancient Indian society, he earns his keep by doing things that are despised by *dvijas* (the "twice-born" members of the top three classes) (*Mānavadharmaśāstra* 10.17, 46). According to *Mānavadharmaśāstra* 10.47, his occupation entails horse training and chariot driving. Although the law tome does not associate him explicitly with any poetic activity, I think that there are two reasons why poesy can be considered a part of his repertoire. First, he appears in the same four verses of the law book (*Mānavadharmaśāstra* 10.11, 17, 26, 47) as does the *māgadha* (another figure seen as a poet in the *Arthaśāstra*)—as though the *Mānavadharmaśāstra* pairs these practitioners by their poesy, in spite of overtly assigning the *māgadha* only trade

15 The *Arthaśāstra*'s attribution of the *sūta*'s existence to his king's unrighteousness conflicts with a more general principle presented in *Mānavadharmaśāstra* 8.304, viz. the king's shouldering of one-sixth of his subjects' unrighteousness (and its karmic consequences) if he fails to protect them. Thus, in the *Mānavadharmaśāstra* the ruler is punished if he misbehaves, whereas in the *Arthaśāstra* only the subject suffers social stigma for his ruler's misdeeds (particularly this king's condoning of contraindicated interclass commingling). The *Arthaśāstra* example may make more sense if the word *rājan* (which I, like Kangle, have construed as "king") actually is synonymous here with the word *kṣatriya*, and thus denotes a member of the warrior class, perhaps the warrior who—by entering an irregular, hypogamous marriage—failed to fulfill his class duty and fathered the *sūta*. Yet the *sūta*'s father is designated in *sūtra* 3.7.28 by the term *kṣatriya*, so if he were involved in *sūtra* 3.7.30 I would think that he would be labeled in the same way. Hence I keep the king here—a reading rendered all the more intelligible by the fact that the productiveness of other *pratiloma* unions (i.e. those involving husbands who are *śūdras* or *vaiśyas* [the latter being members of the merchant and farmer class that occupies the second-lowest tier of ancient Indian society's hierarchy]) is blamed on this ruler as well (*Arthaśāstra* 3.7.26–27, 30).

(*Mānavadharmaśāstra* 10.47). Second, this legal text is roughly coeval with the Sanskrit epics, where *sūta* and *māgadha* alike are poets.[16]

As an outcast as well as an artist, the *sūta* cannot qualify for a minister's post, of which a key criterion—as the *Arthaśāstra* indicates—is "noble birth" (*abhijana*) (*Arthaśāstra* 1.8.26, 1.9.3). Yet the statecraft manual does ascribe high status to one sort of *sūta*: "The *sūta* and the *māgadha* featured in legends, however, are something else, a special kind separate from priests and rulers" (*paurāṇikas tv anyaḥ sūto māgadhaś ca, brahmakṣatrād viśeṣaḥ*) (*Arthaśāstra* 3.7.29). Following two of the *Arthaśāstra*'s modern commentators, Sastri and Kangle,[17] I render *paurāṇikas* as "featured in legends" rather than as "versed in legends," because the *Arthaśāstra* here is elevating a certain type of *sūta* and *māgadha* above all other *sūtas* and *māgadhas*. The basis for this elevation is not poetic ability, which the work regards all the outcast practitioners belonging to these two occupational groups as possessing, but their exemplary members' appearances as characters in the kinds of narratives that *sūtas* and *māgadhas* normally only perform. But the *Arthaśāstra*'s text itself is problematic here, as Kangle comments in the note to his translation of it: "[T]he s. [i.e. the *sūtra*] is suspicious. *viśeṣaḥ* or *viśeṣataḥ* [the alternative preserved in the *Bhāṣāvyākhyāna*, an anonymous twelfth-century Malayalam commentary] cannot be properly construed in the sentence. The s. appears to be a late marginal comment that has got into the text."[18] Even so, the *sūtra* invites inquiry into what warranted the *sūtra*'s composition. In my opinion, the *Arthaśāstra* here treats a specific *sūta*: Saṃjaya.

Although initially only the charioteer of King Dhṛtarāṣṭra of Hāstinapura, Saṃjaya becomes the *Mahābhārata*'s most prominent epic poet as well. Just as war is about to break out between the factions fighting for the Kuru family's fatherland, Saṃjaya obtains omniscience through divine intervention. The immortal sage Vyāsa—who, later in the text, is identified with the deity Nārāyaṇa—offers to enable blind Dhṛtarāṣṭra to see the events of the war (*Mahābhārata* 13.18.31, 12.334.9, 6.2.6). But, after Dhṛtarāṣṭra decides that he would rather hear about than see the fighting, Vyāsa—the *Mahābhārata*'s mythological author—bestows his boon on Saṃjaya (*Mahābhārata* 6.2.7–8), telling Dhṛtarāṣṭra that "this man, Saṃjaya, ... has been endowed with divine vision / [and] will narrate the war to [him] ..." (*cakṣuṣā saṃjayo ... divyenaiṣa samanvitaḥ / kathayiṣyati te yuddhaṃ ...*) and that, by means of this vision, "Saṃjaya will know everything" (*sarvaṃ vetsyati saṃjayaḥ*) (*Mahābhārata* 6.2.10, 11d). As a result, both Vyāsa—who has the same "eye of knowledge" (*jñānacakṣuṣā*) that he has given to Saṃjaya—and

16 For epic references to these performers, see Brockington 1998:19–20.

17 Kangle 1969–1972, critical and explanatory notes to pt. 2:3.7.29n.

18 Kangle 1969–1972, critical and explanatory notes to pt. 2:3.7.29n.

this charioteer are characterized as "knowing what [was], what [i]s, and what w[i]l[l] be" (*bhūtabhavyabhaviṣyavit*) and as "seeing [things] as though they [a]re right in front of [them]" (*pratyakṣadarśī*) (*Mahābhārata* 12.327.23, 6.5.8, 6.2.2d, 6.14.1). With these capabilities, Saṃjaya can see and detail for Dhṛtarāṣṭra the fighting that already has occurred,[19] current geography and astronomy, and events to come during the Losing Age (*Mahābhārata* 6.14–9.33; 9.54–61, 63–64; 10.1–9; 6.5.3–6.10.74; 6.12–13; 6.11.7, 12–13).

Just as Saṃjaya is no mere bard but a poet par excellence, he reaches unprecedented heights in the *sūta*'s even older role as one of his king's companions. Whereas the *Arthaśāstra*—by marginalizing almost every such bard—distances him from his ruler, the *Mahābhārata* potentially brings each *sūta* even closer to his king than were the late Vedic *ratnins* to theirs, by recommending that every king appoint as one of his ministers a *sūta* "versed in legends" (*paurāṇikaṃ*) (*Mahābhārata* 12.86.8). Acting in this capacity, Saṃjaya speaks to Dhṛtarāṣṭra incredibly freely, unstinting in criticism and comfort. Saṃjaya holds Dhṛtarāṣṭra responsible for the epic's central internecine conflict and the ensuing carnage (*Mahābhārata* 2.72.5; 6.58.7; 6.72.1–2; 6.79.8; 7.90.1, 4; 7.110.24; 7.122.37, 86, 88; 7.127.26; 8.1.29; 8.4.57; 8.22.27; 9.15.37; 9.22.41), because the king turned a deaf ear to his advisors' entreaties to stop Duryodhana from making war with the Pāṇḍavas, his cousins (*Mahābhārata* 6.61.21–22, 6.85.9–13, 6.99.45, 7.110.25, 8.1.30–31, 8.4.56, 8.22.26). Moreover, Dhṛtarāṣṭra seems to accept Saṃjaya's critique, for the ruler assumes responsibility for his family's destruction (*Mahābhārata* 7.10.47, 7.113.1). Yet Saṃjaya, despite his disappointment in Dhṛtarāṣṭra, offers solace to the king as he laments his soldiers' slaughter. For example, Saṃjaya calms and comforts Dhṛtarāṣṭra as the monarch bemoans his slain sons, the *sūta* himself having wept when he saw how sad his employer was when he first learned that his sons were dead (*Mahābhārata* 11.11.20, 9.1.46).

When Dhṛtarāṣṭra's line is cut off, Saṃjaya's poetry becomes superfluous: as soon as the sovereign's eldest and sole surviving son—Duryodhana—dies in battle, the *sūta* loses his divine vision (*Mahābhārata* 10.9.58), because his ability to see into the past, present, and future no longer is required now that the near extinction of his aging patron's dynasty ensures an absence of demand for the poet's epic accounts. The lines of epic transmission and dynastic descent that are parallel through most of the *Mahābhārata* stem from the same source: the epic's mythological author, Vyāsa, who fathers the fathers of the Kauravas and the Pāṇḍavas and passes down the poem to his disciple Vaiśaṃpāyana, who—at

19 The *Mahābhārata*, in its first chapter, revisits, yet reverses, the poet/patron relationship of Saṃjaya and Dhṛtarāṣṭra, seeing that one of the devices that the epic employs here to outline its contents—as Mangels (1994:141) has remarked—is the king's summary of the epic events of which he, lacking vision, could only hear from the divinely sighted charioteer (*Mahābhārata* 1.1.95–159).

Vyāsa's request—tells the epic in its main frame story (*Mahābhārata* 1.100.13, 21; 1.54.21–24). Without the celestial sight conferred by this spry progenitor, Saṃjaya continues and ends his career as a charioteer. Ultimately leaving Dhṛtarāṣṭra's vehicle to accompany him when—some sixteen years after the intrafamilial fighting has ceased and the fallen's final rites have been completed—he retires from courtly life and goes into the forest for good, Saṃjaya there serves, on foot, as the king's guide (*Mahābhārata* 14.3.9–12; 14.14.1–8; 14.71.1–7; 14.85.23; 15.1.4–7; 15.5.9–23; 15.8.9–18; 15.22.4; 15.45.10–11, 17).

Yet Dhṛtarāṣṭra precedes Saṃjaya in decease: when the king, Gāndhārī (his queen), and Kuntī (his sister-in-law) are trapped in a forest fire, he urges his charioteer to save himself (*Mahābhārata* 15.45.22–23). This *sūta*'s survival, which precludes the problem of an outcast being cremated with members of the warrior class, signifies the persistence of poetic memory long after heroes have died. Indeed, Saṃjaya does spend some time surrounded by a group of ascetics on a bank of the Ganges River, and thus prefigures the bard featured in the *Mahābhārata*'s outermost frame story, namely, Ugraśravas (who recites the epic to a group of ascetics in the Naimiṣa Forest, located on a bank of the Gomatī River, which runs east of and roughly parallel to the Ganges before becoming tributary to it) (*Mahābhārata* 15.45.32, 12.343.2).

Although Saṃjaya is not constrained by the social strictures binding *sūta*s in the śāstric texts, his seems to be an exceptional case in the epic. For the most part, the *Mahābhārata* reinforces its measured recapitulation of the śāstric restrictions by shunning the *sūta* in the manner of ancient Indian society. Certainly the epic resonates with its contemporaries as it ordains: "On a woman of the priestly class, a warrior fathers a *sūta*, an outcast by whom sacrifices must not be offered and whose occupation is the performance of praise poetry" (*ayājyaṃ kṣatriyo vrātyaṃ sūtaṃ stomakriyāparam*) (*Mahābhārata* 13.48.10ab).

Moreover, the *Mahābhārata* keeps the *sūta* on society's fringes in three more specific ways. First, the text treats as an aberration any intellectual talent that the *sūta* has. For instance, the epic explains away the ability of the *sūta* Bandin to best *brāhmaṇa*s in knowledge contests as the consequence of his being the son of the water god Varuṇa (*Mahābhārata* 3.134.24). Furthermore, once Bandin himself has been outwitted by the *brāhmaṇa* Aṣṭāvakra, the ocean drowning of the *sūta*'s earlier opponents—including Aṣṭāvakra's father, Kahoḍa—is reversed. Just before these former competitors, who have witnessed a sacrifice for Varuṇa, return, Aṣṭāvakra orders Bandin to be drowned, and thus to be sent back to his divine father (*Mahābhārata* 3.134.23, 25, 30–32).

Second, the epic allows the apparent and actual *sūta*s who dare to assume power—i.e. Karṇa and Kīcaka—to be put in their place. Although Karṇa, a commander of the Kaurava army, actually is a *kṣatriya* and the Pāṇḍavas' elder half-brother, they know him only as a *sūta*—until after his death at the hands of Arjuna (*Mahābhārata* 8.1.11; 11.27.6–13; 8.67.24, 31–32). Before then, the Pāṇḍavas call Karṇa a "son of a *sūta*" (*sūtaputra*). Because the Pāṇḍavas assume that Karṇa shares the lowliness of his adoptive father, the *sūta* Adhiratha (*Mahābhārata* 1.104.14), their appellation becomes a slur, much like today's "son of a bitch." Yet the rubric *sūtaputra*—which, by far, is Karṇa's most common qualifier in the *Mahābhārata*—also is a means by which the epic signals his *kṣatriya* status, for only by virtue of having been adopted by a *sūta* can Karṇa be claimed as such. Indeed, in the *Karṇaparvan*, the *Mahābhārata* book where Karṇa is most prominent, he is said to be a *sūta* only on those two occasions when he wrongs *brāhmaṇas*. To his arms instructor, Rāma Jāmadagnya, Karṇa himself admits that he is a *sūta* who has posed as a *brāhmaṇa* so as to obtain a divine weapon; and, in response, this aggrieved instructor identifies Karṇa as a *sūta* while angrily imprecating upon him the failure of his newly found familiarity with the celestial missile at the hour of his mortality (*Mahābhārata* 8.29.3–4, 5–7). Additionally, a *brāhmaṇa* calls Karṇa a *sūta* in the course of cursing him to suffer fearfully the intractable sinking of his chariot wheel in battle, because Karṇa accidentally has killed the calf of the *brāhmaṇa*'s ceremonial cow amid practicing at archery (*Mahābhārata* 8.373*; 8.29.33; 8.376*; 8.29.31, 37).

In both of these interactions with *brāhmaṇas*, the priests' ire appears to be aggravated by their disgust at Karṇa's ostensible social dissembling. He actually hazards such fateful encounters by choosing, out of love for his adoptive parents, to retain his *sūta* status while alive, and thereby to refuse the opportunity to assume his rightful station as a warrior (*Mahābhārata* 5.139.5–10). Because Karṇa appears to be an outcast, Yudhiṣṭhira's brother Bhīma does not deign to become angry with him when he taunts Draupadī after she has been staked and lost at a dice game (*Mahābhārata* 2.63.1–5). Instead, Bhīma avows: "I am not getting mad at the son of a *sūta*, ... for this really is the morality of slaves that has come into play" (*nāhaṃ kupye sūtaputrasya ... eṣa satyaṃ dāsadharmaḥ praviṣṭaḥ |*) (*Mahābhārata* 2.63.7). Here, Bhīma implies that the elders presiding over the dicing have empty ethical stores, if a mere *sūta* can scorn a warrior's wife. This behavior of Karṇa's outrages Draupadī in particular, who—while venting her anger to Kṛṣṇa—attributes her resentment to her humiliation by one of the "lowly" (*kṣudrair*) members of her society (*Mahābhārata* 3.13.113).

Yet, once Karṇa's *kṣatriya* status is revealed after his death, he is regarded very differently. For example, Yudhiṣṭhira, before knowing of Karṇa's true birth, praises him in terms of only his military prowess (*Mahābhārata* 3.37.18, 8.46.25–26), which hampers the Pāṇḍavas' ability to defeat their Kaurava cousins. But, after learning that Karṇa was a born warrior, Yudhiṣṭhira becomes more generous in his assessment of his elder half-brother, praising not only Karṇa's fighting skills but also his intelligence, compassion, generosity, and observance of vows (*Mahābhārata* 12.1.19).

In addition to Karṇa, the Pāṇḍavas put down an actual *sūta*. The five brothers and their wife are required to go unrecognized for a year, in order to fulfill the terms of the dice game that Yudhiṣṭhira has lost to Duryodhana, and thus to return to Indraprastha. To this end, the Pāṇḍavas and Draupadī complete an incognito stay at the court of King Virāṭa of Matsya. While the Indraprasthan exiles are living at this court, the *sūta* Kīcaka (Virāṭa's brother-in-law and army commander) propositions the disguised Draupadī, even though he knows that she is married (*Mahābhārata* 4.13.3–21, 4.15.1–6). When she tries to flee his second sexual advance, he chases her into Virāṭa's assembly hall, grabs her by the hair, throws her on the floor, and kicks her (*Mahābhārata* 4.15.6–7). Kīcaka's degradation of Draupadī evokes her humiliation at Karṇa's hands. This time, Draupadī, in her outcry to Virāṭa, utters the angry refrain "Me, the highly esteemed wife of those men, a *sūta*'s son has struck with his foot!" (*teṣāṃ māṃ māninīṃ bhāryāṃ sūtaputraḥ padāvadhīt ||*) five times—once for each of her five husbands—so as to stress her ignominy at having to endure again such disrespect from someone of such low social status (*Mahābhārata* 4.15.15cd, 16cd, 17cd, 18cd, 19cd).

Karṇa's and Kīcaka's mistreatments of Draupadī represent the indifference of bards toward people who are no longer praiseworthy, including rulers who fall from power. By the time Karṇa vilifies Draupadī in Dhṛtarāṣṭra's assembly hall, a dice throw has already demoted her from queen (*devī*) to slave (*dāsī*) (*Mahābhārata* 2.58.31, 2.60.37). Similarly, when she is subject to Kīcaka's advances, she is merely a maidservant (*sairandhrī*) to another queen (*Mahābhārata* 4.13.13). However, despite Draupadī's demotion, Kīcaka's harassment of her is not condoned, as her subsequent complaints spur Bhīma to kill him (*Mahābhārata* 4.16.8–10, 4.17.1–4.19.28, 4.21.59–60). Nevertheless, Kīcaka has much in common with Karṇa. Like Karṇa, and in spite of being an accomplished fighter (as Karṇa is), Kīcaka dies at a Pāṇḍava's hands. Like Karṇa, and in spite of being a *sūta* (as Karṇa appears to be), Kīcaka is prized for his fighting skills by a ruler (as Karṇa is, by Duryodhana) and therefore is named an army commander (*Mahābhārata* 4.24.2, 4.13.5, 1.126.12–14, 8.1.11). But—because military might can save neither soldier—the message that the *Mahābhārata* sends apropos of Kīcaka and Karṇa alike is that no *sūta* can succeed for long, since he is sure to be forced out of the spotlight that ill suits someone of his humble origins.

The epic itself obscures the *sūta* in a third way: by excluding him from contexts that could have called for his appearance. Although three characters, besides Saṃjaya and Nala, serve as charioteers and as storytellers—namely, King Śalya of Madra (who narrates to Yudhiṣṭhira before driving Karṇa), and the warriors Kṛṣṇa (who narrates to Arjuna while driving him) and Uttara (who narrates to his father, Virāṭa, after driving Arjuna) (*Mahābhārata* 5.8.29–5.18.24; 7.121.6, 16–29; 4.41.1; 4.64.19–29; 4.66.11–14)—none of these three is termed a *sūta*. Rather, the generic word *sārathi* (a "charioteer," or—more literally—a "man having to do with a man with a chariot")—which, unlike *sūta*, does not denote an outcast position—is applied to Śalya, Kṛṣṇa, and Uttara, as well as to Mātali, Indra's immortal charioteer (*Mahābhārata* 5.8.29, 7.121.6, 4.41.1, 3.164.36). There are two reasons why the three men are not transformed into *sūtas*. First, none of these *kṣatriyas* experiences a reversal of fortune that would necessitate his degradation. Simply in the course of fulfilling their military obligations do these soldiers tell stories and drive chariots. Second, all three of these characters are related—at least by marriage—to Yudhiṣṭhira, the epic's hero: Śalya is the maternal uncle of Yudhiṣṭhira's half-brothers Nakula and Sahadeva (who too were reared by Kuntī); Kṛṣṇa is Yudhiṣṭhira's first cousin; and Uttara is the brother of the soon-to-be daughter-in-law of Yudhiṣṭhira's brother Arjuna.

Even Nala, whose fortune has fallen and who is unrelated to Yudhiṣṭhira, spends only a short time as a stunted *sūta*—certainly no more than about three years, the duration of Nala's separation from his wife, Damayantī, if he was transformed soon after abandoning her (*Mahābhārata* 3.59.24–25; 3.63.1–12; 3.75.11–12, 25). Moreover, Nala's metamorphosis, from its onset, is marked as reversible. Karkoṭaka—the snake king by whose bite Nala has become Bāhuka—tells him immediately afterward how to regain his kingdom and normal form. According to Karkoṭaka, Nala will not be affected by the snake venom, which will disable and torture Kali (the demon dwelling in Nala's body), Nala will be able to reclaim Niṣadha by serving as *sūta* to Ṛtuparṇa (who will teach him how to win at dice), and Nala will return to normal when he wears the celestial set of clothes that the snake gives him (*Mahābhārata* 3.63.18, 16, 14–15, 19–23).

In the *Mahābhārata*, then, a *sūta*'s lot is a mixed bag, a combination both of proximity to royal power and of distance from social superiors. The complexity of the *sūta*'s social situation, as well as the reversibility of Nala's transformation into such a charioteer-bard, raises the question of why the epic takes the trouble to double Nala's role in this regard. In response, I offer three reasons why he must change into a *sūta*.

The first is that, by serving as a *sūta*, Nala is able to obtain the information that he needs to retake his throne. Nala learns from Ṛtuparṇa how to excel at dicing, because the Ayodhyan ruler has the ability to count instantaneously what he sees, and knows how to apply this talent to dicing (*Mahābhārata* 3.70.7–10, 23). Ṛtuparṇa agrees to share his knowledge with Nala, but only if Nala shows him how to handle horses so well—a skill that he knows Nala has, because Nala has driven him at the speed of flight (*Mahābhārata* 3.70.26, 3.69.21–22, 3.70.1).

Thus, as Ṛtuparṇa's *sūta* (and *sārathi* [*Mahābhārata* 3.72.9]), Nala is close enough to the king to barter for what only this ruler can provide. And—as Ṛtuparṇa's confidant—Nala is privy not simply to the secret of the dice, but also to the fact that the Ayodhyan is on his way to the kingdom of Vidarbha so that he can woo Nala's wife, Damayantī, at the sham ceremony that she has set up supposedly to select another husband for herself (*Mahābhārata* 3.69.1–2).

While Nala is disguised as Bāhuka, he seems to become the *sūta* to his own successor. Ṛtuparṇa does not actually usurp his servant's former kingdom, but figuratively replaces Nala as Niṣadha's king. Shortly before the displaced Nala—as Bāhuka—approaches Ṛtuparṇa for employment, the Ayodhyan hires Nala's former *sūta* (and *sārathi*), Vārṣṇeya (*Mahābhārata* 3.57.9, 19, 23). By giving Vārṣṇeya cause to reside in Ayodhyā instead of Niṣadha, Ṛtuparṇa symbolically supersedes this *sūta*'s erstwhile employer, who—rather than being the ruler of Niṣadha—now is only an outcast in the Ayodhyan monarch's employ. This symbolic supersession accounts for the king's having both charioteer-bards at his beck and call. Furthermore, Ṛtuparṇa—the only, and hence most eligible, invited king present at Damayantī's second *svayaṃvara* (bridegroom-choice ceremony)—plays the front-runner role assigned first to Nala when Damayantī decided to choose him as her husband before even seeing any of the other kings who wanted to marry her (*Mahābhārata* 3.71.22, 3.53.11). Even though Bāhuka accompanies Ṛtuparṇa to Vidarbha for the repeat *svayaṃvara*, Nala—in the physical form familiar to his wife—is nowhere in sight.

Moreover, even as Bāhuka, Nala chooses not to stay too close to Ṛtuparṇa in Vidarbha, but to lie low enough there to test Damayantī in the ways that Doniger has discussed.[20] Thus, Bāhuka finds useful his temporary identity as an outcast, for he is subordinate to Ṛtuparṇa's other servants as well as to the ruler himself. After Ṛtuparṇa arrives in Vidarbha, he and his retinue—including Vārṣṇeya—are accommodated in the royal guest house (*Mahābhārata* 3.71.27), a place that positions them to interact readily with their hosts. But Bāhuka, though seated—in Ṛtuparṇa's place—in the pit of Ṛtuparṇa's chariot, stays in the stable (*Mahābhārata* 3.71.29, 19, 28). Because Bāhuka has been hired by Ṛtuparṇa as his "horse supervisor" (*aśvādhyakṣo*) and has been charged with tasks including the chariot driving that the *Mānavadharmaśāstra* specifies for *sūtas*, Bāhuka is to earn for his work "one hundred hundreds" (*śataṃ śatāḥ*)—100 *śatamānas* (32,000 rattis), which is the weight of 1000 *paṇas*, the annual salary stipulated for *aśvādhyakṣa* and *sūta* alike in the *Arthaśāstra*, which contains an entire chapter about the *aśvādhyakṣa*'s duties (*Mahābhārata* 3.64.6; *Arthaśāstra* 5.3.13, 2.30). While the *Arthaśāstra* does not include chariot driving among these duties, the *Mahābhārata*—in Bāhuka's

20 Doniger 1999:152–153.

case—blurs the boundary between *sūta* and *aśvādhyakṣa*, so that Bāhuka can be a charioteer-bard, yet also serve a somewhat different function from that of his fellow *sūta*, Vārṣṇeya. Even though Ṛtuparṇa decrees that Vārṣṇeya will assist Bāhuka, the *Mahābhārata* takes pains to stress that Bāhuka somehow is socially inferior to Vārṣṇeya—who rides on Ṛtuparṇa's chariot driven by Bāhuka (*Mahābhārata* 3.64.7; 3.69.18, 20) and who resides with Ṛtuparṇa, apart from Bāhuka, in the Vidarbha guest house—because the Niṣadhan king and the Niṣadhan *sūta*'s temporary inversion evinces the effectiveness of Nala's exilic disguise.[21]

In this disguise, Nala can remain remote from Vidarbha's royal-family members, who—in order to reach him—either have to send servants to speak with him where he is, or have to summon him to the palace (*Mahābhārata* 3.71.34, 3.74.6). At this distance from his wife and in-laws, a divide that symbolizes the social breach between the subservient *sūta* and his royal superiors, Nala is at less risk of being recognized before he wants to be. Indeed, he maintains his masquerade until he is convinced of Damayantī's fidelity. At this point, Nala doffs his disguise by donning the heavenly garments supplied by the snake king (*Mahābhārata* 3.75.16–17).

Nala's lowly *sūta* status, despite helping the Niṣadhan to return to his queen and kingdom, does not stem solely from strategic advantage. Nala also needs this disguise, precisely because it contrasts with his peerless prowess as a ruler (*Mahābhārata* 3.50.2), yet symbolizes the types of kingly instruction that have enabled him to make the most of his personal talents in such areas as horse managing and chariot driving. When Nala is masked as Bāhuka, someone who lacks stature and power but who is seeking a king's knowledge, Nala evokes his own childhood experience of learning how to rule.

The *Arthaśāstra* elucidates such a boy's royal education: "During the earlier part of the day, [the prince] should be trained in the arts of riding elephants and horses, driving chariots, and wielding weapons. During the later part of the day, he should be instructed in *itihāsas*[22]" (*purvam aharbhāgaṃ*

21 For a different interpretation of the unusually asymmetrical relationship between Nala and Vārṣṇeya—an interpretation that likens them to the *Bhagavadgītā*'s Arjuna and Kṛṣṇa, respectively—see Hiltebeitel 2001:218–219, 225–226, 232–236, 238.

22 At the time of the *Arthaśāstra*, *itihāsa*s included some form of the *Mahābhārata* as well as older stories of the same type. Although *Arthaśāstra* 1.5.14 contains a different definition ("The term *itihāsa* refers to the Purāṇas, Itivṛtta [the two epics, etc., according to Śaṅkarārya's *Jayamaṅgalā*, a fourteenth-century Sanskrit commentary], Ākhyāyikā [a kind of prose narrative], Udāharaṇa [a type of panegyric], Dharmaśāstra, and Arthaśāstra" [*purāṇam itivṛttam ākhyāyikodāharaṇaṃ dharmaśāstram arthaśāstraṃ cetītihāsaḥ* //]), this more inclusive notion appears to have been retrojected into the *Arthaśāstra*, as Kangle (1969–1972, critical and explanatory notes to pt. 2:1.5.14n) speculates in the note to his own translation of this *sūtra*: "It is not unlikely that [*sūtra* 1.5.]14 is a marginal gloss (in explanation of Itihāsa occurring in [*sūtra* 1.5.]13) which later got into the text."

hastyaśvarathapraharaṇavidyāsu vinayaṃ gacchet | paścimam itihāsaśravaṇe |) (*Arthaśāstra* 1.5.12–13). Accordingly, every prince learned from two kinds of teachers. His military trainers were other *kṣatriyas*. But the instructors who introduced him to heroic accounts were *brāhmaṇas*. Even though the *Mahābhārata* portrays the *sūtas* Saṃjaya and Ugraśravas as epic authors (*Mahābhārata* 6.2.10, 1.2.29), and even though *sūtas* may have had a hand in the *Mahābhārata*'s making, the epic's main authors were *brāhmaṇas*,[23] who—by virtue of their familiarity with Vedic and non-Vedic texts and ability to convey their lessons—had become fixtures at the courts of *kṣatriyas*. Thus, every king-in-the-making was steeped in the traditions of both the bookish, stereotypically effete *brāhmaṇa* and the aggressive, stereotypically virile *kṣatriya*. Who better, then, than a *sūta*—son of a *brāhmaṇī* and a *kṣatriya*—to symbolize this dual educational heritage?

This twofold royal training not only is represented by Bāhuka's *sūta* identity, but also accounts for Nala's knowledge of his horse lore before he becomes Bāhuka. Such equine expertise would have helped an ancient Indian ruler—whether he had been on tour or the warpath. Indeed, such a king was already connected so closely to his horse and his chariot, both of which enabled him physically to protect his domain, that he swore by these vehicles—as well as by his weapons—whenever he made an oath (*Mānavadharmaśāstra* 8.113). So, Nala, at the beginning of his story, is said to be "skilled with horses" (*aśvakovidaḥ*), and the telltale sound that his chariot makes while he drives nearly gives him away a couple of times during his concealment (*Mahābhārata* 3.50.1, 3.69.23–32, 3.71.4–8). Yet he still has a lot to learn, and his physical transformation allows him to progress to the point where he can rule his own realm successfully again. When Nala (as Bāhuka) acquires Ṛtuparṇa's dicing expertise, Kali is cast out of Nala's disguised body; and, later (after resuming his normal form), the Niṣadhan can win back his kingdom from Puṣkara (*Mahābhārata* 3.70.27, 3.77.18–19). Then King Nala, Queen Damayantī, and their twins, Princess Indrasenā and Prince Indrasena, live happily ever after (*Mahābhārata* 3.57.20, 21; 3.78.3).

However, in order to arrive at this deceptively happy literary resolution—the third motivation behind Nala's transformation into a *sūta*—Nala himself has to behave like a bard. Disguised as the dwarf Bāhuka, Nala voices in curtailed verse his dislocation and isolation on three occasions, in response to the inquiries of other people. His first story unfolds in Ayodhyā as he mourns Damayantī's absence:

> *sa tatra nivasan rājā vaidarbhīm anucintayan |*
> *sāyaṃ sāyaṃ sadā cemaṃ ślokam ekaṃ jagāda ha ||*

[23] Like Hiltebeitel (2001:19, 21–22, 27–28), I believe—pace Brockington (1998:19–21)—that the *Mahābhārata* was composed not by *sūtas* first and by *brāhmaṇas* only later, but by *brāhmaṇas* from the start.

kva nu sā kṣutpipāsārtā śrāntā śete tapasvinī |
smarantī tasya mandasya kaṃ vā sādyopatiṣṭhati ||
evaṃ bruvantaṃ rājānaṃ niśāyāṃ jīvalo 'bravīt |
kām enāṃ śocase nityaṃ śrotum icchāmi bāhuka ||
tam uvāca nalo rājā mandaprajñasya kasyacit |
āsīd bahumatā nārī tasyā dṛḍhataraṃ ca saḥ ||
sa vai kenacid arthena tayā mando vyayujyata |
viprayuktaś ca mandātmā bhramaty asukhapīḍitaḥ ||
dahyamānaḥ sa śokena divārātram atandritaḥ |
niśākāle smaraṃs tasyāḥ ślokam ekaṃ sma gāyati ||
sa vai bhraman mahīṃ sarvāṃ kvacid āsādya kiṃcana |
vasaty anarhas tadduḥkhaṃ bhūya evānusaṃsmaran ||
sā tu taṃ puruṣaṃ nārī kṛcchre 'py anugatā vane |
tyaktā tenālpapuṇyena duṣkaraṃ yadi jīvati ||
ekā bālānabhijñā ca mārgāṇām atathocitā |
kṣutpipāsāparītā ca duṣkaraṃ yadi jīvati ||
śvāpadācarite nityaṃ vane mahati dāruṇe |
tyaktā tenālpapuṇyena mandaprajñena māriṣa ||
ity evaṃ naiṣadho rājā damayantīm anusmaran |
ajñātavāsam avasad rājñas tasya niveśane ||

While the [Niṣadhan] king was living there, his thoughts kept
returning to the lady from Vidarbha,
and, every evening, he always recited this one verse:
"Where, in the world, is that wretched, weary woman going to bed,
hungry and thirsty,
with that dolt on her mind? And whom is she serving now?"
One night, as the king was saying this, Jīvala [Bāhuka's other assistant] said:
"Who is that woman whom you always are lamenting? I want to hear
about her, Bāhuka."
King Nala replied: "Some half-wit
had a woman of whom he thought highly, and she had an even
higher opinion of him.
Something separated that dunce from her,
and, in his deprivation, that dullard is wandering around, gripped by
grief,
being burned by sorrow day and night, without respite.
At night, he remembers her and sings his single verse.
That man wandered the world over, found something somewhere,

and is living there unworthily, remembering his anguish over her
more and more.
That woman went after that man—even into the frightful forest—
but, having been abandoned by that man of little merit, she hardly
can be alive.
Alone, young, not knowing her way around, unaccustomed to and
undeserving of all of this,
and seized by hunger and thirst—she hardly can be alive.
That man of little merit, that half-wit, abandoned her
in the huge, horrid forest, where predators always are on the prowl,
my friend."
This is how the king of Niṣadha remembered Damayantī
as he hid in that [other] king's home.

Mahābhārata 3.64.9–19

There are two ways in which to interpret this tale that Nala tells while he is in Ayodhyā. This city is the central site of the power struggle portrayed in the *Rāmāyaṇa*, and the story of its hero, Rāma, is retold in a shorter form in the *Mahābhārata*, when Yudhiṣṭhira asks whether any man has been more unfortunate than he (*Mahābhārata* 3.258–275, 3.257.10). This eliciting question echoes the one that Yudhiṣṭhira has used to induce the narration of Nala's story, but allows for the sharing of a tale of even greater pathos—for Yudhiṣṭhira here asks to hear not of any king in straits direr than his own, but of any man so afflicted. This very man, Rāma, suffers two great losses. First, although he is older than his three half-brothers, and thus is his father's heir, Rāma is displaced from Ayodhyā's throne before he has even a chance to ascend it, because his stepmother Kaikeyī schemes successfully to have her son, Bharata, supersede him (*Mahābhārata* 3.261.24–27). She has Rāma exiled to the forest, where he sustains his second loss, when Rāvaṇa kidnaps Sītā (*Mahābhārata* 3.262.40).

Like Rāma, Nala has lost both his kingdom (to his younger brother) and his wife (as the result of a demon's act). These broad thematic correspondences suggest that the *Rāmāyaṇa*'s authors and the authors of Nala's story (the *Nalopākhyāna*) were aware of one another's works, a possibility also evidenced when Sanskritist V. S. Sukthankar evinced syntactic connections between these texts.[24] Although the *Rāmāyaṇa*'s Rāvaṇa is a *rākṣasa* rather than an *asura* (such as the *Nalopākhyāna*'s Kali), and thus belongs to a baser class of demons (namely, shape-shifters most famous for being monstrous man-eaters), this *rākṣasa* king,

24 Sukthankar 1939:295–300.

by force of his own austerities, becomes for a time the most powerful being in the universe and is dreaded by gods as well as humans.[25]

Nala, for his own part, is possessed by the *asura* Kali. As a result, the Niṣadhan is driven both to gamble away his throne to Puṣkara and to discard Damayantī (*Mahābhārata* 3.59.24–25), who has followed her husband to the forest. But, once Nala is bitten by Karkoṭaka and becomes Bāhuka, Kali can no longer delude him. Consequently, Nala can tell his story, with a clear head, if not conscience. This tale is twofold: in addition to bemoaning his wife, he bewails his kingdom. Although he is a bard as he relates the narrative, while doing so, he is called a "king" (*rājan*) four times (*Mahābhārata* 3.64.9a, 11a, 12a, 19a). When thus recast in his earlier role, his very person underscores the supplementary significance of his story of lament. He takes himself to task explicitly for failing his wife and implicitly for failing his people, narratively comparing his kingdom to his wife, because he is supposed to be the foremost protector of both. But he has been deprived of both, by the intervening Kali, who engineered the dicing downfall that left the king realmless, and condemned him to the forest exile during which he forsook his queen (*Mahābhārata* 3.55.12–13). Under Kali's influence, Nala failed to fulfill his dual royal obligations. He left his faultless queen, Damayantī, to fend for herself in a disorienting, predator-ridden forest (*Mahābhārata* 3.60.5, 12–14, 18, 17; 3.64.12, 16, 17, 18). When forsaken similarly, yet even earlier, by her righteous prime provider, Nala's kingdom, Niṣadha, herself seems to experience hunger and thirst—as represented tropaically by the only half-grown grain on the desiccated land about to be irrigated to which Damayantī is compared just before she receives Nala's seed, after his three-year absence (*Mahābhārata* 3.58.6; 3.61.46–48, 88; 3.54.38; 3.75.26–27; 3.64.10, 17). These states of deprivation, considered together with Niṣadha's vulnerability to usurpers such as Puṣkara, compose a negative for the positive print of a kingdom kept safe—Yudhiṣṭhira's realm of Indraprastha early in the epic (*Mahābhārata* 3.58.1; 3.64.18; 2.30.1–3).

Nala's twin losses inform his subsequent bardic efforts as well. In response to two nearly identical inquiries, he—as the *sūta* Bāhuka—relates two almost identical stories. On the first occasion, a *brāhmaṇa* named Parṇāda—whom Damayantī's father, King Bhīma (not to be confused with Yudhiṣṭhira's brother), has dispatched from Vidarbha to find Nala—repeats to Bāhuka, in Ayodhyā, this behest of Damayantī's (*Mahābhārata* 3.67.6–8, 3.68.1–6):

> *kva nu tvaṃ kitava chittvā vastrārdhaṃ prasthito mama |*
> *utsṛjya vipine suptām anuraktāṃ priyāṃ priya ||*
> *sā vai yathā samādiṣṭā tatrāste tvatpratīkṣiṇī |*
> *dahyamānā bhṛśaṃ bālā vastrārdhenābhisaṃvṛtā ||*

[25] For further discussion of the distinction between *asuras* and *rākṣasas*, see O'Flaherty 1976:84.

tasyā rudantyāḥ satataṃ tena śokena pārthiva |
prasādaṃ kuru vai vīra prativākyaṃ dadasva ca ||

Where in the world are you, gambler, now that you have cut off half of my garment and have gone away,
now that you have left your beloved wife asleep in the forest, my love?
That young woman covered with half of a garment—she sits waiting for you there as she was ordered to,
being tormented too much.
To that woman constantly crying with that sorrow, king,
be gracious and give your reply, hero.

Mahābhārata 3.67.9–11

On the second occasion, in Vidarbha, Damayantī sends a woman named Keśinī to make a similar request of Bāhuka, with almost the same words that Damayantī asked Parṇāda to utter (*Mahābhārata* 3.72.1–4):

kva nu tvaṃ kitava chittvā vastrārdhaṃ prasthito mama |
utsṛjya vipine suptām anuraktāṃ priyāṃ priya ||
sā vai yathā samādiṣṭā tatrāste tvatpratīkṣiṇī |
dahyamānā divārātraṃ vastrārdhenābhisaṃvṛtā ||
tasyā rudantyāḥ satataṃ tena duḥkhena pārthiva |
prasādaṃ kuru vai vīra prativākyaṃ prayaccha ca ||

Where in the world are you, gambler, now that you have cut off half of my garment and have gone away,
now that you have left your beloved wife asleep in the forest, my love?
Covered with half of a garment, she sits waiting for you there as she was ordered to,
being tormented day and night.
To that woman constantly crying with that sorrow, king,
be gracious and give your reply, hero.

Mahābhārata 3.72.18–20

Yet Keśinī changes Parṇāda's message in three places, replacing the phrase *bhṛśaṃ bālā* (too much, the young woman) in *Mahābhārata* 3.67.10 with *divārātraṃ* (day and night) in *Mahābhārata* 3.72.19, and substituting for *śokena* (with sorrow) and *dadasva* (give) in *Mahābhārata* 3.67.11 their respective synonyms, *duḥkhena* and *prayaccha*, in *Mahābhārata* 3.72.20.

Keśinī's first modification indicates the different imports of these approximately duplicate missives. The first message has been sent by Vidarbha's king, Bhīma, who forged an alliance with Niṣadha's throne when its prior occupant, Nala, married Bhīma's daughter, Damayantī. Accordingly, this communiqué sponsored by Bhīma, the senior sovereign, implicitly compares Niṣadha to a "young woman" (*bālā*) because Nala ruled Niṣadha for no more than twelve years before Kali's overcoming of him caused him to desert his kingdom (*Mahābhārata* 3.67.10, 3.56.2).[26] (Just as Nala left Niṣadha not long [i.e. a number of days rather than of months] prior to leaving Damayantī [*Mahābhārata* 3.58.6–7, 10; 3.244*; 3.58.11; 3.59.6–8, 24–25], so too had he ascended Niṣadha's throne presumably only recently when he wedded Damayantī, given that the *Mānavadharmaśāstra* urges rulers to marry as soon as they have moved into their palaces [*Mānavadharmaśāstra* 7.77].) The second message, by contrast, is more personal than political, and therefore is delivered by a lady in waiting, rather than by an agent of state. Fittingly, this dispatch accentuates the extent of Damayantī's round-the-clock grieving for Nala, rather than Damayantī's age (*Mahābhārata* 3.72.19, 3.67.10). Although she was a "young woman" (*bālā*) when he abandoned her three years earlier—a separation that came some twelve years after this couple's wedding, which had occurred soon after Damayantī had matured into a *bālā*—she probably is too old to be termed a *bālā* when Keśini delivers her message (*Mahābhārata* 3.60.1, 13; 3.50.11, 13; 3.51.7; 3.72.17–22). (Indeed, assuming that Damayantī, in accordance with *Mānavadharmaśāstra* 9.90, got married three years after her menarche, eighteen years now have elapsed since she started to menstruate.) Hence, Keśini calls Damayantī a *nārī* (woman), and not a *bālā*, just before relaying her request to Bāhuka (*Mahābhārata* 3.72.17).

The two tales that Parṇāda's and Keśini's requests elicit from Bāhuka begin as one account that then bifurcates. It opens with the following lines:

26 Likewise, the ongoing connection to his kingdom that a king has is represented as a marital bond in the *Rāmāyaṇa*, where "royal proprietorship of the land is so often ... expressed through sexual metaphors (the king is 'husband' of the earth, 2.1.28, for instance, and his death leaves the earth a widow, 2.45.12, [2.]97.11)" (Pollock 1986:15n15). The reasons why "[t]he king was considered to be the symbolic husband of the Earth, who was his wife," have been enumerated by historian John W. Spellman (1964:209), who also explains why the king's relinquishing of his kingdom would have been regarded as a problem in ancient India: "The king protected the Earth as a husband does his wife. The king was held responsible for the fertility of the earth. Depending upon his dharma, rain or drought would afflict the Earth. By his paying for sacrifices, the king ensured the well-being of the Earth. The king was required as 'Lord of the Earth' to fulfill these functions to his symbolic bride. It is significant to note that however many other rights ancient Indians had over their wives, they could not legally or morally give them away, at least in the days of developed Hinduism. It may be that the objections in the legends in which the king attempts to give away the Earth stem from this reasoning."

vaiṣamyam api saṃprāptā gopāyanti kulastriyaḥ |
ātmānam ātmanā satyo jitasvargā na saṃśayaḥ | / ||
rahitā bhartṛbhiś caiva na krudhyanti kadācana || / |

Noble families' women protect themselves by themselves, even if they have fallen into distress.
These virtuous women win heaven, no doubt about it.
They never get angry, even though they have been forsaken by their lords.

Mahābhārata 3.68.8, 3.72.25–26ab

From this point, however, Bāhuka tailors his poems to their contexts. To Parṇāda, Bhīma's envoy, Bāhuka declares:

viṣamasthena mūḍhena paribhraṣṭasukhena ca |
yat sā tena parityaktā tatra na kroddhum arhati ||
prāṇayātrāṃ pariprepsoḥ śakunair hṛtavāsasaḥ |
ādhibhir dahyamānasya śyāmā na kroddhum arhati ||
satkṛtāsatkṛtā vāpi patiṃ dṛṣṭvā tathāgatam |
bhraṣṭarājyaṃ śriyā hīnaṃ śyāmā na kroddhum arhati ||

If she has been abandoned by a dejected fool fallen on hard times,
then she ought not to get angry.
A beautiful woman ought not to get angry with a sustenance seeker whose garment has been snatched by birds
and who is being tormented by his thoughts.
Well treated or not, a beautiful woman ought not to get angry after seeing her lord in such a state—
deprived of his kingdom and wanting for wealth.

Mahābhārata 3.68.9–11

But Bāhuka implores Keśinī, Damayantī's confidante:

prāṇāṃś cāritrakavacā dhārayantīha satstriyaḥ ||
prāṇayātrāṃ pariprepsoḥ śakunair hṛtavāsasaḥ |
ādhibhir dahyamānasya śyāmā na kroddhum arhati ||
satkṛtāsatkṛtā vāpi patiṃ dṛṣṭvā tathāgatam |
bhraṣṭarājyaṃ śriyā hīnaṃ kṣudhitaṃ vyasanāplutam ||

Encased in their commendable conduct, these good women now keep themselves alive.

> A beautiful woman ought not to get angry with a sustenance seeker
> whose garment has been snatched by birds
> and who is being tormented by his thoughts,
> once she, well treated or not, has seen her lord in such a state—
> deprived of his kingdom, wanting for wealth, hungry, and overwhelmed by vice.
>
> *Mahābhārata* 3.72.26cd–28

Though three lines are common to Bāhuka's doublet of compositions (*Mahābhārata* 3.68.10ab, 3.72.27ab; 3.68.10cd, 3.72.27cd; 3.68.11ab, 3.72.28ab), his works differ in tone. The first work attempts to appease Nala's angry ex-subjects in Niṣadha by thrice sounding the refrain "she ought not to get angry" (*na kroddhum arhati*), and thereby evoking the Niṣadhans' impatience with their king's vice of reckless dicing (*Mahābhārata* 3.68.9d, 10d, 11d; 3.56.13), a sensitive topic that Bāhuka does not mention explicitly herein. By contrast, his second work seeks to soothe Damayantī (by complimenting her conduct) and to appeal to her sympathy (by citing her husband's hunger and his lack of control over his gambling vice) (*Mahābhārata* 3.72.26cd, 28d).

Thus, these episodes of request and response—which have been regarded recently as riddles about the alien self,[27] about shared memories,[28] and about self-recovery[29]—occasion Bāhuka's truncated accounts of Nala's misfortune. These poetic narratives express the frustration that Nala feels as he fails to fulfill the demands of *dharma*, and thereby implicitly interrogate the attainment of this ideal. Accordingly, his stories—poems as short as the dwarf who composes them—vary, in form, from the epic of the *Rāmāyaṇa*'s poetic rulers. Unlike the affirmative account offered by Kuśa and Lava, Nala's poems appear effaced of four features of the Sanskrit epics. Hence, the Niṣadhan's compositions

1. are not attributed to a divine source;
2. each consist of a mere fragment instead of an expansive, embedding whole;
3. are anonymous, naming neither hero nor heroine; and
4. take on a plaintive, rather than celebratory, tone.

[27] Shulman 2001:142.
[28] Doniger 1999:152–153.
[29] Hiltebeitel 2001:230–236.

Nala's Bardic Compositions: Prolepses of Yudhiṣṭhira's Hindered *Dharma*

Nala's works are so morose because they express the despair that Yudhiṣṭhira feels even after he hears about Nala. Like Nala, Yudhiṣṭhira learns Ṛtuparṇa's reckoning technique (*Mahābhārata* 3.78.17), but it does not cast Kali out of the Pāṇḍava's life. Even though Yudhiṣṭhira uses his dicing skill to support his brothers and wife during the year that he spends with them in disguise, and even though he reminds his opponents that the terms of the agreement he and Duryodhana made at their last dicing match have been satisfied, Duryodhana reneges and refuses to relinquish Indraprastha (*Mahābhārata* 4.12.4–5; 5.5.18; 5.20.1, 9–11; 5.125.22–26). While Yudhiṣṭhira eventually takes over the earth—in the aftermath of the war that ushers in the Kali Age—the king does so at a human cost that is all too easy for a man of his counting expertise to quantify (*Mahābhārata* 11.26.9–10).

Ultimately, when the losses of the Kali Age become too hard for Yudhiṣṭhira to bear, he leaves his land and ascends into heaven (*Mahābhārata* 17.1.2–3). He does not heed the scoldings of his sorrowful subjects, who—without swaying him—have to return to their homes, and thus are akin to their counterparts in Nala's stronghold of Niṣadha, who are ignored by their Kali-possessed king as he lets go of his land (*Mahābhārata* 17.1.15–17, 23–24; 3.56.15–18). When Vārṣṇeya tells Damayantī that Nala should be informed that all his subjects are waiting to see him on business and are not putting up with his dice vice (*Mahābhārata* 3.56.12–13), she sugarcoats the *sūta*'s message for his king. She veils Vārṣṇeya's plain words with deference, telling her husband that his subjects are demonstrating their devotion to him, rather than that they are not tolerating his behavior (*Mahābhārata* 3.56.15, 13). After he fails to respond, the queen—preparing for Nala's dethronement—sends Vārṣṇeya away from Niṣadha, so that the *sūta* can seek employment elsewhere; and he sorrowfully finds it at Ṛtuparṇa's court, in Ayodhyā (*Mahābhārata* 3.57.17–18, 23).

Although Vārṣṇeya does not recite poetry during the *Nalopākhyāna*, the story seems to symbolize his involvement in such activity, by portraying him as the protector of Nala's legacy. As Damayantī dismisses Vārṣṇeya, she asks him to harness Nala's favorite horses to his chariot, to drive her twin children to her family's home in Vidarbha, and to leave the princess and prince, the horses, and the chariot there (*Mahābhārata* 3.57.17–18). Thus, Damayantī—acting on the knowledge that Nala "could be ruined" (*vinaśed*) by losing his kingdom (*Mahābhārata* 3.57.16)—assures the continuity of his line. But, because Nala's dynasty has been displaced from its ancestral realm, there is no need to retain a *sūta* so as to reinforce this lineage's reputation there. Consequently, Vārṣṇeya decides to leave the Niṣadhan royal family's employ, even though Damayantī has given him the option to remain in Vidarbha with her relatives (*Mahābhārata* 3.57.18).

Some of the words that Nala himself puts together to appease his people and queen after abandoning them would be appropriate for Yudhiṣṭhira to use, if he were to try to soothe his own subjects. Recognizing that, in his day, righteousness has been dimmed and diminished by the passage of time (*Mahābhārata* 17.1.16), Yudhiṣṭhira—by virtue of his paternity—cannot help but be affected by this turn of events. In this degenerate age, this man who is the deity Dharma's son, and who also is known as King Dharma, is himself someone who, like Nala, has "fallen on hard times" (*viṣamasthena*) and has been "overwhelmed by vice" (*vyasanāplutam*) (*Mahābhārata* 1.114.1–3, 3.68.9, 3.72.28).

Yudhiṣṭhira is burdened as well by a distress parallel to that which Nala expresses in his first poem as he laments the loss of his beloved. Like Nala, Yudhiṣṭhira, who circumambulated the earth on his way heavenward, has "'wandered the world over'" (*bhraman mahīṃ sarvāṃ*) (*Mahābhārata* 17.1.44, 3.64.15a). In fact, heaven is what Yudhiṣṭhira has "'found'" (*āsādya*), so the other "king" (*rājñas*) to whose "home" (*niveśane*) the Pāṇḍava has resorted is Indra, the gods' ruler (*Mahābhārata* 18.1.4; 3.64.15, 19; 17.3.30–33). Yudhiṣṭhira, in the absence here of his wife and brothers, feels guilt and "'anguish'" (*duḥkhaṃ*) akin to Nala's (*Mahābhārata* 18.2.1–12, 3.64.15). Just as Nala was followed by Damayantī but left her "'abandoned'" (*tyaktā*), Yudhiṣṭhira was trailed by his loved ones on his trek to heaven, but, without looking back, left his near and dear by the wayside when they were felled by their moral flaws (*Mahābhārata* 3.64.16, 17.2). Now that Yudhiṣṭhira's loved ones no longer are "'alive'" (*jīvati*), they are "'seized by hunger and thirst'" (*kṣutpipāsāparītā*) while dwelling "'in the huge, horrid forest'" (*vane mahati dāruṇe*) of hell, and thus experience an extreme version of the dire fate that Nala fears has befallen his wife in his absence (*Mahābhārata* 3.64.16, 17, 18b). In the inferno, some trees have swords for leaves, while other trees have sharp thorns (*Mahābhārata* 18.2.23, 25). Nothing can grow there for Yudhiṣṭhira's relatives to eat, because the ground is covered with corpses, and the mud is made of flesh and blood (*Mahābhārata* 18.2.18, 17). Moreover, hell's river has hot water that is hard to drink (*Mahābhārata* 18.2.23). The "'predators always ... on the prowl'" (*śvāpadācarite nityaṃ*) in hell actually are scavengers: iron-beaked crows and vultures, and needle-mouthed ghosts (*Mahābhārata* 3.64.18a, 18.2.20). When Yudhiṣṭhira himself has to go there to find his family members, he feels that they—like the blameless Damayantī of Nala's memory—are "'undeserving of all of this'" (*atathocitā*) (*Mahābhārata* 18.2.44, 3.64.17), even though King Dharma was the one who enumerated their failings on his way to heaven.

Despite these dire scenes, the epic does have a happy ending. Soon after Yudhiṣṭhira arrives in the inferno, it disappears and a cool, gentle, fragrant wind wafts in with the gods—hell breezes over (*Mahābhārata* 18.3.1–8). It turns out to have been an illusion designed to deceive him because he had allowed Droṇa, his former military instructor, to be deceived before his death (*Mahābhārata* 18.3.14). Now, this and the other improper acts that led Yudhiṣṭhira and those dear to him to hell have been redressed (*Mahābhārata* 18.3.16). After he finally gives up his human body, he and his relatives all reenter the deities from whom they have issued (*Mahābhārata* 18.3.39, 18.4.2–7, 18.5.9–22). Moreover, the account of his life, the *Mahābhārata*, comes to be classified as an *itihāsa*, as had the tale told about Nala (*Mahābhārata* 18.5.31, 3.78.10).

But all is not well that ends well. The vague glimpses of heaven that the *Mahābhārata* offers to its audience do not displace the epic's vivid depictions of hell, no matter how unreal these infernal scenes may be. By the same token, the poem's main military victory does not mitigate the unfathomable bloodshed that such success has exacted. In my mind, the best bearer of the *Mahābhārata*'s moral standard is the Yudhiṣṭhira who stands in what seems to him to be hell, questioning the fate that has befallen his family, "with his senses confounded by concern" (*cintāvyākulitendriyaḥ*) (*Mahābhārata* 18.2.49d), and who goes on to censure the gods and *dharma* itself (*Mahābhārata* 18.2.15–16, 42–44, 46–50). King Dharma's doubts, which are encapsulated in Nala's interrogative narratives,[30] reveal the *Mahābhārata* to be an epic that has misgivings about the righteousness upon which the *Rāmāyaṇa* resolves.

The distinct tacks that these works take toward *dharma* lead their heroes' efforts to achieve this ideal to appear to be different, despite the fact that these men must fulfill several of the same obligations. As rulers (*kṣatriyas*), they must protect their peoples and realms; as householders (*gṛhasthas*), they must marry and have children; and, as husbands (*patis*), they must guard their wives. In addition to meeting these requirements, Rāma and Yudhiṣṭhira are expected to uphold comprehensive, or *sāmāsika*, *dharma*, which comprises five duties incumbent on all four of ancient Indian society's classes: nonviolence (*ahiṃsā*); truth (*satya*); curbing anger (*akrodha*); purification (*śauca*); and suppression of the senses (*indriyanigraha*) (*Mānavadharmaśāstra* 7.35, 110; 3.4, 45; 9.3; 10.63).

As kings, Rāma and Yudhiṣṭhira cannot help but confront *dharma*'s conflicting demands, for the monarchs cannot defend their kingdoms while refraining from violence and its attendant impurities. And, in certain situations,

[30] In spite of the disparate sets of circumstances in which Nala and Yudhiṣṭhira find themselves, the similar sorrows that the sovereigns experience vitiate John D. Smith's (1992:13) assertion that the *Nalopākhyāna* "is essentially light reading, a happy-ever-after tale standing in sharp contrast to the grimness of the epic narrative which surrounds it."

the kings can commit to warfare only at the cost of their honesty. But their compromises are portrayed very differently.

In the *Rāmāyaṇa*, Rāma fights unfairly when he ambushes and kills Vālin, the monkey king, even though Vālin already is dueling with his brother, Sugrīva. Yet Rāma comes off very well, both before and after his deceitful deed, which he has done primarily to obtain Sugrīva's support in the search for abducted Sītā. Prior to Rāma's sneak attack, Vālin's wife Tāra warns him of Rāma's inexorability and integrity, likening Rāma not only to "the fire at the end of an age" (*yugāntāgnir*), but also to "a tree that is a refuge for moral people" (*nivāsavṛkṣaḥ sādhūnām*) (*Rāmāyaṇa* 4.15.15, 16a). In addition, once the attack has occurred, only Vālin himself voices outrage in response. Moreover, as soon as Rāma justifies his subterfuge as a means of punishing Vālin for taking Sugrīva's wife Rumā, Vālin asks Rāma to forgive his outburst (*Rāmāyaṇa* 4.17.12–45; 4.18.2–39, 42). In fact, Vālin goes so far as to say that Rāma "knows right from wrong" (*dharmajña*) (*Rāmāyaṇa* 4.18.44)—a remarkable reversal! Rāma is not even reproached by soon-to-be-widowed Tāra, who simply goes on to recognize that Rāma, in slaying her husband, has performed "a great act" (*mahat karma*) (*Rāmāyaṇa* 4.20.18).

Like Rāma, Yudhiṣṭhira deploys deception to kill a powerful enemy. Yet, even though Yudhiṣṭhira does so much less directly in the *Mahābhārata* than does Rāma in the *Rāmāyaṇa*, the Indraprasthan incurs much more of a reprisal than does the Ayodhyan. At the urging of Kṛṣṇa, Yudhiṣṭhira deliberately misleads Droṇa into thinking that Droṇa's son, Aśvatthāman, has died. Yudhiṣṭhira does so, because Droṇa, even at the age of eighty-five, has enough prowess to imperil Yudhiṣṭhira's army. Yudhiṣṭhira's half-truth, however, ultimately disheartens Droṇa so much that he sets aside his arms and gives up his life, just before being beheaded by Yudhiṣṭhira's brother-in-law Dhṛṣṭadyumna (*Mahābhārata* 7.164.62–69, 105–106; 7.165.98–107, 32–47).

Yet, unlike Rāma, Yudhiṣṭhira is not praised for his improbity. Yudhiṣṭhira himself is ambivalent about duping Droṇa, having decided to do so "with much difficulty" (*kṛcchreṇa*) (*Mahābhārata* 7.164.70). Moreover, as soon as Yudhiṣṭhira equivocates, his chariot drops to the earth, from an elevation of four fingerbreadths (*Mahābhārata* 7.164.107).

Yudhiṣṭhira's deceit, unlike Rāma's deceit, has disastrous effects. Aśvatthāman, upon learning how Droṇa died, denounces Yudhiṣṭhira's "ignoble and extremely wicked act" (*anāryaṃ sunṛśaṃsaṃ ca*) and pledges not only to destroy Dhṛṣṭadyumna and his family, the Pāñcālas, but also to shed Yudhiṣṭhira's blood (*Mahābhārata* 7.166.19e [in one Kaśmīrī (K_4), six Devanāgarī ($D_{2.3.5-8}$), and both Telugu manuscripts], 27–29). Rather than achieve these aims on the battlefield by day, Aśvatthāman bides his time and ambushes his marks in their camp at night (*Mahābhārata* 10.8.9–139). Although he cannot target the absent Yudhiṣṭhira, Aśvatthāman does slay many of this monarch's blood relatives when they should be asleep (*Mahābhārata* 10.11.1–2). And, as Aśvatthāman exits from the camp, he is the one who is compared to "the fire at the end of an age" (*yugānte ... pāvakaḥ*) (*Mahābhārata* 10.8.137). Yudhiṣṭhira, though unscathed by Aśvatthāman's fury, eventually has to face hell's flames and other horrors for a few moments, as punishment for his prevarication (*Mahābhārata* 18.2.15–18.3.19).

To say that Yudhiṣṭhira has a much harder time than Rāma is to make a literal, as well as a colloquial, statement. Yudhiṣṭhira has more difficulty fulfilling his dharmic obligations, because he lives at a time when the cosmos' *dharma* has devolved from its condition in Rāma's day. According to the *Mahābhārata*, Rāma and Yudhiṣṭhira live at different points of a cycle comprising four ages whose names, which refer to progressively unluckier throws of dice, reflect *dharma*'s decline over the ages' course. While Nārāyaṇa, a form of the deity Viṣṇu, declares that he is born as Rāma between the Trey Age (*tretāyuga*) and the Deuce Age (*dvāparayuga*), the Mahābhārata war—and therefore the lives of its participants, including Yudhiṣṭhira—is said to take place during the transition from the Deuce Age to the Losing Age (*kaliyuga*) (*Mahābhārata* 12.326.78, 1.2.9).

Yet the *Rāmāyaṇa* does not locate Rāma's lifetime so precisely. If the Losing Age overshadows the *Mahābhārata*, no period casts such a pall over the *Rāmāyaṇa*. While Yudhiṣṭhira's expanded kingdom is checked quite quickly by the creep of the *kaliyuga*, Rāma's realm flourishes for about ten millennia. Furthermore, the *Rāmāyaṇa* creates the impression that this thriving is inevitable—by presenting its prediction by Nārada, and its repeated realization in the epic that Kuśa and Lava recite.

The fate of Rāma's followers—that is, their unimpeded prosperity on earth and in heaven alike—reinforces the *Rāmāyaṇa*'s main idea, namely, that Rāma is impeccable despite doing apparently dubious deeds. The *Mahābhārata*, however, is not so single-minded in assessing its hero. Yudhiṣṭhira's achievements, while bearing some resemblance to Rāma's, are both questioned and championed in one breath.

Like Rāma, Yudhiṣṭhira defeats his primary enemy, but—even so—Yudhiṣṭhira does not deem this victory worthy of praise. After the death of Duryodhana—who was the reincarnation of a part of Kali (*Mahābhārata* 10.9.55, 1.61.80), the demon embodying the *kaliyuga* (who had possessed Nala)—there is no serious opponent to Yudhiṣṭhira's universal sovereignty. Yet, a major means by which kings expanded their land holdings, the horse sacrifice (*aśvamedha*), has a different character in Yudhiṣṭhira's story than in Rāma's. In the *Rāmāyaṇa*, the horse sacrifice carries positive connotations: Rāma is renowned for having horse sacrifices performed regularly, and these rites index his riches and authority.

In the *Mahābhārata*, however, the horse sacrifice takes on a negative tenor: the ritual's overriding emphasis is not power augmentation but purification. By the time Yudhiṣṭhira sponsors such a sacrifice, at the dawn of the *kaliyuga*, this king already has conquered the earth (*Mahābhārata* 14.90.17–14.91.41, 14.1.7). But he needs the expiation provided by this rite—which is known, both in the *Mahābhārata* and in the *Mānavadharmaśāstra*, for expunging the effects of all evildoing (*Mahābhārata* 14.70.16; *Mānavadharmaśāstra* 11.261)—so that he can make up for bringing about the deaths of so many of his mentors and relatives. Yet, despite discharging the *aśvamedha*, Yudhiṣṭhira rules the world for a total of only thirty-six years (*Mahābhārata* 16.1.1).

Unlike Rāma, whose realm thrives throughout his lengthy reign, Yudhiṣṭhira actually seems worse off for winning the war against his Kaurava cousins. Before this conflict, Yudhiṣṭhira has success in his sovereignty, Indraprastha:

> *rakṣaṇād dharmarājasya satyasya paripālanāt |*
> *śatrūṇāṃ kṣapaṇāc caiva svakarmaniratāḥ prajāḥ ||*
> *balīnāṃ samyag ādānād dharmataś cānuśāsanāt |*
> *nikāmavarṣī parjanyaḥ sphīto janapado 'bhavat ||*
> *sarvārambhāḥ supravṛttā gorakṣaṃ karṣaṇaṃ vaṇik |*
> *viśeṣāt sarvam evaitat saṃjajñe rājakarmaṇaḥ ||*
>
> As a result of King Dharma's protection, his defense of the truth,
> and his destruction of his enemies, his subjects were devoted to their own occupations.
> As a consequence of accurate tax collection and lawful rule,
> it rained as much as everyone wanted and the country throve.
> All undertakings went smoothly—especially cow-tending, agriculture, and commerce.
> All this arose from the king's activity, in particular.
>
> *Mahābhārata* 2.30.1–3

At the end of the war, Yudhiṣṭhira rules the whole world, but it is in a sorry state of near depopulation. By Yudhiṣṭhira's own reckoning, 1,660,020,000 men have died in the fighting, while only 24,165 men have survived (*Mahābhārata* 11.26.9–10). If a man is judged by the kingdom he keeps, then—by the end of the epic—Yudhiṣṭhira's reputation is diminished rather than enhanced.

Two other *Mahābhārata* events also highlight the limits of Yudhiṣṭhira's righteousness. First, even though his father is the deified form of *dharma* itself, Yudhiṣṭhira is taught how to reign righteously—by his great-uncle Bhīṣma in the war's wake and by his uncle Dhṛtarāṣṭra still afterward. Second, Yudhiṣṭhira ascends into heaven alone (*Mahābhārata* 12.56–159, 15.9.7–15.12.23, 17.3.24). While Rāma leads all of his righteous subjects right to their celestial reward, Yudhiṣṭhira cannot keep the few humans who accompany him—i.e. his wife and his four brothers—from falling first to hell, as recompense for their moral failings (*Mahābhārata* 17.2.3–25, 18.2.40–41, 18.3.15).

Thus, Rāma and Yudhiṣṭhira experience *dharma* differently. Rāma readily spreads *dharma* through his realm because he is a human manifestation of Viṣṇu. This deity has descended to earth expressly to restore *dharma* to the universe, by ridding it of Rāvaṇa, the demon whose austerities have made him invulnerable to all other supernatural beings (*Rāmāyaṇa* 6.105.25–26, 1.1.13, 7.10.17). Rāma's righteousness, then, continues from his kingdom to the cosmos. In contrast to Rāma, Yudhiṣṭhira is merely a man descended from divine Dharma and has to struggle simply to lay down the law in his domain as unrighteousness ravages the universe. In Yudhiṣṭhira's trying time, the destabilizing decline of *dharma* in the cosmos hinders his efforts to keep his kingdom intact, both physically and morally.

The Sanskrit epics offer in Rāma and Yudhiṣṭhira alternative exemplars of uprightness. In addition to embodying the different perspectives that these poems have on *dharma*, the monarchs, by heeding royal poets either directly or indirectly, demonstrate the distinct ways in which the *Rāmāyaṇa* and the *Mahābhārata* instill this ideal in their audiences.

The different, yet complementary, approaches that the *Rāmāyaṇa* and the *Mahābhārata* take to *dharma* will come into even clearer focus as I consider the ways in which these works resemble and contrast with their Greek counterparts. As I complete this comparative study, by applying modern theories of self and social psychology, I will refine the epic category into which all four poems have been placed, and thus I will illuminate their enduring appeal as religious resources.

Conclusion

Affirmative and Interrogative Epics

SO FAR, I HAVE DISCUSSED the Greek and Sanskrit epics largely separately. In Chapters 1 and 2, I examined the ways in which the Greek poems and their Sanskrit counterparts classified themselves, and I considered the effects that the reclassification of each pair of poems, as epics, had on their subsequent interpretation. In Chapters 3 and 4, I showed that each epic's approach to its core religious ideal of either Archaic Greek *kléos* or ancient Indian *dharma* was encapsulated by one or more poems that were embedded in the epic and were related by one or more poetic rulers.

But now I will intertwine these two lines of inquiry into an analogical meta-comparison. As I compare my comparisons of the *Iliad* and the *Odyssey* and of the *Rāmāyaṇa* and the *Mahābhārata*, I aim both to explain the variations that occurred between the epics' embedded royal poems within and across the Greek and Indian traditions and to theorize the intertraditional similarities between these royal poems and between the epics that embed them. In doing so, I will reconsider briefly the epic pairs' respective cultural contexts and then will reflect at greater length on the human psychology that informs all four works. I will emphasize their intercultural commonalities over their intracultural ones, in order to develop a conception of epic that illuminates the analogous types of religious instruction that, from their inception to the present, the Greek and Sanskrit poems—human compositions that present themselves as having been authored divinely—have offered to their audiences. My new notion of epic will help account for the enduring appeal of the *Iliad*, *Odyssey*, *Rāmāyaṇa*, and *Mahābhārata*.

The Intercultural Boundaries between Greek and Indian Royal Poems

Even as the epic category subsumes the Greek and Indian rulers' verse works (as well as the poems that embed them), they remain separate culturally in three regards: the embedded poems are performed by Greek heroes, but are presented to Indian ones; Greek poetic rulers evince brevity in ascendancy and expansiveness in debasement, but Indian royal poets are prolix in success and concise in shame; and the Greek kings use implicit and explicit prolepses in their triumphal and woeful poems, respectively, but the converse holds true in the case of the Indian monarchs.

Royal poems are related *by* the heroes of the *Iliad* and *Odyssey*, but *to* the heroes of the *Rāmāyaṇa* and *Mahābhārata*, because of the different religious ideals on which the Greek and Indian works center. The epic pairs promote *kléos* and *dharma* as solutions to two different existential problems. The *Iliad* and *Odyssey*, by demonstrating how heroic glory may be achieved, assuage their audiences' anxiety about the uncertainty of the afterlife—the fate that befalls human beings when they die, but that is unknowable before that moment. Yet, the *Rāmāyaṇa* and *Mahābhārata*, by illustrating the attainment of righteousness under adverse circumstances, ease their audiences' misgivings about behaving morally in the face of increasing immorality.

The different natures of the epic pairs' religious ideals affect their expressions by poetic rulers. *Kléos* is what constitutes Archaic Greek epic poetry itself. To be remembered and celebrated in such song, and thereby to acquire poetic, if not physical, immortality, a hero has to do exceptional deeds of his own. Although he is likely, before attaining fame, to have heard of others who already have done so, he need match their exploits only in magnitude and not in specifics. Indeed, the Greek poetic tradition allows its leading men to be exceptional in quite individual ways, depending on the particular talents that divinities bestowed on these protagonists when they were born. Consequently, the tradition tends to portray its heroes striving for their own glory rather than assuring that it accords with that of their predecessors. So, in the *Iliad* and *Odyssey*, the royal poetry that appears is articulated by the epics' heroes themselves, in anticipation of the distinctive impressions that they will leave on their shared poetic tradition.

By contrast, the royal poems that the *Rāmāyaṇa*'s and *Mahābhārata*'s heroes hear convey to them the ways in which ancient Indian society expects kings to realize their *dharma*. Because this type of righteousness requires rulers to behave morally both toward and in behalf of a great many others, the kings have much to glean from the experiences of their antecedents. Hence, the epics represent their heroes listening to stories that look not only ahead to these heroes' own fulfillments of righteousness, but also back to the moral achievements of preceding kings of the sort featured in other pieces of *dharma* literature.

In addition to treating different religious ideals, the Greek and Sanskrit epics' royal poets wax wretched and triumphant to different extents. Achilles evokes his future victory only briefly in a rhapsody that the *Iliad* hardly characterizes, but Kuśa and Lava elaborate on the rise of Rāma in a poem that occupies almost the entire *Rāmāyaṇa*. Conversely, Odysseus delineates at length in the *Odyssey* the travails of his travels, whereas Nala depicts elliptically the woes that Yudhiṣṭhira will face at the close of the *Mahābhārata*.

The opposite relationships between affect and length in the Greek and Indian royal poems may stem from their embedding epics' distinct genre designations. The traditional Archaic Greek categorization of the *Iliad* and *Odyssey* as the glories of two men implies both that the mere mention of Achilles' singing of *kléa andrôn* is enough to suggest that his own fame is nigh, and that the extended portrayal of Odysseus eloquently lamenting his lost fame-gaining opportunities provides him with the poetic disguise that he needs so as to sow his renown. Yet, given the traditional ancient Indian classifications of the *Rāmāyaṇa* as a *kāvya* and of the *Mahābhārata* as an *itihāsa*, Kuśa and Lava take pains to ensure that their rendering of the *Rāmāyaṇa* contains as many of the emotional initial lows and final highs as does that of its composer, Vālmīki, while Nala—who composes vivid poems only about his present failures and not about the past successes of other heroes—cannot craft accounts anywhere near as monumental as the epic in which they fleetingly appear.

The works of Achilles and Odysseus and those of Kuśa and Lava and Nala differ interculturally in still a third respect, namely, in the poetic rulers' use of prolepses. In the case of the Greek kings, Achilles' rhapsodic recitation on his lyre from Thebe is an implicit prolepsis of the warrior's preordained triumph-to-come in Troy, while Odysseus' bardic compositions incorporating or evoking the prophecies of Teiresias and Theoclymenus are explicit prolepses of the homecomer's perilous return to and restoration of Ithaca. In the instance of the Indian rulers, however, Kuśa and Lava's rhapsody, including their prophecy of Rāma's success on earth and in heaven, is an explicit prolepsis of this hero's accomplishments, whereas Nala's abbreviated compositions capturing the losses that will afflict Yudhiṣṭhira on his way to heaven and hell and back are implicit prolepses of this hero's difficulties.

The Greek and Indian royal poets may use implicit and explicit prolepses differently because prophets occupy disparate positions in these rulers' societies. In Archaic Greek literature, the prophet is a stock character whose predictions tend to challenge an oppressive status quo in favor of a new order engineered by a hero. Where the hero's victory, like that of the Iliadic Achilles, is a foregone conclusion, overt prophecy of his success is unnecessary to include in his poetry. But, where the hero's success is more precarious, as is that of the Odyssean Odysseus, its prediction in prophecies incorporated into his poetry reassures his audiences that he will indeed prevail.

In ancient Indian literature, however, prophecy is presented by sages who tend to work from—rather than invert—the status quo, and thus who envision a continuation of present events as they are conditioned by the development or devolution of *dharma*. Therefore, prophecy is present manifestly in the sage Vālmīki's poem, which Kuśa and Lava recite in their certainty of righteous Rāma's terrestrial and celestial victories. Yet, in the poems that the non-sage Nala seems to compose about his own sorrows over the reversal of his fortune, he expresses only vaguely unpleasant presentiments of judicious Yudhiṣṭhira's terminal loneliness.

Although the Greek and Indian royal poems diverge in at least these three ways, the works resemble each other as well. In fact, their striking intercultural similarities allow their embedding epics to be recategorized to reflect the variety encompassed by the epic genre.

The Intercultural Bridges between Affirmative Epics and between Interrogative Epics

The genre (or genres) in which poems like the *Iliad*, the *Odyssey*, the *Rāmāyaṇa*, and the *Mahābhārata* are placed is (or are) important because classification itself is an act of interpretation. Genre, then—to borrow the definition offered by literary critic Alastair Fowler—"is a communication system, for the use of writers in writing, and readers and critics in reading and interpreting."[1] On this view, Fowler recommends that critics distinguish between the genre of a literary work at the time of its composition and this work's genre in the critics' time, and implies that these critics should employ the generic notion that best suits their own analytical purposes: "We identify the genre to interpret the exemplar."[2]

In Chapters 1 and 2, I examined the self-designations of the *Iliad*, the *Odyssey*, the *Rāmāyaṇa*, and the *Mahābhārata*, and I adopted "epic" as an umbrella term for these poems, even as I recognized the reciprocal influences that these works and this rubric had upon each other. Yet my readings of the Greek and Sanskrit epics and of the royal poems that they include (see Chapters 3 and 4) lead me to conclude that the intercultural correspondences between these works warrant refinement of the epic category overspreading them. As a result, I regard the *Iliad* and the *Rāmāyaṇa* as affirmative epics that depict the ready realization of *kléos* and *dharma*, respectively, and the *Odyssey* and the *Mahābhārata* as interrogative epics that portray the difficulties in achieving these religious ideals.

1 A. Fowler 1982:256.

2 A. Fowler 1982:51, 38.

In the past, scholars distinguished the *Iliad* from the *Odyssey*—or the *Mahābhārata* from the *Rāmāyaṇa*—by classifying the former poem of the pair as an epic, and the latter as a romance. Among the earliest interpreters to make this observation of the Sanskrit works, as well as of the Greek ones, were the philologists and spouses Hector Munro Chadwick and Nora Kershaw Chadwick. At first glance, the Chadwicks seem to see romance only in certain segments of the *Odyssey* and the *Rāmāyaṇa*, offering the following characterization of the Indian work: "The rest of the story, contained in Books III–VI, can hardly be regarded otherwise than as romance. In principle it resembles the romantic part of the Odyssey, though it is largely concerned with fighting."[3] But the Chadwicks then infer, from these romantic segments, that the poems comprising them are best categorized as romances, if these critics' assessment of the *Rāmāyaṇa* narrative gives any indication: "The theme is a heroic story which is just passing—or perhaps rather has already passed—into romance."[4]

Classing the *Odyssey* and *Rāmāyaṇa* as romances creates two interpretational problems. The first is that this classification can be based on the assumption that the romantic poems have deviated and devolved from earlier, epic forms of poetry. Such an assumption, which appears to have informed the Chadwicks' aforementioned categorization, was held by Bowra as well, as evidences his discussion of the

> transformation of heroic poetry [in general] ... when it passes into what is conveniently called romance. Romance is a vague term, but at least it suggests anything which is not real or even believed to be real by the poets themselves, who advance it as a charming fancy and ask it to be accepted as such. In other words, while strictly heroic poems claim to deal with a past which once existed, though its date may not be known, romance claims to be nothing but delightful and is quite content to be accepted at its own valuation. ...
>
> When heroic poetry passes into romance, it is touched by a lyrical spirit which dwells on tender emotions and charming scenes and softens the stark outlines of adventure with intervals of ease and pleasure. ... The whole of this transformation into romance may be regarded as the intrusion into narrative of a spirit which likes to linger

3 Chadwick and Chadwick 1932–1940, vol. 2:472. In regard to *Odyssey* 9–12, Hainsworth (1991:67) similarly argues: "[T]hese books have little to do with heroic epic. Blown past Cape Malea, Odysseus sailed into a world of fantasy: the Lotus-Eaters, who lived in blissful oblivion; the Cyclops; the island of Aeolus, god of the winds, and his family of incestuous children; the cannibal Laestrygonians; the witch Circe; the land of the dead; then the Sirens, Charybdis, the Cattle of the Sun, and, for a touch of realism, the final shipwreck."

4 Chadwick and Chadwick 1932–1940, vol. 3:878–879.

> on the elegances of life and belongs to a society which tries to make its customs less brutal and its manners less forthright.[5]

Bowra's rather harsh evaluation of romance—relative to epic—leaves the impression that romance is less honest than fanciful, less momentous than frivolous, and less traditional than recreational. On the first page of his preface, he actually acknowledges his intellectual debt to the Chadwicks, whose "analytical examination of [heroic poetry] shows what it is in a number of countries and establishes some of its main characteristics." But Bowra, despite doing work "continuing the subject [of heroic poetry] where [the Chadwicks] stop," differs from them in "exclud[ing from his study] ... the old Indian epics, in which a truly heroic foundation is overlaid with much literary and theological matter."[6] Even so, his adoption of the Chadwicks' devolutionary view of heroic poetry implies that he may have approved also of the Chadwicks' elevation, on this view, of the *Mahābhārata* above the *Rāmāyaṇa*.

Unfortunately, more current considerations of the *Odyssey* and *Rāmāyaṇa* as romances are nearly as derogatory as are the Chadwicks' and Bowra's assessments. For instance, Hainsworth observes of the *Odyssey*: "Like most folktales, this story is rich in mystery and suspense, and by exploiting these qualities it has grown into a romance. Many [of its] incidents are irredeemably unheroic."[7] Likewise, Sanskritist J. A. B. van Buitenen remarks that the "romance" that is the *Rāmāyaṇa* "is a consciously literary work, and [that] Vālmīki is the First Poet, the *ādikavi*, even though by later standards his composition might be found to be lacking in poetic power, refinement, and precision."[8]

Fortunately, however, even newer views of the *Odyssey* and *Rāmāyaṇa* provide insight into their epic aspects. In the eyes of literary critic David Quint, for instance, the *Odyssey*'s heroic teleology is as patent as this poem's persistent dilatoriness: "While the narrative romances that we are most familiar with, including the *Odyssey* itself, contain seemingly aimless episodes of wandering and digression—*adventures*—they also characteristically are organized by a quest that, however much it may be deferred by adventure, will finally achieve its goal."[9] Similarly suffering from being read solely as a romance is, from Pollock's perspective, the *Rāmāyaṇa*: "[T]hinking of Vālmīki's poem in this way, however justified it may appear to be by certain surface resemblances, ... makes some readers less receptive to the product of a very different literary culture, closing

5 Bowra 1952:543, 548–549.

6 Bowra 1952:v.

7 Hainsworth 1991:35.

8 Buitenen 1974:70, 54.

9 Quint 1993:9.

off instead of providing access to a whole range of topics in which Vālmīki seems to be deeply interested. Adventure, love, and service, staples of romance that have little broad social significance, are certainly part of his poem, but so are those patterns of 'public behavior' that are the central concern of a very different species of literature,"[10] namely, epic, of which heroic exemplarity is a defining characteristic.

Categorizing the *Odyssey* and *Rāmāyaṇa* as romances hampers the poems' interpretation in another way, for this categorization separates these works utterly from their intracultural partners, the *Iliad* and *Mahābhārata.* The disparities between each intracultural pair of poems warrant not the exclusion of the *Odyssey* and *Rāmāyaṇa* from the epic genre, but the genre's reformulation. This work of reworking a literary category is actually the signal contribution that genre criticism can make, and such a reworking is much more significant than simply placing literary works in pre-existing classes. The difference between classification and reclassification has been captured by literary critic Tzvetan Todorov: "By locating the universal features of literature within an individual work, we merely illustrate, to infinity, premises we will have already posited. A study in poetics, on the contrary, must come to conclusions which complete or modify the initial premises." Although these "premises" may require revision, they provide starting points for literary inquiries: "The moment we produce a discourse on literature, we rely, willy-nilly, on a general conception of the literary text; poetics is the site where this conception is elaborated."[11]

The twofold process that Todorov treats exemplifies the two types of category work that occur in an informed comparison. To set up such a comparison, a comparativist sets forth a category that requires her to take for granted that her comparanda have something in common that distinguishes them from the data that she excludes from her analysis. In other words, at this early point in her study, she gives unqualified credence to her category, because she—in order to proceed with her comparative inquiry—"need[s] to assume some stable entity, some reasonable conception, some logic of connections and distinctions." And, by employing such a category, she registers her "recognition of [the] similarity between the instances to which [she] applie[s it]."[12]

As soon as she has compared her comparanda in the manner suggested by her chosen category, she can assess it critically. After approaching her comparanda from the top down (taking no issue initially with her category), she can work from the bottom up (reconstructing her category so that it reflects

10 Pollock 1991:11.

11 Todorov 1977:236, 237.

12 Miner 1990:237; Lloyd 1966:172.

the results of her comparison).[13] The reflexivity[14] of this dual method has been described by Doniger, who remarks that a scholar starts with her "motivating idea [i.e. her category]; but that idea then leads her back to her texts, where she may find unexpected details that will in turn modify the idea of what she is looking for."[15]

I have taken this twofold approach to my metacomparison of the Greek and Sanskrit epics. In Chapters 3 and 4, I first compared the *Iliad* and the *Odyssey* and then the *Rāmāyaṇa* and the *Mahābhārata*, while assuming that all four royal-poem-embedding works were comparable by virtue of having been labeled epics. Now that I have described the ways in which the royal poems within the Greek epics and within the Indian epics differ intra- and interculturally, I will refine the epic category, on the basis of the intercultural similarities between the Greek and Indian poems belonging to this category. By identifying both affirmative epics and interrogative epics across the Homeric and Hindu traditions, I will offer a new explanation of the complementarity that characterizes each tradition's poem pair.

Affirmative and interrogative epics as accounts of intracultural complementarity

A chorus of classicists has characterized the *Iliad* and the *Odyssey* as being "complementary,"[16] with each poem centering on something that is significant, yet that is absent from the other poem. More precisely, each poem is distinguished by its hero's behavior: "Achilles' story is that of a man increasingly isolated from his own society, for even at the end of the wrath he still sits and dines apart from the rest of the host. The *Odyssey* tells of a man and wife reunited, a family and kingdom restored to peace and order."[17]

Yet the distinction between Odysseus' story and the *Iliad* evinces the interaction between, rather than the separation of, these two epic traditions. One way to regard this encounter is as an adversarial one:

13 In advocating that comparativists combine these top-down and bottom-up procedures in their studies, I differ from Freidenreich (2004:90), who presents these approaches as separate methods.

14 According to historian of religions William E. Paden (2000:190), reflexivity comprises "self-awareness of the role of the comparativist as enculturated, classifying, and purposive subject (which does not mean that patterns are fictions without substance); a cleaner [*sic*] sense of the process and practice of selectivity; an exploratory and multileveled rather than hegemonic sense of the pursuit of knowledge; the need for ongoing category critique; and the production of new or revisionary thematic collocations."

15 Doniger 1998:60.

16 Stanford 1963:26; Finley 1978:54; Nagy 1999:21; Mueller 1984:180–181; Beye 1993:33; Rutherford 2001:118; Felson and Slatkin 2004:103.

17 Rutherford 2001:144.

> It has been argued that the *Odyssey* perceives its relation to the *Iliad*, or *Iliads*, or Achilles tradition—whichever is more correct—as competitive. ...
>
> ... For inasmuch as the priorities and organization of epic songs reflect larger cultural preoccupations and values, poetry and poet simultaneously serve as a central means not only of preserving and reproducing these values, but of reformulating and rethinking them as well. It is from this perspective that we must view the *Odyssey*'s confrontation of Achilles and the tradition promoting him.[18]

But poets' efforts to differentiate the ideals and outlooks of the Homeric epics may have been cooperative, not competitive. Certainly, in the case of the epics' central ideal, *kléos*, epic audiences have benefited from having available "two exemplary extremes in conceiving [thei]r relationship with life and death and accordingly two different ways of writing and circumventing [thei]r anxiety about death."[19] The authors of the *Iliad* and of the *Odyssey*, then, may have strived to provide alternative models of *kléos* between which their audiences could choose: one model affirming such glory so fervently that its destructive achievement is expressed as a kind of easy creativity, but the other model interrogating such fame so intently that its productive attainment is threatened continually by ruin. Perhaps, in order to cover both poles of human experience (and thus everything in between them), these epic poets actually agreed to make their respective protagonists, Achilles and Odysseus, disagree.[20]

Like the *Iliad* and the *Odyssey*, the *Rāmāyaṇa* and the *Mahābhārata* have been described as being "complementary," but have been recognized primarily for their disparities rather than for their interrelationship. Thus, the *Rāmāyaṇa* is ascribed to a "'poetics of perfection,'" which populates the poem with exemplary players who, through their unwavering actions and interactions, reach the aesthetic acme of the "lyrical universe" that they inhabit. By contrast, the *Mahābhārata* is attributed to a "'poetics of dilemma,'" which recreates the actual world with imperfect actors who struggle to find their rightful places in a show stalled by indecision and stolen by ruin.[21]

Onto this perfection/dilemma dichotomy, Shulman maps a breach between the idealistic *Rāmāyaṇa* and the realistic *Mahābhārata*. As a *kāvya* (or sung poem), the *Rāmāyaṇa* "achieves a perfection of form in the telling" and correspondingly portrays "cultural ideals in the near stillness of their presumed perfection." Yet,

18 A. T. Edwards 1985:92, 93.

19 Pucci 1987:173.

20 Earlier versions of the following three paragraphs have appeared in Pathak 2006:141–142.

21 Shulman 2001:22, 24, 31, 36, 37, 26.

the mythic history (or *itihāsa*) of the *Mahābhārata* operates as a "vehicle of ... 'realistic' insight" that has a "structure of ongoing dilemmas ... that is amazingly supple and absorptive, to the point where the world itself is seen as held within this frame."[22] Similarly, historian of religions Gregory D. Alles differentiates from the *Rāmāyaṇa* "the other great Indian epic, the *Mahābhārata*, renowned for 'telling it like it is,' not as it ought to be."[23]

But both the *Rāmāyaṇa* and the *Mahābhārata* may be understood as being idealistic rather than realistic. Both works are the spheres of "idealized"[24] heroes who demonstrate the ideal of *dharma*. Yet, even though *dharma* is the focus of both the *Rāmāyaṇa* and the *Mahābhārata*, poems that expanded at about the same time, they treat this ideal differently. Whereas the *Rāmāyaṇa* "affirm[s] ... the centrality of *dharma* to all right endeavor," the *Mahābhārata* "explores the problems of acting in accordance with *dharma*" and thus displays "the questioning of *dharma* by those who are obliged to uphold it."[25] In depicting *dharma*, then, the *Rāmāyaṇa* is an affirmative epic,[26] while the *Mahābhārata* is an interrogative one. As the epics together present their audiences with alternative approaches to *dharma*, the poems' "complementarity" is not simply "contrastive,"[27] but additionally collaborative.

The *Rāmāyaṇa* and the *Mahābhārata*—in their different, though complementary, approaches to inculcating *dharma*—resemble the *Iliad* and the *Odyssey*, works that together affirm and interrogate *kléos* in a continuing effort to impress this ideal's importance upon the minds of their attenders. The influences that the four epics have had on individuals open to the poems' cultural instructions can be comprehended by recourse to modern theories of self and social psychology.

The self and social psychologies of affirmative and interrogative epics

One way to assess the influences of the epics as religious instructors is to study the texts and practices of the communities in which the epics arose and persisted. But such sociological analysis constitutes only one of several stories that interpreters of the epics can tell about their educational role. My own account will center on the ways in which individuals who turned to the religious teachings of the epics interacted implicitly with these texts. Because I am

22 Shulman 2001:22, 39, 26, 28.
23 Alles 1994:71.
24 Sutherland 1989:77, 72.
25 Brockington 2004:656, 1998:242; Bailey 1983:124.
26 In its later retellings, however, the *Rāmāyaṇa* comes to question Rāma's *dharma*, as the contributors to three edited collections have shown (Richman 1991, 2001; Bose 2004).
27 Shulman 2001:39.

interested in a set of psychological processes that are not attested outside of the epics themselves, my exegetical tale is, by necessity, hypothetical. Even so, this tale can explain in part the patent popularity and persistence of the ancient poems at this tale's heart, much as contemporary fiction can shed light on the actual human condition.

At the core of my interpretative story, I contend that the epics' heroes show, by their own example, how the epics' audiences took to heart and put into practice these texts' religious instructions. To actualize the religious ideals of the epics, the heroes first heed traditional tales whose protagonists demonstrate the epics' ideals, tales that the heroes themselves tell (as in the case of the Greek epics) or that other displaced rulers tell (as in the case of the Sanskrit epics). Then the heroes follow in the footsteps of the tales' protagonists.

These acts of internalization and imitation[28] can be understood better by referring to modern self- and social-psychological theories—specifically, the life-story metaphor of identity psychologist Dan P. McAdams and the mastery and coping models of behavior therapist Donald H. Meichenbaum.[29]

The first of these frameworks focuses on the formation of the self. McAdams equates identity with a "life story," a "personal myth" that an individual invents over the course of his late adolescence and adulthood so as to make sense of the events of his past, present, and future. Although this narrative is inside him, it incorporates elements from his social environment. Among these elements are the stories that he hears being passed down as part of his cultural tradition.[30]

To any extent that internalization occurs—that is, to any extent that a person integrates outside stories into the life story of his identity—this process promises that he will enact the external tales that he has made his own. More specifically, the life story that he has created from the substance of the tales that he has heard serves as a script for his future action. He thus "live[s] according to [the] narrative assumptions" of this personal myth.[31] Because the myth is made from the accounts that his society has made available to him, "to live the myth [in the aforementioned manner] is [both] to connect to the grand narratives of [his] social world" and, by realizing them in some way, to contribute to the actual world from which these narratives emerge.[32]

28 In positing these processes of internalization and imitation, I elaborate on the events that religion scholar Arti Dhand (2002:360) describes as she identifies the Sanskrit epics as aids to moral development: "Ultimately, one aspires not simply to emulation of epic characters, but to an active re-creation or grafting of the epic narrative onto one's own individual life."

29 Earlier versions of the following three paragraphs have appeared in Pathak 2006:145, 146.

30 McAdams 1985:v, 17–19, 25, 29, 120, 252; 1993:5, 11–12, 232, 94–95, 265, 268–269, 13.

31 McAdams 1985:v.

32 McAdams 1993:265, 37.

If the internalization of traditional tales has real-world influence—that is, if certain of their components are assembled into a life story whose creator can actualize them—then the content of this life story is crucial. The most important impulses behind a personal myth's plot are the need for "power," an urge to obtain authority over one's environment, and the need for "intimacy," a desire for close interpersonal interaction. These two motives manifest and absent themselves most overtly in what are, for better or for worse, the myth's most emotionally intense episodes, its "peak and nadir experiences."[33]

To imagine how these narrative highs and lows affect their authors' communities in the manner in which McAdams implies, I turn to Meichenbaum's models of mastery and coping. In advancing these models, Meichenbaum, like the social psychologist Albert Bandura before him, assumes that observers imitate more easily models who seem to be like them.[34] So those who hear a person relating his peak or nadir experiences, and who find that these experiences resemble their own, are more likely to imitate his subsequent actions.

Those audience members who identify most closely with and mirror a person who achieves his aims easily, a "mastery model," probably are those people whose own lives have been eased by frequent peaks of pleasure. But those audience members who empathize most strongly with and emulate a person who attains his goals only by struggling, a "coping model," probably are those people whose lives often have descended to nadirs of misery. Yet the memberships of these two groups may be identical, given that all human beings are likely to live through both highs and lows. The same people, depending on their moods, may respond to mastery models at certain times and to coping models at other times.

In any case, combining McAdams' metaphor and Meichenbaum's models illuminates both the influences that a mythical character can have on an individual and the influences that this individual in turn can have on those who hear the life story that he has put together, in part from the myths that he has heard. This influence chain itself has been depicted in the Greek and Sanskrit epics. In each of these four epics, a displaced ruler hears a myth that he himself (or his proxy) learns to tell and that he enacts eventually as an exemplar for others. Yet the emphases that each of the two epic pairs places on the processes of internalization and imitation depend on the pair's particular religious ideal.

The *Iliad* and *Odyssey* accent the ability of their heroes to perform poetry themselves because Greek epic verse consists in, and thus preserves, the ideal

33 McAdams 1985:62, 77, 83–84, 136–137, 161–162. McAdams' notions of peak and nadir experiences derive from the ideas of humanistic psychologist Abraham H. Maslow (1959; 1968:84n1, 103–114) and of psychiatrist and clinical psychologist Frederick C. Thorne (1963).

34 Meichenbaum 1971:298; Bandura 1969:171.

that allays anxiety about an uncertain afterlife, namely, *kléos*. Accordingly, the Greek epics stress their successful protagonists' identification with the poets who would celebrate them. Especially important in the *Iliad* and *Odyssey*, then, is internalization, the operation whereby the epics' heroes anticipate their own poetic immortalization. Only by performing poems on their own, in the manner of traditional poets, can these heroes provide themselves with the proper scripts to perform unforgettably up to their potential as heroes and thus to take their rightful places on their culture's stage of commemorated players.

By contrast, the *Rāmāyaṇa* and *Mahābhārata* highlight heroes who hear poems from other displaced rulers because the Sanskrit epics teach their ideal of *dharma* by example. Hence these works' heroes not only hear about exemplarily righteous rulers, but also hear from monarchs who embody the hard choices that doing right requires in an age of increasing immorality. Because the *Rāmāyaṇa* and *Mahābhārata* underscore rightdoing, these poems spotlight their heroes' imitation of dharmic paragons, rather than the heroes' internalization of admirable episodes (which presumably precedes the heroes' good deeds).

Although the Greek and Sanskrit epics, in accordance with their respective religious ideals, accentuate internalization and imitation differently, the epic pairs adopt analogous approaches to instill those ideals. In each pair, one epic features a hero who tells or hears a triumphal tale punctuated by peak experiences and who, by enacting this story, acts as a mastery model for the audience of the epic. The epic affirms its core ideal by exhibiting the ease with which this ideal is achieved to peak perfection both in the epic's embedded tale and in the epic's main story. But the poem with which this affirmative epic is partnered interrogates the same ideal. The interrogative epic focuses on a hero who relates or listens to melancholy accounts laden with nadir experiences and who, like the plaintive protagonist of the encapsulated narratives, attains his ideal with a great deal of difficulty. Consequently, he serves as a coping model for the epic's audience.

The heroes of the affirmative and interrogative epics serve as such different exemplars by virtue of having internalized differently the tales of their traditions. Achilles and Odysseus, for instance, both surely have attended to the *kléa andrôn* since childhood, but have drawn from these glorious deeds of men distinctively while crafting personal myths.

By the time that Achilles—sitting in the camp that his countrymen have pitched before battling the Trojans—takes up the lyre that he has looted from Thebe, he sings of the famous acts of his antecedents, even as he is poised to procure similar glory for himself (*Iliad* 9.185–189). Although the *Iliad* does not specify about whom Achilles is singing, its classification of his song among the *kléa andrôn*—the designation that this epic, like the *Odyssey*, employs implicitly for itself (*Iliad* 9.519–526, *Odyssey* 8.72–78)—suggests that Achilles is singing his own life story in advance of its celebrated completion. His story has little suspense even when he is absent from the Trojan War, for, during this nonfighting phase, Achilles cannot help but set in motion the divine machinery that fixes his own future fame. He asks Thetis to ask Zeus to help the Trojans so that Agamemnon will suffer enough losses to be punished for dishonoring Achilles, who has left the fray in protest. Moreover, even before Patroclus' death draws Achilles back into battle to slay Hector and other Trojans soon before dying himself—and to obtain everlasting fame as a result—Phoenix foresees the Phthian king's glorious trajectory, comparing Achilles to men who have been immortalized in past poems (*Iliad* 1.407–412, 335–344; 18.114–116; 9.412–413, 519–526). Hence, Achilles articulates at Troy a life story that probably consists of peak experiences and, in its emphasis on glory, corresponds to the full actualization of destructive power that Achilles himself is destined to accomplish there.

But the internalization of *kléa* does not appear to come nearly so easily to Odysseus, for—unlike Achilles—Odysseus does not overtly incorporate earlier glories into his own stories. Even though he has heard his own wartime exploits sung by Demodocus, Odysseus dwells on his defeats as he looks back on his life and tells of having hit rock bottom repeatedly, dogged by nadir experiences at almost every one of his many turns. At this lowly position, the Ithacan laments his lost opportunities to exert authority over his subjects and to enjoy intimacy with his loved ones. Yet, his strategic performances of such harrowing stories are the means by which the hero will be restored to royal power and close associations atop his society. He acquires the economic resources requisite to this reascent by sharing narratively with generous Phaeacians not only past sorrows, but also happy prospects guaranteed by Theban Teiresias. And Odysseus lives up to Teiresias' prophecy by ascertaining poetically the sympathies of his Ithacan herdsman and queen, telling each of the two a tale that is false on its distorted face, but true to Odysseus' sincere intent to reconnect with the people who have made—and who will make—his productive rule possible (*Odyssey* 8.73–74, 511–515; 9.1–12.453; 14.191–359; 19.164–202, 220–248, 268–299).[35]

A similar difference in internalization is at work in the Sanskrit epics. On their surface, the poems portray their heroes hearing traditional tales being told by bardic monarchs. Whereas Rāma listens to the *Rāmāyaṇa* recited by Kuśa and Lava, Yudhiṣṭhira hears Nala's narratives secondhand (or second-ear) (*Rāmāyaṇa* 1.5.1–7.100.25; *Mahābhārata* 3.64.9–19, 3.68.8–11, 3.72.25–28). On closer inspection, these accounts that the epics embed reveal themselves as the life stories that Rāma and Yudhiṣṭhira would tell, were the sovereigns

[35] Earlier versions of the following three paragraphs have appeared in Pathak 2006:145–146, 146.

too to take poetic turns. This symbolic significance of the encapsulated tales is brought out by their royal tellers' close resemblances to the epics' heroes. Kuśa and Lava look just like Rāma, and the tale that the twins tell is the story of their father's life. Although the Ayodhyan king and princes have more in common than do Yudhiṣṭhira and Nala, the Niṣadhan monarch's circumstances are much the same as those of his Indraprasthan counterpart.[36] Consequently, the sorrow and shame that Nala expresses in his accounts are shared by Yudhiṣṭhira and probably would color any story that Yudhiṣṭhira would tell about his own life.

At the same time that the Sanskrit epics portray internalization, the poems' distinct depictions of this process imply that it comes more easily to some characters than to others. Rāma, for instance, hears a *dharma*-affirming account directly from its princely performers. Their physical similarity to him, as well as the fact that they actually are recounting a story about him, suggests that he could take over for them and render his life story readily—a fitting outcome for a ruler to whom righteousness is always apparent. In contrast, Yudhiṣṭhira listens only indirectly when a bardic king laments losses that interrogate whether *dharma* can be attained at all. Yudhiṣṭhira's lack of a blood relationship to this ruler, Nala, and Yudhiṣṭhira's distance from Nala's life (which is described to Yudhiṣṭhira by an intermediary, Bṛhadaśva, rather than by Nala himself) would limit Yudhiṣṭhira's ability to reproduce Nala's poems as his own—an appropriate problem on the part of a King Dharma who is unsure of how to act rightly.

While peak and nadir experiences alike appear in the royal poems that represent Rāma's and Yudhiṣṭhira's life stories, the experiences are distributed differently in these personal myths, which accordingly paint strikingly different portraits of the monarchs at the myths' centers. Rāma, according to Kuśa and Lava's *Rāmāyaṇa* recitation, suffers greatly when he is separated from Sītā through her abduction and interment. Even so, Rāma's is much less a tale of lost intimacy than of power won, as his sovereign success attests. By contrast, the Yudhiṣṭhira seen in the shadows of Nala's woeful tales has cause to lament the losses of his own land and family, even as he remains their ruler. The limited power in Yudhiṣṭhira's possession does little to offset his lost opportunities for intimacy.

In comparison with Odysseus and Yudhiṣṭhira, Achilles and Rāma internalize their respective societies' stories of glory and morality more readily because the affirmative *Iliad* and *Rāmāyaṇa* offer a different type of exemplar than the interrogative *Odyssey* and *Mahābhārata* do. Both Achilles and Rāma

36 While I have shown, in Chapter 4, how Nala's narratives speak to Yudhiṣṭhira's ultimate situation, a number of other parallels between Nala's and Yudhiṣṭhira's experiences have been pointed out by Indologist Madeleine Biardeau (1984, 1985), Shulman (2001:131–158), and Hiltebeitel (2001:215–239).

masterly model their religious ideals. Achilles, in effect, recites his fated fame as though it has long been a part of his society's poetic repertoire. And Rama hears a tale about how he himself has done and will do right decisively, an account that represents the ease with which he will put into practice what he has heard and thus will imitate the king whom Kuśa and Lava limn. Odysseus and Yudhiṣṭhira, however, cope with adversity as they struggle to model *kléos* and *dharma*, respectively. Odysseus can realize his renown only after his narratives have moved Alcinous, Eumaeus, and Penelope to aid him in his effort to regain his throne. And Yudhiṣṭhira—after hearing the abbreviated narratives in which long-gone Nala questions whether he himself can do right by his kingdom and queen—treks uphill to heaven, while accompanied not just by Dharma but also by self-doubt.

By presenting these mastery and coping models simultaneously, the affirmative and interrogative epics increase the appeal of their ideals to their audiences, whose differential abilities to realize glory and to realize righteousness are implied by the disparities between the Greek paragons and between the Indian ones. While Achilles and Rāma demonstrate the mastery with which *kléos* and *dharma* may be achieved, Odysseus and Yudhiṣṭhira cope with the difficulties in the attainment of these ideals. Taking clear and occluded paths to reach their ideals, the affirmative and interrogative heroes allow contrasting kinds of audience members—those to whom the ideals come readily and those for whom the ideals are hard won—to follow in the footsteps of the corresponding heroes and to apply the lessons of their lives.

The effectiveness of the affirmative and interrogative epics as instructors explains their persistence and prominence now as in the past. These poems transcend the times and places of their makings, by meeting religious needs that human beings still have today. Whenever they encounter the epics, audiences can find existential comfort as their heroes counter by *kléos* the uncertainty that death threatens and defeat by *dharma* the forces of increasing immorality, whether these exemplars achieve their ideals easily or not. And audience members, by internalizing the stories of these rulers and by imitating their endeavors to some extent, can incorporate into their own identities those ancient narratives and paragons.

Bibliography

Classical Sources

Greek

Aelian

Dilts, Mervin R., ed. 1974. *Claudii Aeliani Varia Historia*. Leipzig.

Herodotus

Hude, Karl, ed. 1927. *Herodoti Historiae*. 3rd ed. 2 vols. Oxford.

Hesiod

West, M. L., ed. 1966. *Hesiod. Theogony*. Oxford. Repr., 1997.

Homer

Allen, Thomas W., ed. 1917–1919. *Odyssey*. 2nd ed. Vols. 3–4 of *Homeri opera*. Oxford.

Monro, David B., and Thomas W. Allen, eds. 1920. *Iliad*. 3rd ed. Vols. 1–2 of *Homeri opera*. Oxford.

Homeric Hymns

Allen, T. W., W. R. Halliday, and E. E. Sikes, eds. 1936. *The Homeric Hymns*. 2nd ed. Oxford.

Pindar

Bowra, C. M., ed. 1935. *Pindari carmina cum fragmentis*. Oxford.

Drachmann, A. B., ed. 1903–1927. *Scholia vetera in Pindari carmina*. 3 vols. Leipzig.

Lattimore, Richmond, trans. 1976. *The Odes of Pindar*. 2nd ed. Chicago.

Snell, Bruno, and Herwig Maehler, eds. 1971–1975. *Pindari carmina cum fragmentis*. 2 vols. Leipzig.

Sanskrit

Arthaśāstra

Kangle, R. P., ed. and trans. 1969–1972. *The Kauṭilīya Arthaśāstra*. 2nd ed. 2 pts. Bombay.

Dhvanyāloka

Ingalls, Daniel H. H., Jeffrey Moussaieff Masson, and M. V. Patwardhan, trans. 1990. *The* Dhvanyāloka *of Ānandavardhana with the* Locana *of Abhinavagupta*. Ed. Daniel H. H. Ingalls. Cambridge, MA.

Krishnamoorthy, K., ed. and trans. 1974. *Dhvanyāloka of Ānandavardhana*. Dharwar.

Śāstrī, Paṭṭābhirāma, ed. 1940. *The Dhvanyāloka of Śrī Ānandavardhanāchārya with the Lochana and Bālapriyā Commentaries by Śrī Abhinavagupta and Paṇḍitrājā Sahṛdayatilaka Śrī Rāmaśāraka*. Benares.

Kāvyamīmāṃsā

Dalal, C. D., and R. Anantakrishna Shastry, eds. 1916. *Kāvyamīmāṃsā of Rājaśekhara*. Baroda.

Parashar, Sadhana, ed. and trans. 2000. *Kāvyamīmāṁsā of Rājaśekhara: Original Text in Sanskrit and Translation with Explanatory Notes*. New Delhi.

Sharma, Madhusudan, ed. 1931–1934. *The Kāvyamīmāṃsā of Rājaśekhara Edited with the Madhusūdanī Commentary by Sāhityāchārya Paṇḍit Madhusūdana Miśra*. 3 pts. Benares.

Mahābhārata

Fitzgerald, James L. 2004a. *See under* Contemporary Sources *below*.

———, trans. and ed. 2004b. *Book 11: The Book of the Women; Book 12: The Book of Peace, Part One*. Vol. 7 of *The Mahābhārata*. Ed. J. A. B. van Buitenen and James L. Fitzgerald. Chicago.

Sukthankar, Vishnu S., S. K. Belvalkar, and P. L. Vaidya, eds. 1933–1966. *The Mahābhārata*. 19 vols. Poona.

Maitrāyaṇī Saṃhitā

Schroeder, Leopold von, ed. 1881–1886. *Maitrāyaṇī Saṃhitā: Die Saṃhitā der Maitrāyaṇīya-Śākhā*. 4 vols. Leipzig. Repr., Wiesbaden, 1970–1972.

Mānavadharmaśāstra

Olivelle, Patrick, ed. and trans. 2005. *Manu's Code of Law: A Critical Edition and Translation of the* Mānava-Dharmaśāstra. With the editorial assistance of Suman Olivelle. Oxford.

Nāṭyaśāstra

Krishnamoorthy, K., ed. 1992. *Nāṭyaśāstra of Bharatamuni with the Commentary Abhinavabhāratī by Abhinavaguptācārya.* 4th ed. Vol. 1. Vadodara.

Nagar, R. S., ed. 1981–1984. *Nāṭyaśāstra of Bharatamuni with the Commentary Abhinavabhāratī by Abhinavaguptācārya.* With the assistance of K. L. Joshi and M. A. Vedalankar. 4 vols. Delhi.

Rāmāyaṇa

Bhatt, G. H., and U. P. Shah, eds. 1960–1975. *The Vālmīki-Rāmāyaṇa.* 7 vols. Baroda.

Goldman, Robert P., and Sally J. Sutherland Goldman, eds. 1984–2009. *The Rāmāyaṇa of Vālmīki: An Epic of Ancient India.* With the assistance of Leonard E. Nathan and Kristi L. Wiley. Trans. Robert P. Goldman, Rosalind Lefeber, Sheldon I. Pollock, Sally J. Sutherland Goldman, and Barend A. van Nooten. 6 vols. Princeton.

Śatapatha Brāhmaṇa

Upadhyaya, Ganga Prasad, ed. 1998. *Śatapatha-Brāhmaṇam.* New Delhi.

Taittirīya Brāhmaṇa

Mitra, Rājendralāla, ed. 1855–1870. *The Taittirīya Brāhmaṇa of the Black Yajur Veda.* With the assistance of several learned *paṇḍitas.* 4 vols. Calcutta. Repr., Osnabrück, 1981.

Taittirīya Saṃhitā

Sontakke, N. S., and T. N. Dharmadhikari, eds. 1970–1990. *Taittirīya Saṃhitā with the Padapāṭha and the Commentaries of Bhaṭṭa Bhāskara Miśra and Sāyaṇācārya.* 3 vols. Poona.

Contemporary Sources

Alles, Gregory D. 1994. *The* Iliad, *the* Rāmāyaṇa, *and the Work of Religion: Failed Persuasion and Religious Mystification*. University Park, PA.

Amory, Anne. 1963. "The Reunion of Odysseus and Penelope." In *Essays on the* Odyssey*: Selected Modern Criticism*, ed. Charles H. Taylor, Jr., 100–121. Bloomington.

Andersen, Øivind. 1992. "Agamemnon's Singer (*Od.* 3.262–272)." *Symbolae Osloenses* 67:5–26.

Athanassakis, A. N. 1987. "Penelope's Dream in the Context of the Eagle against Serpent Motif." *Hellenika* 38:260–268.

Austin, Norman. 1975. *Archery at the Dark of the Moon: Poetic Problems in Homer's* Odyssey. Berkeley.

Bailey, Gregory. 1983. "Suffering in the *Mahābhārata*: Draupadī and Yudhiṣṭhira." *Puruṣārtha* 7:109–129.

Bal, Mieke. 1997. *Narratology: Introduction to the Theory of Narrative*. Trans. Christine van Boheemen. 2nd ed. Toronto.

Bandura, Albert. 1969. *Principles of Behavior Modification*. New York.

Beardsley, Monroe C. 1962. "The Metaphorical Twist." *Philosophy and Phenomenological Research* 22:293–307.

Beye, Charles Rowan. 1993. *Ancient Epic Poetry: Homer, Apollonius, Virgil*. Ithaca.

Bhatt, B. N. 1986. "Vālmīki's Skill in the Delineation of Sentiments." *Journal of the Oriental Institute, Baroda* 36:55–60.

Biardeau, Madeleine. 1984. "Nala et Damayantī, héros épiques." *Indo-Iranian Journal* 27:247–274.

———. 1985. "Nala et Damayantī, héros épiques." *Indo-Iranian Journal* 28:1–34.

Black, Max. 1962. *Models and Metaphors: Studies in Language and Philosophy*. Ithaca.

Bose, Mandakranta, ed. 2004. *The* Rāmāyaṇa *Revisited*. Oxford.

Bowra, C. M. 1952. *Heroic Poetry*. London. Repr., 1961.

Brockington, John. 1998. *The Sanskrit Epics*. Leiden.

———. 2004. "The Concept of *Dharma* in the *Rāmāyaṇa*." *Journal of Indian Philosophy* 32:655–670.

Buchan, Mark. 2004. *The Limits of Heroism: Homer and the Ethics of Reading*. Ann Arbor.

Buitenen, J. A. B. van. 1974. "The Indian Epic." In *The Literatures of India: An Introduction*, ed. Edward C. Dimock, Jr., Edwin Gerow, C. M. Naim, A. K. Ramanujan, Gordon Roadarmel, and J. A. B. van Buitenen, 47–80. Chicago.

Bulfinch, Thomas. 1912. *The Age of Fable*. Rev. ed. London. Repr., 1942.

Burgess, Jonathan S. 2001. *The Tradition of the Trojan War in Homer and the Epic Cycle*. Baltimore.

———. 2005. "The Epic Cycle and Fragments." In Foley 2005:344–352.

———. 2009. *The Death and Afterlife of Achilles*. Baltimore.

Burkert, Walter. 1985. *Greek Religion*. Trans. John Raffan. Cambridge, MA.

———. 2001. "The Making of Homer in the Sixth Century BC: Rhapsodes versus Stesichorus." In Cairns 2001:92–116.

Butchvarov, Panayot. 1966. *Resemblance and Identity: An Examination of the Problem of Universals*. Bloomington.

Bynum, David E. 1976. "The Generic Nature of Oral Epic Poetry." In *Folklore Genres*, ed. Dan Ben-Amos, 35–58. Austin.

Cairns, Douglas L., ed. 2001. *Oxford Readings in Homer's* Iliad. Oxford.

Carlier, Pierre. 1984. *La royauté en Grèce avant Alexandre*. Strasbourg.

Chadwick, H[ector] Munro, and N[ora] Kershaw Chadwick. 1932–1940. *The Growth of Literature*. 3 vols. Cambridge. Repr., 1968.

Chantraine, Pierre. 1984–1990. *Dictionnaire étymologique de la langue grecque: Histoire des mots*. New ed. 4 vols. Paris.

Crotty, Kevin. 1994. *The Poetics of Supplication: Homer's* Iliad *and* Odyssey. Ithaca.

D'Aulaire, Ingri, and Edgar Parin d'Aulaire. 1962. *Book of Greek Myths*. Garden City, NY.

Derrida, Jacques. 1974. "White Mythology: Metaphor in the Text of Philosophy." Trans. F. C. T. Moore. *New Literary History* 6:5–74.

Detienne, Marcel, and Jean-Pierre Vernant. 1978. *Cunning Intelligence in Greek Culture and Society*. Trans. Janet Lloyd. Atlantic Highlands.

Dhand, Arti. 2002. "The *Dharma* of Ethics, the Ethics of *Dharma*: Quizzing the Ideals of Hinduism." *Journal of Religious Ethics* 30:347–372.

Dimock, George E. 1989. *The Unity of the* Odyssey. Amherst.

Dodds, E. R. 1951. *The Greeks and the Irrational*. Berkeley.

Doniger, Wendy. 1998. *The Implied Spider: Politics and Theology in Myth*. New York.

———. 1999. *Splitting the Difference: Gender and Myth in Ancient Greece and India*. Chicago.

———. *See also* O'Flaherty, Wendy Doniger.

Drews, Robert. 1983. *Basileus: The Evidence for Kingship in Geometric Greece*. New Haven.

Duckworth, George Eckel. 1933. *Foreshadowing and Suspense in the Epics of Homer, Apollonius, and Vergil*. Princeton.

Edwards, Anthony T. 1985. *Achilles in the Odyssey*. Königstein im Taunus.

Edwards, Mark W. 1987. *Homer: Poet of the* Iliad. Baltimore.

Erbse, Hartmut. 1972. *Beiträge zum Verständnis der Odyssee*. Berlin.

Felson, Nancy. 1997. *Regarding Penelope: From Character to Poetics*. Norman.

Felson, Nancy, and Laura M. Slatkin. 2004. "Gender and Homeric Epic." In R. Fowler 2004:91–114.

Finley, John H., Jr. 1978. *Homer's* Odyssey. Cambridge, MA.
Fitch, Edward. 1924. "Pindar and Homer." *Classical Philology* 19:57–65.
Fitzgerald, James L. 1991. "India's Fifth Veda: The *Mahābhārata*'s Presentation of Itself." In *Essays on the Mahābhārata*, ed. Arvind Sharma, 150–170. Leiden.
———. 2004a. "*Dharma* and Its Translation in the *Mahābhārata*." *Journal of Indian Philosophy* 32:671–685.
———, trans. and ed. 2004b. *See under* Classical Sources *above*.
Foley, John Miles. 2004. "Epic as Genre." In R. Fowler 2004:171–187.
———, ed. 2005. *A Companion to Ancient Epic*. Malden.
Ford, Andrew. 1992. *Homer: The Poetry of the Past*. Ithaca.
Foucault, Michel. 1977. "What Is an Author?" In *Language, Counter-Memory, Practice: Selected Essays and Interviews*, ed. Donald F. Bouchard and trans. Donald F. Bouchard and Sherry Simon, 113–138. Ithaca.
Fowler, Alastair. 1982. *Kinds of Literature: An Introduction to the Theory of Genres and Modes*. Cambridge, MA.
Fowler, Robert, ed. 2004. *The Cambridge Companion to Homer*. Cambridge.
Freeman, Edward A. 1873. *Comparative Politics*. London.
Freidenreich, David M. 2004. "Comparisons Compared: A Methodological Survey of Comparisons of Religion from 'A Magic Dwells' to *A Magic Still Dwells*." *Method & Theory in the Study of Religion* 16:80–101.
Frontisi-Ducroux, Françoise. 1986. *La cithare d'Achille: Essai sur la poétique de l'*Iliade. Rome.
Genette, Gérard. 1980. *Narrative Discourse: An Essay in Method*. Trans. Jane E. Lewin. Ithaca.
Goldman, Robert P. 1976. "Vālmīki and the Bhṛgu Connection." *Journal of the American Oriental Society* 96:97–101.
———. 1977. *Gods, Priests, and Warriors: The Bhṛgus of the* Mahābhārata. New York.
———. 1989. "Tracking the Elusive *Ṛkṣa*: The Tradition of Bears as Rāma's Allies in Various Versions of the *Rāmakathā*." *Journal of the American Oriental Society* 109:545–552.
Goldman, Robert P., and Sally J. Sutherland Goldman, eds. 1984–2009. *See under* Classical Sources *above*.
Graziosi, Barbara. 2002. *Inventing Homer: The Early Reception of Epic*. Cambridge.
Griffin, Jasper. 1977. "The Epic Cycle and the Uniqueness of Homer." *Journal of Hellenic Studies* 97:39–53.
———. 1987. "Homer and Excess." In *Homer: Beyond Oral Poetry; Recent Trends in Homeric Interpretation*, ed. J. M. Bremer, I. J. F. de Jong, and J. Kalff, 85–104. Amsterdam.
Haft, Adele J. 1984. "Odysseus, Idomeneus and Meriones: The Cretan Lies of *Odyssey* 13–19." *Classical Journal* 79:289–306.

———. 1990. "'The City-Sacker Odysseus' in *Iliad* 2 and 10." *Transactions of the American Philological Association* 120:37–56.

Hainsworth, J. B. 1991. *The Idea of Epic*. Berkeley.

Hamilton, Edith. 1942. *Mythology*. Boston. Repr., New York, 1969.

Harsh, Philip Whaley. 1950. "Penelope and Odysseus in *Odyssey* XIX." *American Journal of Philology* 71:1–21.

Havelock, Eric A. 1963. *Preface to Plato*. Cambridge, MA.

———. 1978. "The Alphabetization of Homer." In *Communication Arts in the Ancient World*, ed. Eric A. Havelock and Jackson P. Hershbell, 3–21. New York.

Hiltebeitel, Alf. 1990. *The Ritual of Battle: Krishna in the* Mahābhārata. Albany.

———. 2001. *Rethinking the Mahābhārata: A Reader's Guide to the Education of the Dharma King*. Chicago.

———. 2005. "Not without Subtales: Telling Laws and Truths in the Sanskrit Epics." *Journal of Indian Philosophy* 33:455–511.

Hopkins, E. Washburn. 1901. *The Great Epic of India: Character and Origin of the Mahabharata*. New York. Repr., Delhi, 1993.

———. 1915. *Epic Mythology*. Strassburg. Repr., Delhi, 1974.

How, W. W., and J. Wells. 1912. *A Commentary on Herodotus*. 2 vols. Oxford. Repr., 1979–1980.

Huberman, Eric A. 1994. "Who Is Vālmīki?: The *Ādi-kavi* and the Origins of Lyric Poetry." *Journal of Vaishnava Studies* 2:17–30.

Huxley, G. L. 1969. *Greek Epic Poetry from Eumelos to Panyassis*. Cambridge, MA.

Ingalls, Daniel H. H., Jeffrey Moussaieff Masson, and M. V. Patwardhan, trans. 1990. *See under* Classical Sources *above*.

Jong, Irene J. F. de. 2001. *A Narratological Commentary on the* Odyssey. Cambridge.

Kane, P. V. 1966. "The Two Epics." *Annals of the Bhandarkar Oriental Research Institute* 47:11–58.

King, Katherine Callen. 1987. *Achilles: Paradigms of the War Hero from Homer to the Middle Ages*. Berkeley.

Kirk, G. S. 1962. *The Songs of Homer*. Cambridge.

Laine, James W. 1989. *Visions of God: Narratives of Theophany in the Mahābhārata*. Vienna.

Lattimore, Richmond, trans. 1976. *See under* Classical Sources *above*.

Lévi-Strauss, Claude. 1963. *Structural Anthropology*. Trans. Claire Jacobson and Brooke Grundfest Schoepf. New York.

Liddell, Henry George, Robert Scott, and Henry Stuart Jones, eds. 1940. *A Greek-English Lexicon*. 9th ed. Oxford.

Lincoln, Bruce. 1994. *Authority: Construction and Corrosion*. Chicago.

———. 1999. *Theorizing Myth: Narrative, Ideology, and Scholarship*. Chicago.

Lloyd, G. E. R. 1966. *Polarity and Analogy: Two Types of Argumentation in Early Greek Thought*. Cambridge.

Lynn-George, Michael. 1988. *Epos: Word, Narrative and the* Iliad. Basingstoke.

Mallory, J. P. 1989. *In Search of the Indo-Europeans: Language, Archaeology and Myth*. London.

Mangels, Annette. 1994. *Zur Erzähltechnik im Mahābhārata*. Hamburg.

Maslow, Abraham H. 1959. "Cognition of Being in the Peak Experiences." *Journal of Genetic Psychology* 94:43–66.

———. 1968. *Toward a Psychology of Being*. 2nd ed. Princeton.

Masson, J. 1969. "Who Killed Cock Krauñca? Abhinavagupta's Reflections on the Origin of Aesthetic Experience." *Journal of the Oriental Institute, Baroda* 18:207–224.

Masson, J. L., and M. V. Patwardhan. 1969. *Śāntarasa and Abhinavagupta's Philosophy of Aesthetics*. Poona.

Matilal, Bimal Krishna. 1989. "Moral Dilemmas: Insights from Indian Epics." In *Moral Dilemmas in the Mahābhārata*, ed. Bimal Krishna Matilal, 1–19. Shimla.

McAdams, Dan P. 1985. *Power, Intimacy, and the Life Story: Personological Inquiries into Identity*. Homewood, IL.

———. 1993. *The Stories We Live By: Personal Myths and the Making of the Self*. New York.

Meichenbaum, Donald H. 1971. "Examination of Model Characteristics in Reducing Avoidance Behavior." *Journal of Personality and Social Psychology* 17:298–307.

Miller, Barbara Stoler. 1973. "The Original Poem: *Vālmīki-Rāmāyaṇa* and Indian Literary Values." *Literature East and West* 17:163–173.

Miner, Earl. 1990. *Comparative Poetics: An Intercultural Essay on Theories of Literature*. Princeton.

Minkowski, Christopher Z. 1989. "Janamejaya's *Sattra* and Ritual Structure." *Journal of the American Oriental Society* 109:401–420.

———. 2001. "The Interrupted Sacrifice and the Sanskrit Epics." *Journal of Indian Philosophy* 29:169–186.

Mitter, Partha. 1992. *Much Maligned Monsters: A History of European Reactions to Indian Art*. 2nd ed. Chicago.

Moriarty, Michael Eugene. 1971. *The Uses of Analogy: An Essay in the Methodology of Comparative Literature*. PhD diss., Indiana University.

Mueller, Martin. 1984. *The Iliad*. London.

Murnaghan, Sheila. 1987. *Disguise and Recognition in the* Odyssey. Princeton.

Nagy, Gregory. 1990a. *Pindar's Homer: The Lyric Possession of an Epic Past*. Baltimore.

———. 1990b. "Ancient Greek Poetry, Prophecy, and Concepts of Theory." In *Poetry and Prophecy: The Beginnings of a Literary Tradition*, ed. James L. Kugel, 56–64. Ithaca.

———. 1996a. *Poetry as Performance: Homer and Beyond*. Cambridge.

———. 1996b. *Homeric Questions*. Austin.

———. 1999. *The Best of the Achaeans: Concepts of the Hero in Archaic Greek Poetry*. Rev. ed. Baltimore.

———. 2005. "The Epic Hero." In Foley 2005:71–89.

Nisetich, Frank J. 1989. *Pindar and Homer*. Baltimore.

Nooten, Barend A. van. 1978. "The Sanskrit Epics." In *Heroic Epic and Saga: An Introduction to the World's Great Folk Epics*, ed. Felix J. Oinas, 49–75. Bloomington.

O'Flaherty, Wendy Doniger. 1973. *Asceticism and Eroticism in the Mythology of Śiva*. Oxford.

———. 1976. *The Origins of Evil in Hindu Mythology*. Berkeley.

———. *See also* Doniger, Wendy.

Olson, S. Douglas. 1995. *Blood and Iron: Stories and Storytelling in Homer's* Odyssey. Leiden.

Oxford English Dictionary. 1989–2013. Ed. J. A. Simpson, E. S. C. Weiner, and Michael Proffitt. Oxford. http://dictionary.oed.com.

Paden, William E. 2000. "Elements of a New Comparativism." In *A Magic Still Dwells: Comparative Religion in the Postmodern Age*, ed. Kimberley C. Patton and Benjamin C. Ray, 182–192. Berkeley.

Pathak, Shubha. 2006. "Why Do Displaced Kings Become Poets in the Sanskrit Epics? Modeling *Dharma* in the Affirmative *Rāmāyaṇa* and the Interrogative *Mahābhārata*." *International Journal of Hindu Studies* 10:127–149.

———. 2013. "'Epic' as an Amnesiac Metaphor: Finding the Word to Compare Ancient Greek and Sanskrit Poems." In *Figuring Religions: Comparing Ideas, Images, and Activities*, ed. Shubha Pathak, 35–62. Albany.

———. Forthcoming. "The Divine Character of Poetic Creativity in Rājaśekhara's *Kāvyamīmāṃsā*." In *Poetry, Drama and Aesthetics*, ed. Mandakranta Bose, David Gitomer, and David Smith. Vol. 6 of *Papers of the 13th World Sanskrit Conference*. Delhi.

Pfeiffer, Rudolf. 1968–1976. *History of Classical Scholarship*. 2 vols. Oxford.

Podlecki, Anthony J. 1967. "Omens in the *Odyssey*." *Greece & Rome*, 2nd ser., 14:12–23.

Pollock, Sheldon I. 1984. "The Divine King in the Indian Epic." *Journal of the American Oriental Society* 104:505–528.

———. 1985. "The Theory of Practice and the Practice of Theory in Indian Intellectual History." *Journal of the American Oriental Society* 105:499–519.

———. 1986. Introduction to *Ayodhyākāṇḍa*, trans. Sheldon I. Pollock and ed. Robert P. Goldman, 1–76. Vol. 2 of Goldman and Goldman 1984–2009.

———. 1991. Introduction to *Araṇyakāṇḍa*, trans. Sheldon I. Pollock and ed. Robert P. Goldman, 1–84. Vol. 3 of Goldman and Goldman 1984–2009.

———. 2003. "Sanskrit Literary Culture from the Inside Out." In *Literary Cultures in History: Reconstructions from South Asia*, ed. Sheldon Pollock, 39–130. Berkeley.

Poole, Fitz John Porter. 1986. "Metaphors and Maps: Towards Comparison in the Anthropology of Religion." *Journal of the American Academy of Religion* 54:411–457.

Preminger, Alex, T. V. F. Brogan, Frank J. Warnke, O. B. Hardison, Jr., and Earl Miner, eds. 1993. *The New Princeton Encyclopedia of Poetry and Poetics*. 3rd ed. Princeton.

Pucci, Pietro. 1987. *Odysseus Polutropos: Intertextual Readings in the* Odyssey *and the* Iliad. Ithaca.

Quint, David. 1993. *Epic and Empire: Politics and Generic Form from Virgil to Milton*. Princeton.

Raghavan, V. 1967. *The Number of Rasa-s*. 2nd ed. Madras.

Redfield, James M. 1983. "The Economic Man." In *Approaches to Homer*, ed. Carl A. Rubino and Cynthia W. Shelmerdine, 218–247. Austin.

———. 1994. *Nature and Culture in the* Iliad: *The Tragedy of Hector*. Expanded ed. Durham.

Richards, I. A. 1936. *The Philosophy of Rhetoric*. Oxford.

Richman, Paula, ed. 1991. *Many Rāmāyaṇas: The Diversity of a Narrative Tradition in South Asia*. Berkeley.

———, ed. 2001. *Questioning Ramayanas: A South Asian Tradition*. Berkeley.

Ricoeur, Paul. 1977. *The Rule of Metaphor: Multi-disciplinary Studies of the Creation of Meaning in Language*. Trans. Robert Czerny, with Kathleen McLaughlin and John Costello. Toronto.

Rutherford, R. B. 2001. "From the *Iliad* to the *Odyssey*." In Cairns 2001:117–146.

Schein, Seth L. 1984. *The Mortal Hero: An Introduction to Homer's* Iliad. Berkeley.

Scherer, Wilhelm. 1893. *Kleine Schriften zur altdeutschen Philologie*. Ed. Konrad Burdach. Vol. 2 of *Kleine Schriften*. Ed. Konrad Burdach and Erich Schmidt. Berlin.

Schmiel, Robert. 1987. "Achilles in Hades." *Classical Philology* 82:35–37.

Scott, John A. 1921. *The Unity of Homer*. Berkeley.

Segal, Charles. 1994. *Singers, Heroes, and Gods in the* Odyssey. Ithaca.

Seidensticker, Bernd. 1978. "Archilochus and Odysseus." *Greek, Roman, and Byzantine Studies* 19:5–22.

Shulman, David. 2001. *The Wisdom of Poets: Studies in Tamil, Telugu, and Sanskrit.* Oxford.

Slatkin, Laura M. 1991. *The Power of Thetis: Allusion and Interpretation in the* Iliad. Berkeley.

Smith, G. Gregory. 1905. "Some Notes on the Comparative Study of Literature." *Modern Language Review* 1:1–8.

Smith, John D. 1980. "Old Indian (The Two Sanskrit Epics)." In *The Traditions*, ed. A. T. Hatto, 48–78. Vol. 1 of *Traditions of Heroic and Epic Poetry*. London.

———. 1992. "The Hero as Gifted Man: Nala in the *Mahābhārata*." In *The Indian Narrative: Perspectives and Patterns*, ed. Christopher Shackle and Rupert Snell, 13–31. Wiesbaden.

Smith, Jonathan Z. 1978. *Map Is Not Territory: Studies in the History of Religions.* Leiden. Repr., Chicago, 1993.

———. 1990. *Drudgery Divine: On the Comparison of Early Christianities and the Religions of Late Antiquity*. Chicago.

Snell, Bruno. 1953. *The Discovery of the Mind: The Greek Origins of European Thought.* Trans. T. G. Rosenmeyer. Oxford.

Spellman, John W. 1964. *Political Theory of Ancient India: A Study of Kingship from the Earliest Times to* circa *A.D. 300*. Oxford.

Stanford, W. B. 1963. *The Ulysses Theme: A Study in the Adaptability of a Traditional Hero*. 2nd ed. Oxford.

Sukthankar, V. S. 1939. "The Nala Episode and the Rāmāyaṇa." In *A Volume of Eastern and Indian Studies Presented to Professor F. W. Thomas, C. I. E., on his 72nd birth-day 21st March 1939*, ed. S. M. Katre and P. K. Gode, 294–303. Bombay.

Sullivan, Bruce M. 1990. *Kṛṣṇa Dvaipāyana Vyāsa and the Mahābhārata: A New Interpretation*. Leiden.

Sutherland, Sally J. 1989. "Sītā and Draupadī: Aggressive Behavior and Female Role-Models in the Sanskrit Epics." *Journal of the American Oriental Society* 109:63–79.

Sutton, Nicholas. 2000. *Religious Doctrines in the Mahābhārata*. Delhi.

Taplin, Oliver. 1980. "The Shield of Achilles within the *Iliad*." *Greece & Rome*, 2nd ser., 27:1–21.

———. 1992. *Homeric Soundings: The Shaping of the* Iliad. Oxford.

Thalmann, William G. 1984. *Conventions of Form and Thought in Early Greek Epic Poetry*. Baltimore.

Thompson, Stith. 1946. *The Folktale*. New York.

Thorne, Frederick C. 1963. "The Clinical Use of Peak and Nadir Experience Reports." *Journal of Clinical Psychology* 19:248–250.

Todorov, Tzvetan. 1977. *The Poetics of Prose*. Trans. Richard Howard. Ithaca.

Tracy, David. 1981. *The Analogical Imagination: Christian Theology and the Culture of Pluralism*. New York.

Tylor, Edward B. 1878. *Researches into the Early History of Mankind and the Development of Civilization*. New York.

Vaudeville, Charlotte. 1961. "A Further Note on *Krauñca-vadha* in Dhvanyāloka and Kāvyamīmāṃsā." *Journal of the Oriental Institute, Baroda* 11:122–126.

Vernant, Jean-Pierre. 1991. "A 'Beautiful Death' and the Disfigured Corpse in Homeric Epic." Trans. Andrew Szegedy-Maszak. In *Mortals and Immortals: Collected Essays*, ed. Froma I. Zeitlin, 50–74. Princeton.

Weisstein, Ulrich. 1973. *Comparative Literature and Literary Theory: Survey and Introduction*. Trans. William Riggan, in collaboration with Ulrich Weisstein. Bloomington.

Whitman, Cedric H. 1958. *Homer and the Heroic Tradition*. Cambridge, MA. Repr., New York, 1965.

———. 1982. *The Heroic Paradox: Essays on Homer, Sophocles, and Aristophanes*. Ed. Charles Segal. Ithaca.

Whitney, William Dwight. 1889. *Sanskrit Grammar*. 2nd ed. Cambridge, MA.

Wieniewski, Ignace. 1924. "La technique d'annoncer les événements futurs chez Homère." *Eos* 27:113–133.

Wilson, Donna F. 2002. *Ransom, Revenge, and Heroic Identity in the* Iliad. Cambridge.

Wyatt, William F., Jr. 1989. "The Intermezzo of Odyssey 11 and the Poets Homer and Odysseus." *Studi Micenei ed Egeo-Anatolici* 27:235–250.

Zarker, John W. 1965. "King Eëtion and Thebe as Symbols in the *Iliad*." *Classical Journal* 61:110–114.

Index of Sources

Index of Subjects